JUN   2012

Discarded

ARAFAT
AND THE
DREAM
OF
PALESTINE

AN INSIDER'S ACCOUNT

BASSAM ABU SHARIF

palgrave
macmillan

All photographs are printed courtesy of Bassam Abu Sharif.

Map of the Middle East is reprinted courtesy of the Library of Congress, Geography and Map Division.

First published in 2009 by PALGRAVE MACMILLAN® in the United States—a division of St. Martin's Press LLC, 175 Fifth Avenue, New York, NY 10010.

Where this book is distributed in the UK, Europe and the rest of the world, this is by Palgrave Macmillan, a division of Macmillan Publishers Limited, registered in England, company number 785998, of Houndmills, Basingstoke, Hampshire RG21 6XS.

Palgrave Macmillan is the global academic imprint of the above companies and has companies and representatives throughout the world.

Palgrave® and Macmillan® are registered trademarks in the United States, the United Kingdom, Europe and other countries.

ISBN–13: 978–0–230–60801–6
ISBN–10: 0–230–60801–9

Library of Congress Cataloging-in-Publication Data
Abu Sharif, Bassam.
    Arafat and the dream of Palestine : an insider's account / Bassam Abu Sharif.
      p.   cm.
    Includes bibliographical references and index.
    ISBN 0–230–60801–9
    1. Arafat, Yasir, 1929–2004.   2. Heads of state—Palestine—Biography.   3. Munazzamat al-Tahrir al-Filastiniyah—Biography.   4. Palestinian Arabs—Biography.   5. Arab-Israeli conflict.   6. Abu Sharif, Bassam.   I. Title.
DS126.6.A67A6   2009
956.95'3044092—dc22
[B]

                                                                                  2008054700

A catalogue record of the book is available from the British Library.

Design by Letra Libre, Inc.

First edition: May 2009
10 9 8 7 6 5 4 3 2 1
Printed in the United States of America.

CONTENTS

Photosection appears between pages 134 and 135.

KEY TERMS AND ORGANIZATIONS

Abtal Al-Awda (Heroes of Return)   An underground organization of fighters set up by the Arab Nationalist Movement in 1964, at the same time that the PLO was being established. After the Arab defeat in 1967, this group was folded into the PFLP.

Al-Hadaf (The Target)   A Lebanese weekly magazine that had wide distribution in many Arab countries as well as areas of the Arab diaspora, including Europe and North, Central, and South America. This was an organ of information for the PFLP.

Al-Yarmouk Camp   The largest Palestinian refugee camp in Syria; it was established by UNRWA (United Nations Relief and Works Agency for Palestine Refugees in the Near East) in 1948.

Amman Agreement   An agreement signed on February 23, 1984, between Arafat and King Hussein of Jordan which called for: (1) Total withdrawal of Israel from lands occupied in 1967; (2) the right of Palestinian self-determination within the confederated states of Jordan and Palestine; (3) a resolution to the Palestinian refugee problem in accordance with previous UN resolutions; and (4) peace negotiations under the auspices of an international conference with the PLO representing the Palestinian people. This agreement was nullified on February 19, 1986, by King Hussein when Arafat refused to recognize UN Resolution 242 because of the language in the document, which only referred to the "settlement of the refugee problem," with no mention of the Palestinians at all. The Amman Agreement was then cancelled permanently by the PNC at the Algiers conference April 20–25, 1987.

Arab League   Representing all Arab countries plus the PLO, this institution carries out the plans and implements decisions of the Arab leaders. Its headquarters are in Cairo, but it has offices all over the world.

Arab Nationalist Movement   A pan-Arab movement established by Dr. George Habash, Dr. Wadi' Haddad, and a group of their colleagues at the American University of Beirut. Founded in part in reaction to the Arab diaspora, this movement called for Arab unity as the only way to restore the rights of the Palestinians.

Bandung Conference (Indonesia)   Conference for the nonaligned countries of India, Indonesia, Yugoslavia, and Egypt.

Bar-Lev Line   A fortification wall built by the Israelis after they had taken the Sinai. It was built all along the Suez Canal and was constructed of earth and concrete, with extra fortifications at likely crossing points.

Belgrade Conference (Yugoslavia) The name of the group of nonaligned countries that included Egypt, India, Indonesia, and Yugoslavia. They tried to form a Third World political power alongside the West (the United States) and the East (the Soviet Union).

Black September The month in 1970 when Jordanian military forces launched a heavy attack against the Palestinian fighters in Jordan, eventually driving them out of the country. The name was later used by a group that carried out missions against the Israelis, one of the most famous being the one in Munich during the 1972 Summer Olympics.

Camp David An American presidential resort where, at the invitation of U.S. president Jimmy Carter, negotiations between Egyptian president Anwar El Sadat and Israeli prime minister Menachem Begin were concluded on September 17, 1978, after twelve days of secret negotiations. The Camp David Accords eventually led to a peace treaty between Israel and Egypt in 1979, as well as to the beginning of negotiations between the Palestinians and the Israelis.

Central Committee of Fateh The highest elected body of Fateh, headed by Yasser Arafat.

Dawson Field An airstrip in the desert east of Amman, Jordan that was used by the British Air Force during World War I. It is where the four hijacked airplanes were brought down by Palestinians on September 6, 1970, and also where they were later blown up. Following this incident, Palestinians continue to refer to this site as "Revolution Airport."

Democratic Front for the Liberation of Palestine (DFLP) One of the Palestinian organizations under the umbrella of the PLO, headed by Nayef Hawatmeh.

Druze A religious community found primarily in Syria, Lebanon, and Israel. It began as an offshoot of Islam, but incorporates other beliefs (i.e., Gnostic, neo-Platonic). They are considered to be Muslims but Muslim scholars do not regard them as such. They call themselves "People of Monotheism or Unitarianism."

Eid Al-Adha The Islamic holiday that comes two months after Ramadan had ended. It is the Feast of Sacrifice that celebrates Abraham's readiness to slaughter his son for God.

Eid Al-Fitr The Islamic holiday that comes one month after Ramadan has begun. It is a celebration of the end of fasting.

Fateh (Palestinian National Liberation Movement) An organization established in 1965 under the umbrella of the PLO, headed by Yasser Arafat. By maintaining leadership of Fateh while he was also president of the PLO, he managed to secure his way in all decisions because Fateh was the most prominent group within the PLO. Having both positions meant that he was able to get his ideas approved through all of the organizations that belonged to the PLO.

Fidayeen (Men of Sacrifice) The name given to all Palestinian freedom fighters who resist Israeli occupation.

General Union of Workers The union that organized the struggle of Palestinian workers throughout Palestine and all other Arab countries. Its leaders are elected every four years.

G8 Countries (Group of Eight Countries) Term used to refer to the richest, most influential countries in the economic and industrial arenas, made up of the United States, Great Britain, France, Germany, Spain, Italy, Belgium, and Russia.

Hezbollah Hezbollah is a Shi'a Islamic political and paramilitary group that first emerged to resist Israel's 1982 invasion of Lebanon.

International Peace Conference (Prague) An international conference held in 1983 that was attended by Palestinians and Israelis. The conference had been called for by an organization in the then C.S.S.R. (Czechoslovak Socialist Republic) known as the Peace Organization, which is dedicated to promoting peace in all regions of the world, including Africa, Asia, and the Middle East.

Intifada The uprising of the Palestinian people against their Israeli occupiers.

Jabotinski-Likud Policy A policy that advocates the complete extermination of the Palestinians as well as the forcible occupation of Palestine by the Jews. This concept of annihilation was developed by Vladimir Jabotinski, a right-wing Zionist who was born in Russia in 1880.

Likud The Israeli extreme Zionist party, now headed by former prime minister Binyamin Netanyahu (in office from June 1996–July 1999), who also served as the finance minister of Israel until 2005.

Lod The Palestinian town where George Habash was born. Israelis confiscated the land and built Ben Gurion Airport on it.

Madrid Conference A Middle East peace conference that was called for by the United States and Russia; the aim was to have Palestinians and Israelis negotiate terms of peace on the basis of the UN Security Council Resolution 242.

Mitchell Report The Mitchell Report, published in 2001, presented the results of a fact-finding committee that investigated the cause for the start of the Al-Aqsa Intifada. The report determined that, despite Israel's claims to the contrary, the Palestinian Authority did not plan the Intifada. The report indicated that, while neither party deliberately instigated the conflict, both bore some responsibility.

Occupied Territories The West Bank and Gaza Strip, which were captured by Israel during the Six Days' War in 1967.

Oslo Accord The agreement signed, on September 13, 1993, by a delegation of the PLO and an Israeli delegation of the ruling Labor Party, which was intended to provide a framework for a permanent resolution to the conflict.

Palestinian Authority The Palestinian Authority was formed in 1994, and governs the Palestinian territories of the West Bank and Gaza Strip. It functions in an administrative capacity within the PLO.

Palestine Liberation Army (PLA) The military organization of the PLO. The Arab League decided to establish the PLA side-by-side with the PLO to recruit Palestinians into one army that would be under the control of the Arab armies.

Palestine Liberation Organization (PLO) The official representative of the Palestinian people. It includes all organizations in its legislative and executive bodies (see PLO chart).

Palestine National Council The Parliament of the Palestinians.

Ramadan The Muslim religious period that takes place every year during the ninth month on the Islamic calendar (lunar). During this month, Muslim adults refrain from all food and drink (and cigarettes) from sunrise until sunset in order to learn about self-sacrifice, patience, and humility. During this holy time, Muslims purify themselves by seeking forgiveness and doing good deeds.

Resolution 242 A unanimous decision taken by the UN Security Council on November 22, 1967, which called for Israel to withdraw from Arab lands it had occupied in June 1967. It also called for the Arab states to recognize the state of Israel and live in peace.

Resolution 338 A confirmation of Resolution 242.

Sabra and Shatilla Two Palestinian refugee camps south of Beirut, the capital Lebanon. The Israelis and extreme right-wing Lebanese Phalangists (the political and military force of the Maronite Church in Lebanon since 1958), attacked the civilians in the camps. Thousands of people were massacred, and then bulldozed under the rubble to hide the extent of the slaughter.

Safad An important Palestinian city overlooking Lake Tiberius. It was also the home of Dr. Wadi' Haddad.

Six Days' War The war waged by Israel on June 5, 1967, against Egypt, Syria, and Jordan. Within six days, Israel had occupied the Sinai and the Gaza Strip in Egypt, the Golan Heights in Syria, and the West Bank of Jordan.

Tanzim A secret or underground military organization.

Tenet Plan A proposal presented on June 10, 2001, by then-CIA director George Tenet, to Israel and the Palestinian Authority in an effort to seek a cease-fire that could eventually

ARAFAT AND THE DREAM OF PALESTINE

lead to a peace settlement between the two parties. Both sides accepted the plan, with some amendments, but Israel never complied.

Troika A committee of three European countries represented by a past president of one of the countries plus an incumbent president of another, and the next president-elect of another one of the countries. They are responsible for steering the affairs of the European Union for a two-year period and they change periodically.

UAE (United Arab Emirates) The strongest and richest Arab Gulf state. It includes Abu Dhabi, Dubai, Qatar, Dubai, Sharja, and Al-Ein.

Waqf An unalienable religious endowment in Islam that was established between the seventh and ninth centuries. It usually denotes a building or a piece of land that is to be used only for Muslim religious or charitable purposes. The Western equivalent would be the common law trust.

PRINCIPAL CHARACTERS

Abu Abbas (Mohammad Abbas) During the 1976 civil war in Lebanon, he and another member of the PFLP, Tala'at Yacoub, led a split in the PLO that was headed by Ahmad Jibril, who had aligned his forces with Syria. Abbas was a charismatic leader who planned many spectacular military operations, the last of which was when he led an attack on the shores of Israel (Tel Aviv) on May 30, 1990. In 1993, he laid down his arms when Arafat signed the Oslo Peace Accord, saying that the time for an armed struggle was over and it was time for Palestinians to concentrate on building Palestine.

Abu Ammar (Father of Ammar) The nickname of Yasser Arafat, head of Fateh and president of the PLO.

Abu Hisham Founding member of Fateh.

Abu Iyad (Salah Mesbah Khalaf) He was in charge of security for the Central Committee of Fateh, and was also the deputy chief and head of intelligence for the PLO. He maintained a bilateral relationship with all European intelligence services. Considered to be part of Arafat's "inner kitchen," he was the number-two man in the PLO after Arafat. He was assassinated in Tunis on January 14, 1991, by an Abu Nidal operative.

Abu Jihad (Khalil Ibrahim Al-Wazir) A leading member of the Central Committee of Fateh. He was in charge of all organizations and activities in the Occupied West Bank and Gaza Strip. He was also one of the leaders of the Intifada. He was assassinated in Tunisia on April 16, 1988 by Israeli Special Forces led by Ehud Barak.

Abu Khaled (Family name: Al-Amla) A colonel in Fateh who split from Arafat in 1982. He was heavily influenced by the Syrians.

Abu Musa (Family name: Maragha) A colonel in Fateh, also heavily influenced by the Syrians, who split from Arafat in 1982 with Abu Khaled.

Abu Nidal (Sabri Khalil Al-Banna) Leader of a radical group of Palestinians who rejected all proposals for a peaceful settlement with Israel. He was responsible for attacks on over twenty countries and for the deaths/injuries of over nine hundred people.

Abu Yousef Abu Najjar A member of the Central Committee of Fateh, he oversaw operations in Lebanon.

Ahmad Jibril He served in the Syrian army from 1956 to 1958. He was kicked out of the army when he was suspected of being a Communist. He founded the Palestine Liberation Front, and in 1967 joined George Habash to found the PFLP. When conflicts arose between Habash and the Syrian government, Jibril, who was loyal to Syria, formed his own splinter group called the PFLP-General Command, which is still based in Damascus.

Ali Doba   A general in the Syrian military who was head of intelligence.

Ali Hassan Salameh (Abu Hassan, also nicknamed "The Red Prince")   Chief of operations for Fateh and for the Black September operation in Munich. He was assassinated by Israelis in Beirut by a car bomb in 1979, as part of their Wrath of God retaliation against his involvement in the Munich killings.

Anwar Sadat   President of Egypt, serving from October 15, 1970 until his assassination on October 6, 1981; close confidant of Gamal Abdel Nasser.

Ariel Sharon   Israeli Prime Minister from March 2001 to April 2006 and former military leader. In 2002, Sharon called for Arafat to be confined to his Muqataa headquarters in Ramallah.

Assad Abdul Rahman   An independent PLO-EC member, formerly in charge of Refugees Affairs Department and chairman of the Palestinian Encyclopedia.

Bachir Gemayel   The son of Pierre Gemayel, he was elected president of Lebanon on August 23, 1982 and was assassinated on September 14, 1982, before he could take office. His brother, Amine Gemayel, served as president of Lebanon from 1982–1988.

Binyamin Netanyahu   Prime minister-designate of Israel as of March 2009. He is chairman of the conservative Likud Party, and was previously the prime minister of Israel from June 1996–July 1999.

Faisal Husseini   One of the Palestinian leaders in Jerusalem who died of a heart attack in the year 2000. He was the son of an important resistance leader, Abdul Khader Al-Husseini, who had protested Jewish immigration during the 1930s and 1940s.

Gamal Abdel Nasser   President of Egypt from 1956 until his death in 1970. He played a major role in founding the Palestine Liberation Organization in 1964.

George Habash   A medical doctor and a graduate of the American University of Beirut, he founded the Arab National Movement and the PFLP. He died of a heart attack at the age of 81, on January 26, 2008, in a hospital in Amman, Jordan.

Ghassan Kanafani   A top Palestinian writer and journalist who was editor-in-chief of the weekly PFLP magazine, *Al-Hadaf.* He also was the author of best-selling novels, many of which are still found in bookstores today. He and his niece were killed in 1972 outside his home in Beirut by a car bomb set by Israeli agents.

Golda Meir   Israeli prime minister from March 1969 to June 1974 and the first Israeli woman to hold this office.

Hafez Al-Assad   President of Syria from 1930 to 2000.

Husni Mubarak   Vice President of Egypt in 1975, and then President beginning on October 14, 1981, following the assassination of President Anwar Sadat.

Jamal Al-Sourani   PLO's former representative in Cairo. He was secretary of PLO-EC (Executive Committee) until April 1996, when he left due to opposition to Oslo.

Kamal Adwan   A member of the Central Committee of Fateh; Adwan was in charge of the West Bank and Gaza.

Kamal Nasser   A member of the Executive Committee of the PLO, he was in charge of information. Nasser was a Christian from Beir Zeit, a village near Ramallah in the West Bank.

Kenneth Kaunda   The first president of Zambia (1964–1991); one of the leaders who fought for and gained independence from the white-dominated Federation of Rhodesia and Nyasaland.

Khaled Hassan   Early adviser of Yasser Arafat, PLO leader and a founder of the Palestinian political and militant organization Fateh.

PRINCIPAL CHARACTERS • xi

King Hussein bin Talal   King of Jordan from the abdication of his father in 1952 until his death in 1999.

Patrice Lumumba   The first legally elected prime minister of the Republic of Congo (June 24, 1960–September 14, 1960). He was deposed in a coup during the Congo crisis that lasted from 1960 to 1965. Lumumba was imprisoned and assassinated on January 17, 1961.

Mohammed Al-Kholi   The Syrian general who was head of the intelligence department for the Syrian Air Force.

Nayef Hawatmeh (Abu An-Nuf)   Born in 1935 in Salt, Jordan. He was the general secretary of the DFLP since its split from the PFLP (which he had helped to found). At the time of this writing, he currently lives in Syria; Israel refuses to allow him to live in Palestine.

Osama Al-Baz   A political advisor to President Husni Mubarak of Egypt.

Philip Habib   The Reagan Administration's special envoy to Lebanon in 1982 during the Israeli invasion. His main goal was to stop the fight and prevent Ariel Sharon from storming Beirut. Habib negotiated the withdrawal of the PLO leadership and the Israelis from Lebanon. The Palestinians complied, while for a long time, the Israelis did not.

Sa'ad Sayel (Abu Walid)   Chief of staff (brigadier general) of the PLO, who was assassinated in 1982 by thirty gunmen as he was on his way to inspect the PLA troops in the Syrian-controlled Beqa'a Valley.

Sari Nusseibeh   The President of Jerusalem University (Al-Quds).

Sheik Zayed   Principal architect of United Arab Emirates (UAE), ruler of Abu Dhabi, and president of the UAE for over 30 years (1971–2004).

Wadi' Haddad   Haddad joined with Dr. George Habash in the establishment of the Arab Nationalist Movement. He became the mastermind of the PFLP's Special Operations Unit. He organized the hijacking of planes as well as such operations as the kidnapping of special Israeli ministers. Israel tried several times to assassinate him by bombing his locations in Beirut. They eventually succeeded through the use of poison.

Walid Jumblatt   The head of the Democratic Progressive Party of Lebanon following the 1973 assassination of his father, Kamal Jumblatt. Jumblatt and his followers have opposed any Syrian intervention in Lebanon's affairs.

Yitzhak Rabin   Prime minister of Israel, serving two terms in office, from 1974–1977 and from 1992 until his assassination in 1995. In 1994, Rabin won the Nobel Peace Prize together with Shimon Peres and Yasser Arafat.

Yitzhak Shamir   Prime minister of Israel from 1983–1984 and again from 1986–1992.

Zaid al-Rifai   Served as prime minister of Jordan twice (May 1973–July 1976, and April 1985–April 1989).

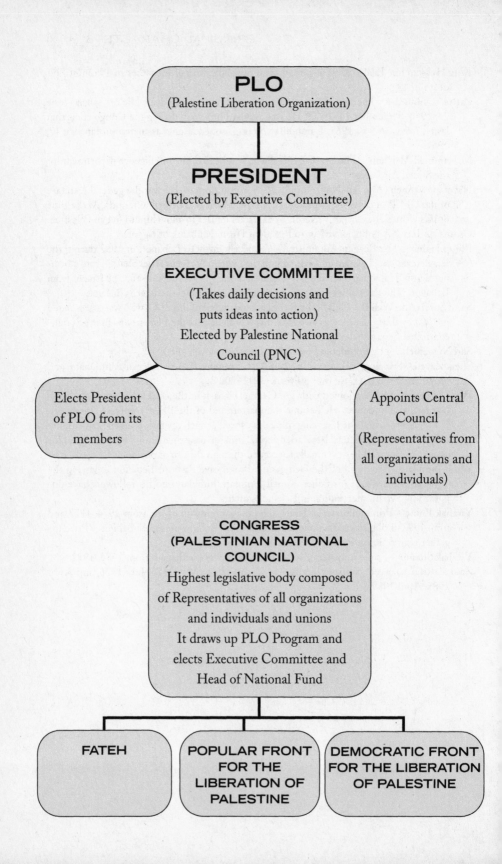

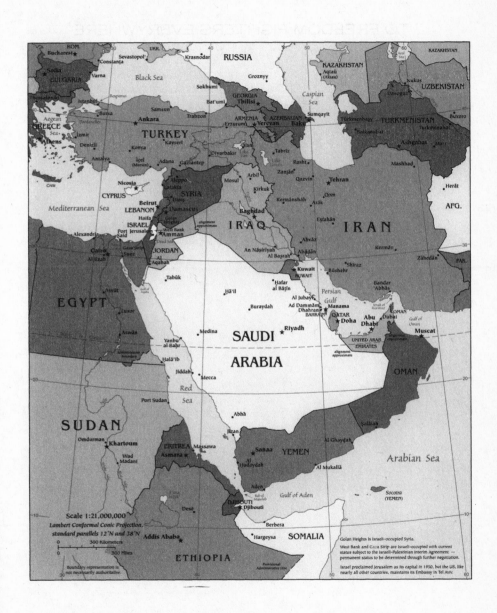

TO FREEDOM FIGHTERS EVERYWHERE

PROLOGUE

T
hough he is not well known, the name Captain Mohammed
Darwish will always remain synonymous in my mind with
great courage. On the evening of April 8, 1993, Darwish and
his copilot, Ghassan Yasseen, were flying a plane that was en-
gulfed in swirling funnels of sand high over the Libyan Desert. Both men knew
that it was impossible to escape the storm. Not only were they unfamiliar with
the land over which they had hoped to land, but most of their instruments had
malfunctioned and they were unable to determine their altitude. Just moments
before, the Romanian aircraft engineer on board the plane had suffered a heart
attack and died, most likely out of sheer terror.

With zero visibility and no chance of making contact with a control tower,
Darwish handed the controls over to Yasseen so that he could go back to the
cabin and confer with their V.I.P. passenger, President Yasser Arafat. According
to the survivors, the captain's words were brief and to the point. "Mr. President,
we are completely isolated. Sandstorms surround us on every side, visibility is nil,
and all our communication devices have malfunctioned. We are somewhere over
the Libyan Desert, not far from the Sara Camp."*

Darwish went on to explain: "We have to make an emergency landing with
no information about the terrain except that it's sand. It could be dunes or flat
plains. Either way, these sandstorms are changing the landscape every second."

Arafat listened and said nothing.

---

* A camp in Libya built for Palestinian troops after they left Lebanon in 1982.

With great composure, Darwish continued: "You must follow my instructions to the letter. Move to the back seat immediately." Arafat did as he was told. Darwish strapped the seat belt tightly around the President, gathered up all the blankets on board, and wrapped them around Arafat's head and body. He ordered Arafat's six bodyguards to surround the president, forming a human shield. They would be attempting to land within minutes; the plane was almost out of fuel.

I can only guess at what Darwish and Yasseen must have felt at that moment, given the gravity of the situation and the importance of their passenger. The future of Palestine was in their hands. Darwish must have known that the only way he could land the plane and ensure Arafat's survival would be to aim the nose of the plane into the ground. That way, the cockpit would receive the full impact of the crash rather than the tail section, where Arafat was strapped down, swathed in blankets and surrounded by several of his loyal men.

When the plane hit the ground, it broke into three separate sections—the tail, the middle, and the cockpit. The cockpit was completely crushed, and both Darwish and Yasseen were killed instantly.

As the stunned survivors climbed out of the twisted metal carcass of the plane, they were blinded by the violent desert storm awaiting them. Sand churned all around them, twisting and turning, biting into everyone's faces, and pushing them along into the howling darkness. Arafat quickly took control. He ordered his bodyguards, who had sustained relatively minor injuries, to search for survivors and to evacuate the plane in case of fire. Besides Arafat and his six bodyguards, there were the three crew members, one who had died earlier and two who were killed instantly upon impact. I was told later that no one could see much of anything due to the darkness and the sandstorm, which made it much more difficult, if not nearly impossible, to locate any potential survivors and tend to their wounds.

When it became clear that the plane was not going to burst into flames, Arafat ordered everyone back into the tail of the plane, worried that predatory desert animals might be drawn to the site by the scent of blood. Guards were set up in shifts to watch for possible attacks.

Arafat ordered that the food and water supplies be checked, but there was not much left of either. Two bottles of water and four oranges were all that had survived the crash. It was decided that these would be carefully rationed. Arafat told the men that although they did not know how long they would have to wait, they needed to prepare for the worst. He asked everyone to save every drop of liquid that they could, which also meant urinating into empty water bottles and then drinking it afterward.

Arafat always carried a survival kit: an army knife, a compass, a needle and thread, a small flashlight, and other gadgets that could prove useful in an emergency situation. Using his flashlight, the president checked the condition of each man, attending to the injuries of many, including Fathi, his closest personal bodyguard. Once he had finished examining everyone, there was not much left to be done except to settle down to wait for a rescue party.

I was working in my office in the Mnazzah Al-Sadis neighborhood of Tunis when I received a call from a ham radio operator, reporting that he had picked up a weak distress signal from Arafat's plane. At first, I thought the call was a prank. Nevertheless, I phoned Libyan officials for news of the president's plane, just in case. I spoke to Abdullah Al-Sanussi, Colonel Muammar Qaddafi's right-hand man, who confirmed that they had lost contact with the plane and were worried because of the intense sandstorm that was still sweeping the area. He assured me that they were trying to get information on the matter from the nearest airport, as well as from their troops in the desert. They had tracked the flight pattern of Arafat's plane in order to determine where his plane might have gone down.

My worst nightmare had happened.

Half an hour later, Al-Sanussi called me back to tell me that they still had not located the plane but that they believed, based on their calculations of flight pattern, speed, and when they had last had contact with the plane, it might have crashed in a desert area near the Sara Camp.

Within hours, the news that Arafat's plane was missing spread like wildfire; reporters began flooding my office. After confirming the news that we had indeed lost contact with the plane, I asked the reporters to wait in the reception area for further developments. I needed to think.

I decided to contact the United States, Britain, and France, the only three countries technically capable of locating the plane—they had the most sophisticated satellites. The Middle East was under surveillance from the satellites these nations had sent up; this was a chance to take advantage of that fact. I knew that it was possible that the satellites could have recorded what happened, and could tell us where the plane was headed and when it went down. That would help us to figure out the coordinates of the possible crash site. I spoke with the director-general of the British Foreign Ministry, and then with the foreign minister himself, informing them both of what had happened and asking for their help in locating the plane. I then called the French foreign minister, asking if the French

Air Force based in Chad might be able to assist us by sending a rescue mission to the site once we had determined the general location of Arafat's plane. Both ministers promised to do their best.

The most important call, however, was to the White House. I asked the receptionist to put me in touch with President Jimmy Carter regarding an urgent matter. I was transferred to the security office and, once my identity was confirmed, I was put on hold as they transferred my call to his residence in Georgia. By the time I had made this call, it was early morning on the East Coast. A few moments later, Mrs. Carter answered the phone and informed me that the president was asleep. But once I explained to her the severity of the situation, she went to wake him up and quickly put the president on the line.

I gave him the preliminary information we had from the Libyans regarding the plane's general whereabouts, and asked whether U.S. satellites, which were undoubtedly monitoring Libya, could be used to help us pinpoint its exact location. The president said that he would do his best, and that he would get back to me in fifteen minutes.

That was the longest fifteen minutes of my life. My hand was on the receiver the entire time, hoping and praying for good news. Finally, the phone rang, and President Carter gave me the coordinates of the plane. I called Al-Sanussi, who was grateful to have the information, but told me that the storm was still raging and visibility remained at zero, which would make starting the search difficult. Since Sara Camp was close to the crash site, I passed the coordinates on to the men at the camp.

As soon as the men at the Sara Camp received the data, patrols headed out into the desert. It was very difficult to move because visibility was still extremely limited and the storm slowed the convoy's progress, forcing them to stop many times along the way to check the compass for directions. Hours passed and they still had not caught sight of the plane. The men were about to give up hope when suddenly a Bedouin emerged from the whirling tornadoes of sand.

"What are you looking for?" he shouted.

Several voices yelled back, "A plane that went down."

The Bedouin volunteered to guide them to the crash site, using his innate desert skills to lead them through the turbulent sandstorms.

The atmosphere in my office was tense. We had no idea what was happening on the ground. All we could do was wait and hope. Hundreds of phone calls came in, all asking about the president. Dozens of radio and television interviews were conducted with local Arabic stations as well as with BBC, CNN, ABC, and

French TV. Even Barbara Walters called. Everyone was speculating about what had happened, and who—if the worst had indeed happened—would succeed Arafat as president.

We rented a small private plane from an Italian company so that Palestinian leaders could fly immediately to Libya, regardless of the outcome of the search. About two hours later, I was informed that the plane had been found and Arafat was being medivacked to the Tripoli Hospital in Libya.

I contacted several leaders of Fateh as well as the PLFP to inform them that a plane was waiting at the airport to take them to the hospital in Libya. No one, including myself, knew yet how badly Arafat may have been injured.

Two hours after I had received the news he had been found, I received a phone call from Arafat. "Thank God, Bassam, I am okay."

I broke down and cried.

INTRODUCTION

I n the 1948 Arab-Israeli War—or *Nakba* (Catastrophe), as it is referred to in the Arab world—armed Zionist gangs like Irgun and Stern, who were supported by British, European, and American Jews, forced hundreds of thousands of Palestinians out of Palestine and into adjacent countries, in defiance of the United Nation's Partition Resolution 181. Passed in 1947, Resolution 181 called for the partition of Palestine into separate states, one for the Jews and one for the Palestinians. This war marked the beginning of the Israeli occupation of Palestine, with the exception of the West Bank and Gaza Strip.

In June 1967, for the first time since 1948, and following the Six Days' War that led to Israel's defeat of the combined Arab forces of Egypt, Syria, and Jordan, the Palestinians had the opportunity to take Palestinian decision making back into their own hands.

During meetings held by Palestinian organizations in Damascus that year, there was talk of establishing a united Palestinian front, aimed at launching an armed struggle against the Israeli occupation. During these meetings, members of Fateh (the Palestinian National Liberation Movement, an organization within the PLO founded by Yasser Arafat) disagreed over who should be their leader. Taking advantage of this situation, Yasser Arafat slipped into the Occupied Territories and spent a long period of time organizing and uniting Fateh associates. When he returned to the PLO's Damascus headquarters, he was elected by his colleagues to be the undisputed leader of Fateh, thus making headlines in the Lebanese press: "Yasser Arafat is the only official Fateh spokesperson." A photograph of him wearing dark glasses was published; this is how observers would always remember Yasser Arafat.

Arafat's rise to power, however, had begun much earlier. He suspended his university studies at the University of King Fuad I (later renamed University of Cairo) to become a volunteer in the Egyptian army during the 1948 war against Israel. In 1956, he joined the Egyptian resistance forces during the Suez Canal War, when the trilateral forces of the British, French, and Israelis attacked the Gaza Strip, Sinai, and the Suez Canal in the hope of gaining control of the canal after it had been nationalized by newly elected Egyptian president Gamal Abdel Nasser.

Upon returning to university, Arafat established the Palestinian Student Union, an organization comprised of Palestinian students enrolled in Egyptian universities, and rented an office that became the working cell for the defense of Palestinian rights. The Union soon grew into a broader organization, the General Union for Palestinian Students, which included all Palestinian students in universities throughout the world.

After graduating from the University of Cairo with a degree in civil engineering in 1956, Arafat headed to Kuwait to work, as did many Palestinian graduates at the time. Because they were highly educated and skilled in such fields as medicine, education, engineering, and economics, to name only a few, these young Palestinians were welcomed into all of the Arab countries. They brought with them the expertise these developing nations needed to build their infrastructures and contributed greatly to the development of the Arab Gulf States.

In Kuwait, Arafat was actively constructing a Palestinian movement aimed at liberating Palestine through armed struggle. He continued working to set up this movement during his stay in Kuwait as well as during his travels to Arab countries to recruit Palestinians for Fateh.

In 1965, the Palestinian National Liberation Movement declared its agenda and initiated military operations against Israel. During that time, Yasser Arafat left Kuwait for Syria and Lebanon, where he and other Palestinian supporters of active resistance to Israel were persecuted and arrested. Because they bordered Israel, Syria and Lebanon were perfect places from which he and his fighters could stage raids against the country. The men kept getting arrested because Arab countries at the time were reluctant to support the Palestinian resistance for fear of Israeli retaliations against any Palestinians residing within their borders. It was common practice for openly rebellious Palestinians like Arafat to be put in jail and/or regularly harassed.

But the Palestinian National Liberation Movement really took off following the Israeli Army's June 1967 defeat of the Arab nations in the Six Days' War. It was then that the security institutions of the neighboring Arab countries changed their tunes. Up to that point they had opposed Palestinian organizations that advocated armed struggle against Israel, but after Israel captured so much Palestinian land, they could no longer practically, morally, or politically justify their persecution of those resistance organizations. Their excuses for "not getting involved" in the Palestine question no longer held up, for Israel now occupied what little remained of Palestine, including the West Bank, the Gaza Strip, the Sinai, and the Golan Heights. The resistance fighters, including Yasser Arafat, seized this opportunity to recruit more fighters and get support from various Arab countries.

Time was of the essence. A network of armed units had to be created within the Occupied Territories and a support base had to be established outside of Palestine.

Three years earlier, in 1964, the League of Arab States had established the Palestinian Liberation Organization (PLO) and the Palestinian Liberation Army (PLA), but these groups still remained under the control of neighboring Arab states (the Arab League) that were making all the decisions concerning the Arab-Israeli struggle. The PLO had obtained the recognition and support of the Arab states, but it still had no right to independent decision making.

The PLO had already established a framework and was recognized by the Palestinians as their legitimate representative, although it was still undecided at the time who would lead the armed struggle. The Popular Front for the Liberation of Palestine (PFLP), founded and led by Dr. George Habash and Dr. Wadi' Haddad in 1968, established in Beirut an axis around which thousands gathered, including Egyptians and, at a later stage, Iraqis. Like Fateh, the PFLP existed under the greater umbrella of the PLO, but it was a more radical group. The PFLP refused to accept any political settlement with Israel whatsoever. Volunteers, many of whom had been smuggled in from the West Bank and Gaza, were taken to training camps in Syria.

Arafat knew that Palestinian control of the PLO would lead to a great push for Fateh and the revolution. The right moment to seize leadership of the PLO came in 1967, when the PFLP refused to take part in the establishment of a new Palestinian National Council, which had the purpose of electing a new Palestinian leader for the PLO. Since the PFLP had a larger membership than Fateh, they could have overturned the elections if they had attended. But the PFLP's absence enabled Arafat to rally followers who supported his presidency, and he was thus elected as the PLO's leader.

Arafat held onto both positions as the political leader of the PLO and the head of the armed struggle on the ground, led by Fateh. This helped him to gain the greatest possible support and protection for the cause. When he was faced with opposition from the general Fateh leadership (the Fateh Central Committee), Arafat could use the Executive Committee of the PLO to exert pressure on them; and when faced with opposition within the Executive Committee, he could then use Fateh to back him up. I always thought this exhibited how clever he was—in order to get what he needed he would play one organization off the other, using his position in each organization to wield the necessary power to accomplish his goal.

Observers in the West never had an accurate impression of Yasser Arafat. They saw him as an unshaven ruffian who couldn't speak English well. He never studied in an Anglo-Saxon nation, so he had not had the opportunity to perfect the language as well as Binyamin Netanyahu, for example, who had grown up mostly in the United States. I noticed that people in the West tend to judge politicians by the way they look and speak, rather than by what they do. Their impressions are often based on physical appearance, which can lead to skewed perspectives. Because Arafat spoke in heavily accented English, people tended to listen not to what he was saying, but how he was saying it. In my opinion, people in the West saw Arafat through the negative propaganda that Israel had spread, which painted Arafat as a terrorist rather than as a freedom fighter. Arafat was easily recognizable by the black and white *hata* he would wear as well as his army fatigues. To Arafat, this meant he was in a constant state of struggle, but to the West, he was seen as scruffy. The West could not help but see him through prejudiced eyes. But those who met Arafat were always struck by his impeccable manners, generous nature, and brilliant mind. He never spoke very much, but when he did he spoke with eloquence and conviction. It was a shame more people couldn't understand his Arabic, because he spoke so fervently in his own language. His sentences were concise, acutely to the point, and factually accurate. He was extremely generous to everyone, helping the poor and sharing his food, even if he had little himself. He was an avid reader and had general knowledge about the world that few ever had the chance to hear. I was privileged to have been able to sit with him on long airplane flights, discussing history and political dialectics with him.

I first met Arafat in Damascus in 1967, when he was campaigning to be elected as the head of Fateh. I was impressed by his high energy and his charisma, and I couldn't help but admire his courage. I noticed that he was hyperactive, unable to sit still for a second. To others, he might have appeared nervous, but I saw in him an unstoppable energy that often consumed him. The first time I heard him say that it was time for us to face our enemy, I saw in his eyes the unwavering spirit of a man who would fight to the death for his beliefs.

Our relationship developed throughout 1970 and 1971 in Jordan, during the events leading up to and following Black September. Arafat was staying in the Ajlun Mountains outside of Jerash, and I had followed him there to discuss our future strategies. I will never forget the sight of him sitting there in that damp cave, the sound of dripping water echoing all around us, while I complained to him about George Habash and the stand he was taking in those difficult times. Even in those harsh surroundings, he retained his dignity and pride. He listened to me expressing my anger with Habash and his inability to see the bigger picture; we both respected Habash but had different views about how we could get Palestine back. Arafat knew that one must fight first, and negotiate later. He knew that concessions would have to be made, whereas Habash did not want to negotiate over even an inch of Palestine. Arafat was always a great inspiration to me.

Our bond grew deeper during the struggles we faced in Beirut from 1972, when Israeli prime minister Golda Meir began her secret war against us with attacks on the Palestinian intelligentsia, including myself, until 1982, when we were forced out of Beirut following the Israeli invasion of Lebanon. Whenever I was going through a rough situation, I would always remember how Arafat never lost sight of his greater vision just because everything appeared to be falling apart all around him. He helped me decide the best path to take when I fell out of favor with the PFLP. He kept me focused when I was feeling angry or confused. He always kept the bigger picture in mind and let the smaller issues slide off his back.

Arafat was a very modest man who lived a monk-like life. I would often find him darning holes in his own socks; he told me that not only did it make them last longer, but when he was darning, he was able to think better. He wore military issue underwear, which was so scratchy I couldn't understand how he could bear it. He told me he wanted to wear the same thing his soldiers were wearing; if military issue underwear was good enough for his men, it was good enough for him. Still, odd as it may sound, whenever I had the chance, I took it upon myself to make sure that Arafat had new socks and good quality underwear.

Arafat was so frugal he would often catch colds in the winter because he didn't see the point of paying good money for a warm coat. I found this rather strange, because Arafat was always cold. Even in the summer, he would always sleep under a warm blanket, while the rest of us were suffering in the heat. Once, when I was in Paris, I bought him a heavy military-style winter coat because I knew he was going on a trip to Moscow. At first he said it was far too expensive and that he couldn't accept it, but he changed his mind once I was able to convince him to try it on. Not only did he like that the coat was just like one Saddam Hussein had, but he especially liked the fact that one of the openings on the side of the coat gave him easy access to his pistol, which he always carried no matter where he went.

Eventually, my official job title became Senior Advisor to the President of Palestine. Arafat sought my advice on everything from major political decisions to how he should handle any domestic disputes he was having with his wife. Although Arafat always treated me as a personal friend, he was often quite tough on me to the point of being unfair. I never resented this, for I understood that I was dear to him because he could see himself in me. We were both Leos, and regardless whether one believes in astrology or not, I found it amusing that we both shared the characteristics that are typically attributed to Leos. We were both enthusiastic about life; we both had broad-minded attitudes about religion, politics, and social issues; both Arafat and I were generous, loyal to our beliefs, and impulsive at times. We both tended to be bossy as well, but somehow we respected each other's boundaries and never tried to overwhelm the other. Both he and I shared the strong ambition to see a state established for Palestine. We both accepted that in this world there were decision makers who needed to be convinced of our vision for our people. I think he liked my adventurous attitude; I was always willing to go into a battle without any thought for myself. He was exactly the same, and perhaps this is what brought us together in our common struggle. Arafat and I were also dialectical in our political vision. On the lighter side, we both enjoyed elegance and admired beautiful women. Because he was hard on himself, he expected the same of me. There were times when I would have little to no food, yet there was always a place for me at his modest table.

I learned a great deal from Arafat. He was very well read and enjoyed sharing his knowledge with me. When we traveled together, I often had the pleasure of hearing him tell the history of the countries we were flying over en route to our destinations. He once told me the history of the Yemeni fleet, which had originated in the *Hadramout* district of Yemen; this area had the most powerful navy in the whole region. He told me how the fleet had reached Indonesia and Singapore. In the hands of the Yemenites, the center of Singapore had become the domain of the Islamic *Waqf* (see Key Terms), which meant that none of the Chinese who came to Singapore could ever own property in that district; it would remain as it had since the days of the Islamic Empire. To this day, the center of Singapore remains a Yemeni Islamic domain.

Once when we were flying over Mozambique, to my delight, Arafat taught me the origins of the name "Mozambique." The Arab leader who had landed on the African nation's beaches was called Mousa bin Shafique, and in time his name and the name of the country became Mozambique. I found that fascinating. I enjoy learning information like that.

Yasser Arafat taught me about the habits and traditions of all the countries he visited. He knew their economic situations, and their social, sectarian, and political problems. For example, he taught me the full history and traditions of the Afghani tribes and the background of the sectarian and tribal conflicts. He knew the names of the tribal princes as well as those of their enemies and the extended family relations between them. It was truly amazing. Traveling with Arafat was always a learning experience I cherished.

What I admired most about Arafat was his iron will, his ability to adapt to change, and his unwillingness to give up no matter how difficult the obstacles might be. His genuine passion for Palestine was what drove him day by day, night by night. He was dedicated to regaining independence for his people. He knew it would be a difficult struggle but he was willing to sacrifice everything he had, including his own life, to achieve his dream of an independent Palestine. Arafat embodied the Palestinians' suffering, their hopes, their dreams, their never-ending fight to achieve their rights as a people who could determine their own futures. His eventual rise to power was based on these characteristics as well as on his uncanny ability to always be in the right place at the right time.

1

THE RISE OF YASSER ARAFAT

On June 5, 1967, Israeli military forces quickly defeated the air forces of Egypt, Syria, and Jordan, and then invaded and occupied the territories of Sinai, the Golan Heights, the West Bank, and the Gaza Strip. Israel had flaunted its aggression against, and forcibly taken, Arab land. An atmosphere of depression, frustration, and humiliation pervaded the Arab world. Thousands of people all over the Middle East took to the streets to express their outrage in huge demonstrations against the United States and Great Britain, whose support and aid to Israel were seen as the main reasons for the Arab defeat.

At the time of the invasion, I was a member of the Arab Nationalist Movement, the purpose of which was the formation of a nationally conscious intellectual elite who would work toward revolutionizing Arab consciousness with the aim of eventually achieving Arab unity and social progress. It had been established decades earlier by two Palestinians, Dr. George Habash and Dr. Wadi' Haddad, along with a number of prominent Arabs from Libya, Egypt, Morocco, Algeria, Jordan, Yemen, Kuwait, and Saudi Arabia. Habash and Haddad were close friends who had studied medicine together at the American University of Beirut (AUB) in Lebanon. Their studies had been interrupted in 1948 by the first Israeli invasion and occupation of Palestine, which established the State of Israel, driving thousands of unarmed Palestinians from their homes. Once the fighting broke out, both men returned to their villages in Palestine—Habash to Lod and Haddad to Safad—to help evacuate their families from the towns in which they had lived for generations. Most of their family members went first to Jerusalem, but then continued on to settle in Lebanon, since the fighting in Jerusalem made it too dangerous for them to settle their families there. When the men finally returned to their classes at AUB and told the other students and their friends about the atrocities they had witnessed, both began advocating for the necessity of resisting in any way they could the Israeli aggression against their people and their homeland.

At AUB, Habash and Haddad had been members of a society at the university called Al Urwa Al-Wuthqa, which had concerned itself mainly with promoting cultural events such as films, folk dancing, and fashion shows. However, following the catastrophe of 1948, Habash and Haddad felt that the society could be more beneficial on campus if it concerned itself with political affairs and helped to bring more awareness to their classmates about some of the social and economic problems the Arab world was facing, with special emphasis on what was taking place in Palestine.

In the early 1950s, they went on to launch the Arab Nationalist Movement, whose members were also university students, in particular those who were planning to return to their homelands when they graduated. Haddad and Habash hoped that this organization would eventually coordinate efforts on a larger scale to serve the Arab cause, which concentrated on unifying the entire Arab world after it had been divided into smaller countries by Britain and France following World War I.

After the Israeli invasion and occupation of Palestine in 1948, the Arab National Movement considered taking the path of armed struggle. Years later, in 1964, the Movement even went so far as to establish a number of militant groups, such as *Shabab Al-Tha'r* (Sons of Revenge) and *Abtal Al-Awda* (Heroes of Return). These groups, however, remained inactive out of respect for the United Arab Republic (U.A.R.), a brief union between Syria and Egypt. Egyptian president Gamal Abdel Nasser, who also served as U.A.R. president, argued that he was not ready to go to war with Israel. Nasser's main agenda item at that time was to establish unity with Iraq, which he hoped would eventually join the U.A.R. Nasser wanted to someday unite the whole of the Arab world under one flag. He had managed to get Syria to join, and was working on Iraq as his next step. Although he was not ready for war, he did promise to train Palestinian fighters and supply them with simple arms in preparation for the eventual fight against the Israeli occupation forces, which was inevitable. He referred to his stand as *fowq al-sifr, taht altawrit* ("above zero and below involvement," also known as "no involvement").

I had officially become a member of the Arab Nationalist Movement in 1963, when I was still a freshman at AUB. That year, I went to Egypt to be trained by Shabab Al-Tha'r as a fighter, and I also received intensive training from the Al-Sa'iqa, the Egyptian special forces.

As Palestinians, our military training took place mainly in camps located in Egypt and Syria. We were taught reconnaissance and learned how to store and camouflage weapons and ammunition inside the Occupied Palestinian Territories. Sometimes we completed observational work for President Nasser by gathering information on Israeli military camps located along the borders with Egypt and Syria. The information included the numbers of troops, types of military equipment, and any troop movements we noticed. During some of these operations members of our groups were shot and killed by Israeli border guards, although what we were doing could not be described as military actions. We were simply involved in normal reconnaissance missions.

The humiliating defeat suffered by the Arab world in the 1967 Six Days' War changed everything for us Palestinians. The Egyptian banner of "no involvement" was soon tossed aside. Dr. Habash and Dr. Haddad took over the leadership of the Palestine branch of the Arab National Movement and began discussions for restructuring it to establish a military unit of fighters from its membership. By then, thousands of young men, including myself, had already been trained as fighters, and strategies to fight the occupation were soon being developed. I was chosen to be a member of the executive committee in charge of the Palestinian branch of the Arab Nationalist Movement along with Dr. Haddad.

The Arab Nationalist Movement Executive Committee met in Beirut in July 1967. Its objective was to decentralize the movement, making each branch independently responsible for its own program, designed specifically for the needs of each country. Previously, the military cells within each branch had been a mishmash of nationalities; there could be a Bahraini, a Qatari, a Palestinian, and a Moroccan in one cell, for example. This was not a good idea since each individual would be looking out for the interests of his own region or nation, very much with a tribal mentality. The Executive Committee now ordered that each individual was to join a cell in his own regional section so that the development of programs would meet the requirements of each individual country. Once members in each cell had been assigned to their regional or country branch, each branch was to draw up its own agenda. A General Secretariat, headed by George Habash, was formed to be in charge of coordinating the decisions made by the national and regional leaders. The Palestinians were therefore placed under a Palestinian leadership and had a new Palestinian agenda. Fateh, Shabab Al-Tha'r, Abtal Al-Awda, and the Palestine Liberation Front (PLF, under Ahmad Jibril) all took part in the Beirut conference.

Fateh was a secret organization that had been founded by Palestinian graduates working in the Arab Gulf States. One of its founders was Yasser Arafat, the son of a Palestinian textile merchant living in Egypt and a Palestinian woman from a well-known family in Jerusalem. After completing his degree in civil engineering from Cairo University in 1954, Arafat moved to Kuwait, where he soon became a successful contractor. He drove sports cars and liked to spend his vacations in Lebanon, like most rich Arabs. By the early 1960s, however, Arafat had started mobilizing and organizing the Fateh movement. Most of its founding members had neither purely secular nor religiously fanatical tendencies.

During the early 1960s there had been serious clashes between Israel and Syria over Israel's plans to divert Syrian water sources to Israel. In particular, the Al-Tawfique region on the border between the two countries experienced heavy artillery fighting in 1964. As a result, the Syrian government decided to allow Palestinian military resistance movements to set up camps in their territory. The Syrians gave Ahmad Jibril, a Palestinian who had joined the Syrian armed forces after the 1948 war and graduated from the Syrian Military Academy as an officer specializing in explosives, the go-ahead to organize the *fidayeen* (which in Arabic can mean either fighters ready to sacrifice their lives, or commandoes) to wage underground military operations against the Israeli army. This resistance movement was initially called the Popular Front for the Liberation of Palestine–General Command (PFLP–GC), but eventually came to be known simply as the General Command. With so many Palestinians joining the PFLP movement, however, Syria began to see it as a possible threat to the regime—unless it could be divided into smaller, less effective splinter groups. Before the end of the year, Syrian intelligence ordered Jibril to split the General Command from the PFLP movement in the hopes that it would severely weaken the PFLP. Since that moment, Jibril remained an obedient officer in the Syrian army, even siding later with the Syrians against his own people during the conflicts in Beirut when the Syrians were vying for control in the 1980s.

In August 1967, the PFLP, Fateh, and other Palestinian organizations such as the Democratic Front for the Liberation of Palestine (DFLP) and the General Command met in Damascus. They agreed that to achieve their common aim of ridding Palestine of its yoke of Israeli occupation, they must unite under the same banner, which was initially known as the National Palestinian Front for the Liberation of Palestine. On the day the announcement was to be made that all Palestinian organizations would join under one umbrella, there were no Fateh representatives in attendance. Why wasn't anyone from Fateh present for the announcement? The reason was really quite simple: Since Fateh had been operating underground for so many years, no real leader had ever been chosen. Since 1965, the members of the Fateh Central Committee, which represented the leadership of the group, had all been considered democratic equals. To be represented in this new federation, however, they would have to name one person as the head of Fateh. The central committee asked local Fateh branches, who were active mainly in the Gulf States, to suggest some names.

Although Yasser Arafat was the most active member of the Fateh leadership (he did everything from recruiting new members, to acquiring arms, to establishing relations between Fateh and the Gulf countries), the other members refused to give him the reins of Fateh. Two days before the Palestinian organizations' announcement, Arafat disappeared. The only trace his colleagues found in his room was a note that said: "The leadership is in the field." The announcement was then modified to include only the members who were present; however, it indicated that the door would remain open to anyone who wanted to join at a later date, leaving the opportunity for Fateh to join the stand of unity once they had selected their leader.

After the committee's decision to blackball him, Arafat decided to infiltrate the Occupied West Bank, which the Israelis had captured during the 1967 Six Days' War. He had thought of doing this before there was any disagreement over who was to lead Fateh, but the timing now was perfect. This way he could prove to one and all that he was a true leader of the group, both politically and in the field. By going to the Occupied Territories of Palestine, Arafat was proving his great courage to face the enemy. He also was proving that he could recruit new members and mobilize his fighters even while they were under occupation. His move was proof that not only was he a brave fighter in the field, but that he also was someone with great political acumen and organizational skills. Right under the noses of the Israelis, he was able to move from place to place to meet with his men in the field without getting caught.

I was later told the details of Arafat's trip to the West Bank by his bodyguard Saleh Nasser, an old fighter from Beit Fourik Village who had traveled with him. According to Nasser, Arafat crossed the Syrian border into Jordan in August 1967, joining up with some of his fighters near the northern city of Irbid. From there, the group headed toward the Jordan River to a prearranged point where it would be easier to cross. Once on the West Bank, they made their way to some caves between the Jordan Valley and the Nablus Mountains, a place considered to be safe by Palestinians who had crossed before.

Arafat pushed the men on relentlessly as they traveled over the rugged terrain by foot. Whenever a member of the group begged for a break, Arafat would usher him along, saying that a fighter never gets tired. Once they reached a prearranged place on the West Bank, Arafat immediately began to make plans. He knew that the Israelis would hear of his presence in the Occupied Territories sooner or later, that he had to make good use of every minute to set up the *tanzim* (military organization), and that, of course, he had to let the fighters know by his presence there that he was their leader. Arafat's entourage spent three weeks sleeping either in caves or under trees while moving from village to village.

One night while they were bivouacked near Ramallah, the roof of their cave began to tremble under the weight of several armored vehicles. They could hear orders being barked out in Hebrew and the heavy boots of soldiers trampling back and forth above them. Arafat signaled his group to remain silent.

For two hours, the Israeli armored vehicles remained parked right above their heads while soldiers searched the area. Finally, the soldiers' voices began to fade into the distance with the diminishing roar of the armored vehicles. Arafat told his men to wait an additional thirty minutes before signaling to Ahmad, a local man who knew the area, to see if it was safe to come out.

When Arafat received the all clear, he turned to one of his men, who knew Hebrew, and asked what the soldiers had said.

"They were looking for you."

Arafat smiled. "Brothers, we are heading for Jerusalem."

Arafat sent some of the men ahead to arrange for the document he was eventually going to need once he decided to leave Israel. The Israeli army had set up increasingly heavy border patrols along the Jordan River. The only way for Arafat to leave was going to be right under their noses.

I was told later by some of the men from Arafat's entourage just how tricky it had been to enter Jerusalem. They had to avoid main roads; they instead traveled along winding side roads that snaked through the surrounding villages. Late at night, they arrived at Anata, a refugee camp located at the entrance to the city. Everything was quiet, lights were out, and no one was in the alleyways.

As they started down one of the alleys, a window creaked open above them.

"Who's there?" a man asked.

"Friends," Arafat answered.

"Do you need help?"

"Do you know where Abu Yousef lives?"

The man pointed to the house opposite his, closed the window, and then disappeared into the shadows of his home.

Abu Yousef, Arafat's maternal uncle, was taken completely by surprise to see Yasser Arafat among the group. He knew that Arafat had entered into the Occupied Territories but he had no idea his nephew would risk entering Jerusalem as well. Abu Yousef was only too aware of the dangers all around them.

"Are you ready, Abu Yousef? We will begin our resistance movement soon. I need you and your men to give your all when the time comes."

"We are all ready."

Arafat looked meaningfully at him. "Is it ready?"

Abu Yousef handed Arafat the Jerusalem ID card that he was going to need to cross through immigration out of Israel into Jordan. The photograph was of someone who looked like Arafat, but the personal details actually belonged to one of Abu Yousef's other relatives. Arafat would leave alone across the Jordan River; most of the men who were with him would return to their own villages.

Early in the morning, Arafat and his men moved toward Jericho, through which he needed to pass in order to enter Jordan. There the men left Arafat to cross through the Israeli immigration checkpoint at the Jordan River on his own, armed only with his fake ID. In 1967, Arafat's face was still relatively unknown, so it was not difficult for him to go through the Israeli checkpoints undetected. Once he made it into Jordan, he headed to Amman, where he spent a few days preparing for a new stage of the armed struggle against the Israeli occupation. He met with the head of the Jordanian branch of Fateh, Kamal Adwan, to plan how arms and ammunition would be smuggled to the fighters on the West Bank. It was obvious that the Jordan River would be the main passageway for the fighters, weapons, and ammunition into the Occupied Territories, but because of increased Israeli patrols along the River, new strategies had to be formulated.

One month later, Arafat returned to Damascus. He took a taxi on his own, and carried a small satchel. Even this time, no one recognized him either as he left Jordan or as he entered Syria. Upon his arrival, he presented to the Central Committee of Fateh a detailed explanation of what he had done inside the Occupied Territories, what the *tanzim* in Palestine needed, and what he had arranged in Jordan. He explained to them how he had managed to meet with several of the *tanzims* in Palestine, and found out what arms they needed and told them what kind of support he was able to get them, both financially and militarily. He then elaborated on how he spent time recruiting new fighters and arranged for any training they required, and how he met with the Fateh fighters in Jordan to discuss plans for transporting ammunitions and arms across the Jordan River, and how various military equipment would be smuggled into Jordan. He told everyone in Damascus that the time to fight had come and that they must all work together.

Arafat had proven his dedication to the cause by taking a huge risk; he personally crossed into Israel at a time when the Israeli authorities were on high alert for any signs of resistance. In addition, his presence in the Occupied Territories had served as a massive morale booster for all the fighters there as well as for all the Palestinians, both inside and outside of the West Bank, who had already lost so much to Israel both in 1948 and again in 1967. The day after Arafat arrived in Damascus, Lebanon newspapers published a short news item alongside what became the iconic photograph of Arafat in dark glasses, announcing him as the sole representative of the Palestine National Liberation Movement (Fateh). This was his first step toward becoming the eventual head of the entire PLO.

Arafat's first order as leader was to gather the weapons and ammunition that had been left in the Golan Heights after the Syrian troops had been ordered to retreat. The area was a prime source for armaments and ammunition. A number of men took on this task, encouraged by Arafat as he drove around in his Volkswagen, pumping enthusiasm into everyone he saw. Once the military hardware had been collected, it was then moved to the Jordan Valley. The larger part of the military hardware would be smuggled into the occupied West Bank; what remained was stored at bases in the Jordan Valley.

Arafat's journey had begun.

2

BLACK
SEPTEMBER

Arafat had been elected head of the PLO in 1968 at the Palestine National Council's elections held in Cairo, but he had not yet secured full control over the group since the PFLP had boycotted the meeting. Arafat had set up some small, unknown Palestinian shadow groups that actually consisted of Fateh members but pretended to represent other groups. These fictitious groups were in attendance in Cairo to secure votes for Fateh's choice for the presidency. Arafat won the election largely thanks to these votes, and to the PFLP's absence from the meeting.

Personally, I believe that Habash, who had depended so heavily on Nasser to defend Palestine, was feeling extremely depressed following the defeat of 1967, and blamed Nasser for his inability to hold up his end of the bargain by failing to stop Israel's occupation of our lands. In my opinion, the reason Habash did not want the PFLP to participate in the PNC elections in Cairo was because he wanted to distance himself from Nasser in any way possible; he no longer trusted him. Although many of us in the PFLP had voted not to boycott the

Cairo elections, Habash managed to get the majority on his side. I believe this was one of Habash's biggest mistakes. The PFLP membership significantly outnumbered that of Fateh; if we had been at the meeting, we would have had the lion's share of the votes. But by boycotting the election, Habash opened the door for Fateh to win the elections, and allowed Arafat the opportunity to take over the PLO leadership with little to no opposition.

Winning the election was a great coup for Arafat since the PLO was already a member of the Arab League, but the organization was still under the control of Syria, Egypt, Jordan, and Iraq. As official head of the PLO, Arafat should have controlled the PLO's official army, the Palestinian Liberation Army (PLA); however, the Arab regimes hosting these brigades maintained control over them. Aside from the obstacles presented by Arab control, the strongest opposition to the notion of a united Palestinian movement was the PFLP, of which I was one of the founders and leaders.

Notwithstanding membership size, the PFLP was stronger than Fateh in many respects. We were better educated than the other Palestinian factions—most of our members were university graduates, which gave us the opportunity to make better contacts with people in powerful managerial and high political positions throughout the region, as well as in the international arena. We were able to communicate well with people from all walks of life because most of us came from middle-class to upper-middle-class backgrounds—we had traveled more extensively and often knew several languages, all of which made it easier for us to contact non-Arabs who supported our cause. In addition, many of our members were not only trained for combat but were experienced tactical officers; this enabled us to accurately plan operations that would inflict greater losses against the Israeli forces and to efficiently coordinate alliances with revolutionary groups.

The mastermind behind the development of advanced technical tools for the planning and execution of these operations was Dr. Haddad. Dr. Habash, however, the secretary general of the PFLP, eventually yielded to Soviet pressure to stop these special operations against Israel. This Palestinian–Soviet relationship had been set up long before 1970, when Nasser had taken Arafat to Moscow to introduce him to the Soviets, and asked them to help Arafat in his struggle against the Israelis. Later, in the 1970s, Habash had been approached by the Soviets, who wanted him to stop all hijacking operations. If he agreed to this condition, they would be willing to set up special arrangements, such as scholarships for students, military training, and arms shipments. Habash liked the arrangement and gave in to their pressure. Wadi' Haddad, however, never acceded to

Soviet entreaties and continued his operations in cooperation with such international allies as the Bader Meinhoff Group (postwar West Germany's most violent and prominent militant left-wing terrorist group), the Red Brigades (a Communist terrorist group in Italy), the Japanese Red Army, and the Irish Republican Army (IRA) in Ireland.

Arafat tried to increase the number of Fateh fighters in the Jordan Valley in order to match the numbers of the PFLP soldiers stationed there. Even though Fateh was leading a growing number of commando attacks on Israeli patrols, military posts, and army camps on the west side of the Jordan River, the Arab world continued to regard the PFLP as the primary organization.

While these operations were taking place in Jordan, the Jordanians were trying to reorganize and rebuild their own army, which had been devastated by the Israelis during the Six Days' War. Because they were concentrating on this effort, neither the Jordanian military nor its intelligence units could stop the growth of Palestinian military bases in the Jordan Valley.

Toward the end of 1969, Israel informed the United States that it was going to strike the Palestinian guerilla bases inside Jordan to stop the incursions they kept making across the Jordan River. Although the United States, seeing Jordan as an ally, did not approve of this action, Israel began making daily air strikes against the bases of the Palestinian *fidayeen*. These sorties, however, failed to deter Palestinian military operations, which actually continued to increase despite the nonstop raids. Palestinian *fidayeen* would cross the Jordan River at night, strike Israeli military targets at dawn, and then withdraw to their bases, which were usually in caves and mountains on the east bank of the Jordan River. In response to this escalation in Palestinian military activity, the Israeli leadership decided to launch a limited invasion of the Jordan Valley, targeting the Palestinian fighter camps. Jordan was powerless to do anything since its army was still in a weakened condition. Civilian villages and camps were being shelled by the Israelis with the hope that Jordanians would see the Palestinians as the reason for the relentless devastation of their homes, and would thus mobilize against them.

It was hard for many of us in the Arab world to believe that we could actually stand up to Israel after our terrible defeat in the Six Days' War. Images of Arab aircraft destroyed while still on the runways, Arab tanks blown to bits, and Arab soldiers being taken prisoner were all burned painfully into our memories. We were still smarting from the humiliation of having lost so much in only six days. And how could we forget how the international media had for months broadcast images of the fighting, and of our defeat, for the whole world to see?

The mainstream media did this, I believe, in order to demoralize the Arab world and to crush not only the Palestinian will to fight against the ongoing Israeli occupation of our lands, but also to serve as an example to all Arab countries what would happen if they decided to stand with us against Israel in our struggle.

Palestinian intelligence in Israel learned that the Israeli military was planning to launch more attacks against our commando bases in the Jordan Valley. The plan was to employ air assaults and land battles to liquidate all of our bases from the north to the south of the Jordan Valley, targeting areas where they believed the Palestinian leadership, especially Arafat, was located, and then withdraw from Jordan. In my opinion, the Israelis must have believed that this operation would be a walk in the park considering how easy the Six Days' War had been.

I had just come from Beirut, where I was establishing the weekly magazine *Al-Hadaf.* I had convinced my friend Ghassan Kanafani to leave his job at a newspaper, *Al-Nahar,* to become the editor-in-chief of our new magazine. After the magazine was safely under Ghassan's watchful eye, I left to meet with Arafat in Jordan, where I was supposed to set up training camps for the volunteers who were coming into the country to join our cause. When I reached Arafat, I found him sitting in a damp cave in the hills of Karameh, a small village located in the middle of the Jordan Valley. Arafat was grappling with a serious question: Shall we confront the Israelis or withdraw? He knew the Israeli army was extremely powerful, and he wondered if we could stand up to them with our limited equipment and numbers. What if we lost? The Arab world was still feeling the pain of the 1967 debacle; another defeat would be a devastating blow and only add to their sadness. But what if we won? That would be a huge jump start to Arab morale. Arafat reasoned that standing up to Israel and giving it our best shot would be better than not doing anything at all. He argued with himself for some time, sharing his thoughts with me as he considered this dilemma. But once he had made up his mind about what he needed to do, he spoke with decisiveness and determination. I will never forget his words: "We will confront them. This is our chance to change the morale of the entire Arab world. We must prove that a small group can stand up to a giant. Even if we die, we will have died trying and thousands more will take our place." He made it clear to all of us that it was immaterial whether we won or lost, for what we were about to do was going to provide a historical turning point in our region.

Some of the fighters disagreed with him and chose to withdraw to the hills, leaving us even more outnumbered, but we remained steadfast. We immediately began to set up defensive lines; some fighters planted mines along the Jordan

River, where the Israelis would have to cross, while others manned the anti-tank weaponry.

When the ground assault began on March 21, 1968, we stood alone against the Israeli forces in Karameh, but not for long. Jordanian forces in Salt, a town in the hills above the Jordan Valley, could see what was happening and informed their headquarters of the attack against Jordan. The Jordanian army received the green light to provide heavy artillery cover for us as we battled the Israeli forces on the ground. When the first tanks crossed the border, we blew them up as soon as soon as they touched Jordanian soil. The Israeli air force began shelling the small villages indiscriminately, leaving many civilians dead and injured in their wake. The Israelis were losing ground troops, so they sent in more troops, which also were bombarded by our forces.

With the Jordanian army pounding the Israelis with their Long Toms and heavy artillery, we had a much better chance of turning them back. Israel had sent in their tanks and armored cars on the ground and they also were attacking from the air with helicopter fire. In addition to the mines we had placed along the roads the Israelis would have to use, we had also stationed ambush patrols all along the Jordan River, right up to the slopes of the Salt Mountains that over-look the Valley, and we stationed anti-tank weaponry in the orchards through-out the Valley. Israeli troops were being hit from all sides; they had to contend with both the Jordanian forces in the mountains and us in the Valley. The battle was long, loud, and fierce. Israel incurred huge losses, something they must not have expected after their easy win in 1967. They had entered into the battle with the arrogance of a victor going on a picnic.

When it was all over, the Israeli soldiers wanted to come in and pick up their dead and wounded. Negotiating through the Red Cross, we granted them per-mission, but only during the daylight hours because we wanted the press to be able to show the world what had happened to the great Israeli army at the Bat-tle of Karameh. Instead of the photographs of victorious Israelis after the Six Days' War, now the international media had something else to show the world: gruesome pictures of dead Israeli soldiers who had been chained to their tanks by their own officers in order to prevent them from deserting; there also were pic-tures of charred and destroyed Israeli weapons and tanks. A handful of Palestin-ian fighters armed with light weapons and backed by the Jordanian artillery had managed to defeat an army many in the Western world considered to be invin-cible. Arafat had been right. With this Palestinian victory at Karameh, Arab pride was revived, and Arabs in the region realized that if they planned well and were united, they could stand up to the Israeli military giant and win. Palestinians had regained their dignity, and Arabs all over the world were no longer ashamed to admit they were Arabs. Donations began to pour in from Arabs and non-Arabs across the globe who supported our cause. Demonstrations took place in many major cities both inside and outside the Arab world that showed solidarity with the Palestinians in our struggle to establish our own country and to secure independence from the occupying forces of Israel.

Thousands of Palestinian and other Arab volunteers began to flood into Jordan to join the fight against the Israeli occupation of Palestine. Operations targeting Israeli military vehicles and soldiers in the Occupied Palestinian Territories increased to an average of ten a day. As a result, the Israelis launched a campaign of arrests of suspected resistance fighters throughout the Occupied Territories. After the Battle of Karameh, the Israelis relied on aerial assaults instead of the land campaigns, for they had discovered that if they faced us on the ground, they would suffer heavy losses.

As daily Israeli air raids intensified against our troops in Jordan, Palestinian troops were forced to retreat into the Salt Mountains. This decreased the size of our fighter bases and the number of our fighters in the Jordan Valley since we had to move farther away from the Jordan River in order to seek cover in the hills. Most of our weaponry was long range enough to just reach the Jordan River from where we were positioned, but the longer distance limited the amount of damage we could inflict on the Israeli forces. When the fighting had intensified between us and the Israeli forces, the Jordanian ground forces joined in, along with their long-range heavy artillery cover. It was very clear to me that Jordan had wanted to make sure Israel would not enter any farther into Jordan under the pretense of attacking our troops.

Once Israel had withdrawn, it was evident to me that Jordan wanted to handle us on their own, with their first show of force taking place in the Jordan Valley. Jordanian roadblocks and army patrols were spread from the north to the south of the valley in order to prevent our *fidayeen* from reaching the Jordan River, where they would have been able to make forays into Israel. These roadblocks and patrols made our operations even more difficult, forcing hundreds of fighters to retreat from the Jordan Valley to refugee camps in and around Amman, such as the Baqa'a camp just north of the city.

As the number of fighters increased both in the Palestinian refugee camps in Amman and in other cities close to the capital, Palestinian groups established their public offices and headquarters in Amman. This was cause for great concern among the Jordanian authorities, who saw the real possibility of Israel targeting Amman and its camps at any time. It was up to Jordan to try to quell the rising numbers of Palestinian fighters who continued to pour into the country from all over the world. If Jordan couldn't stop us from using its borders as a launching pad for our attacks against Israel, then Israel most definitely would, even if it meant occupying Jordan. The ball was now unquestionably in Jordan's court.

3

HIJACKED!

Friction between Palestinian fighters and the Jordanian army increased. The Jordanian government had had three years to work on rebuilding its army, so now the government could concentrate on other domestic issues, which involved the ever-increasing presence of Palestinian fighters in Jordan. They realized that the Palestinian troops themselves had become a force to be reckoned with, and with it the threat of a presence of dual authority in Jordan: the Jordanian government on the one hand, and the PLO leadership on the other. Jordanians wanted to control their own country, and no one could blame them for that. All of the organizations under the umbrella of the PLO wanted desperately to remain strong in Jordan because it was the country that shared the longest border with Israel, making it the perfect place from which to launch operations against Israel. Naturally, the Jordanian government did not want a direct confrontation with Israel concerning the PLO, so it took actions that would keep our fighters' movements to a minimum.

It is only fair here to say that many of the members of our organization started acting quite naive politically by raising signs that featured such anti-Jordanian slogans as "power to the resistance"; this only served to provoke the local regime. To threaten by implication that we wanted to overthrow the Jordanian monarchy was unacceptable to moderates like me. There were also anti-Palestinian groups working under the guise of being Palestinians; they set up illegal roadblocks on the way to certain cities, such as Madaba, where they would stop Jordanian military personnel from going on vacations with their families. Those they had stopped would be arrested and kept as prisoners. These anti-Palestinian groups also spread rumors that we were trying to overthrow King Hussein in order to make Jordan our new Palestine.

The PLO leadership could neither control the juvenile antics that were taking place within its ranks, nor could they put an end to the other anti-Palestinian activities that were making us all look bad. Misunderstandings between the two sides developed, and tensions continued to rise, culminating in the Jordanian authorities' imposition of strict regulations on our movements within the country. Jordan needed to prove to Israel that it was taking strong actions to control us so as to avoid any possible retaliatory air strikes by the Israelis against Jordan. The Jordanians and the Palestinians had tried to come to a middle ground in their negotiations with each other, but they failed time and again.

In June 1970, there was an unprecedented escalation of events. Widespread clashes took place in which the Jordanian army used tanks and heavy weapons against the Palestinian fighters, provoking Palestinian resistance groups to launch counterattacks in the streets of Amman. Members of the PFLP seized control of the Intercontinental Hotel in Amman, taking all the foreign visitors and reporters as hostages. The hostage takers threatened to kill everyone and blow up the hotel unless the Jordanian authorities stopped their assault against the Palestinians.

George Habash called for a press conference at the hotel to list the Palestinian demands. He was willing to release the hostages only if all of the following terms were met: stop the shelling of the camps; release all Palestinian prisoners in Jordanian prisons; and remove the head of the Jordanian army, Zeid Bin Shaker (who was known to be anti-Palestinian). With so many innocent lives at risk, the Jordanian government reluctantly agreed to all of these demands. The shelling stopped.

Jordan was already under a great deal of pressure from Israel to prevent the Palestinian forays across the Jordan River. Israel had threatened to take over the situation in this regard if Jordan didn't. What finally caused Jordan to succumb to this pressure was the PFLP hijacking of four commercial airliners in September 1970.

Masterminded by Dr. Haddad, the plan was for planes of four major air carriers to be hijacked by the PFLP and landed at Dawson's Field, an emergency runway built during World War II by the British in the Zarqa' Desert, east of Amman. All of the flights were destined for New York: A Pan Am flight from Amsterdam; an El Al flight from Amsterdam; a Swissair flight from Zurich; and a TWA flight from Frankfurt. As the PFLP spokesperson, I was responsible for coordinating the landings of all the aircraft while also taking charge of the hostages. This involved selecting the ones we could use for trade, while possibly releasing others who we could not use as bargaining chips. The purpose of these hijackings was twofold: First, hostages who held dual nationalities (Israeli and other), as well as any important diplomats, would be segregated from the others. They would naturally be more important than any of our other hostages because they could be traded to gain the release of Palestinian prisoners held in Israel. Second, and perhaps more important, the hijackings would be an opportunity to bring the plight of the Palestinians to the attention of the whole world.

The El Al hijacking from Amsterdam was not successful; it was foiled by the pilot and authorities. Shortly after takeoff, and once the pilot understood what was happening, he put the plane into a nosedive, which threw the hijackers off balance. Patrick Arguello (a Nicaraguan American hijacker) was hit over the head, beaten, then shot four times in the back by the sky marshal; he died in an ambulance en route to the hospital. One of the Palestinian hijackers, Leila Khaled was beaten, arrested, and sent to London to be imprisoned. The Pan Am plane (which was not initially part of the plan, but hijackers unable to get on the El Al flight out of Amsterdam hijacked it as a target of opportunity) was far too big to land on the airfield, so it was diverted to Cairo and later blown up there once all the passengers had been evacuated. The TWA and Swissair flights were landed safely in the desert. Suddenly, in the midst of all this, we heard about another hijacking, which we had not planned. A call came in to our temporary headquarters on Dawson's Field from a man who said he had hijacked a BOAC airliner leaving from Bahrain, destined for Beirut. He identified himself as Mahmoud Dhaher, a sympathizer to our cause. Dr. Haddad asked him to identify himself better so that he could ascertain if he was a friend or foe, to which the man answered, "Stuffed grape leaves and zucchini." Haddad gave him permission to land at Dawson's Field. The hijacker had mentioned Haddad's favorite dish and only a friend would have known that.

Contrary to the wishes of many of my colleagues, I decided to release all the women and children and anyone else who had nationalities and/or positions that would not have been of use to us in negotiating a prisoner exchange. All hostages deemed liabilities to us, such as children, women, the elderly, and anyone with medical problems, were taken by the Red Cross to Amman, where they were put up at the Intercontinental Hotel. Passengers with dual nationalities (Israeli and something else); anyone who had served as a military pilot in Israel; and diplomats from Switzerland, Israel, Britain, and the United States were held captive.

In the meantime, Israel had detained hundreds of relatives of the PFLP leaders inside the Occupied Palestinian Territories and issued a warning to Jordan that if they did not take action, Israel would conduct a large military operation to free the hostages.

The remaining hostages were moved to a PFLP hideout not far from one of the Palestinian refugee camps just outside of Amman. I made sure they were well fed and had plenty of water. In fact, I made sure the hostages were fed before I allowed my own fighters to eat.

In the United States, President Richard Nixon was informed of the situation; King Hussein discussed what was happening with Egyptian president Gamal Abdel Nasser, who clearly saw the complications of national security and the risks of being attacked by Israel, all of which were arising from the situation. Nasser agreed with King Hussein that in order to avoid Israeli intervention, Jordan would have to carry out a limited military operation alongside Egyptian political efforts to negotiate with the PFLP. Believing that the Jordanian forces would launch a counterattack against us at Dawson Field, we planted explosives in each of the empty planes and blew them up on September 11.

The Jordanian operation, however, was much wider and tougher than originally planned. On September 16, 1970, martial law was declared in Jordan. The formation of a military government was a clear sign that an attack was about to begin. The entire Jordanian task force was put on alert, and curfews were strictly enforced throughout the entire country.

Shortly thereafter, the Jordanian military began intense artillery shelling and tank attacks on PLO offices and Palestinian refugee camps, such as Al-Hussein and Wahdat, in Amman, its suburbs, and other cities, such as Zarqa, Irbid, and Souf. From the onset, Fateh's locations in the suburbs of Jabal Al-Hussein and Al-Hussein refugee camp suffered the greatest military onslaught, leading not only to their fall but to mass arrests of Fateh leaders, among them members of the Central Committee, including such prominent members as Farouq Al-Qadoumi (the chair of the political department of the PLO) and Salah Khalaf (the head of security for the Central Committee of Fateh).

During the attack on Al-Hussein Camp, I was fighting in Wahdat Camp, a Palestinian refugee camp south of Amman, near where the hostages were being kept. We remained in contact with all the fronts. The defense of the camps was carried out by fighters from the PFLP, Fateh, and armed civilians. A united command of Fateh and PFLP leaders was established in every refugee camp to lead the fighters.

Arafat, whose office in Amman had been evacuated, joined the fighters to defend the positions and helped to place barricades at the Maxim Roundabout (now called Firas Roundabout) in Jabal Al-Hussein. The barricades were large enough to at least slow down, if not prevent, Jordanian tanks from entering the Al-Hussein Camp, which was not far from the roundabout. Arafat knew that the barricades were only temporary obstructions, but they would at least give him enough time to move to a more secure location.

Arafat, a group of fighters, and his head of security, Ali Salama, retreated to Al-Hussein Camp and then descended toward Al-Salt Street, which passes the Central Bank of Jordan, taking the long staircase that connected Jabal Al-Hussein to the center of old Amman.

All the streets in that neighborhood were empty. There were no pedestrians, shops were closed, and there were no soldiers or tanks in view. Arafat and his men moved quickly from one alley to the next until they reached the Gold Market near the Grand Husseini Mosque. The location of this mosque in the center of the city is regarded as a pivotal point because it is where all roads in Amman eventually converge. It was nightfall before the men reached the quarters of the forces of Salah Eddin, one of the PFLP officers, who was based at the Al-Ashrafiya refugee camp (to the south of Amman).

A large number of leaders and fellow members of Fateh's Central Committee had already been arrested and killed by the Jordanian army, and it was rumored that Arafat had been one of the victims. In order to dispel the rumor that Arafat had been killed, the Wahdat Refugee Camp was immediately notified that Arafat and his team had arrived at the Al-Ashrafiya Camp safely.

Arafat immediately began to plan where he should set up his new headquarters. It would have to be a place that was both far away from the shelling and unknown to Jordanian security forces. A basement in a deserted building located somewhere between Wahdat and Al-Ashrafeh camps was chosen as a suitable temporary refuge until we could find something better.

The news soon spread among all the fighters and Palestinians throughout the city that Arafat had not been killed and was safe and sound. By midnight, thousands of Amman's inhabitants walked toward the Abu Darwish Mosque, chanting *Allahu Akbar* (God is Great) as they demanded that both sides put an end to the fighting.

The following day, Egyptian president Gamal Abdel Nasser called for an emergency Arab summit to discuss the worsening tragedy in Jordan. Fighting had erupted north of Amman, in the Irbid area, and to the east of Amman, in Zarqa. The U.S. Sixth Fleet had been put on alert. The United States issued a warning to Syria because it had opened its borders to allow Palestinian fighters free passage into Jordan to reinforce the besieged Palestinian troops.

President Nasser wanted the summit to remain in session while a four-member committee of Arab representatives headed to Jordan in an attempt to mediate an agreement between the Jordanian government and the PLO that would end the fighting. Sudanese president Ja'far Al-Nmeiri headed the committee, which also included Sheikh Sa'ad, the crown prince of Kuwait. The committee had been able to contact King Hussein but could not reach Arafat or any of the Palestinian leadership. While the committee was in Amman, Jordanian radio stations continued to broadcast pleas from some of Arafat's colleagues in the Central Committee, asking him to cease fighting as well.

Two days after arriving in Amman, despite its inability to reach Arafat and other members of the Palestinian leadership, the committee issued a statement calling for an end to the bloodshed. They also announced that since they had not been able to mediate a cease-fire, there was no reason for them to remain any longer. The members of the committee would be leaving Amman immediately.

4

ARAFAT'S ESCAPE

With the fighting still continuing and the committee sent by Nasser about to leave Amman, I, along with several of Arafat's inner circle, advised him to contact the committee before they left. We all felt it was advisable for him to give the committee our perspective on the situation we were facing. "And how do you suggest we do that?" he responded. His voice was tense. The Jordanian army had been shelling all of our locations so heavily that it was practically impossible for any one of us, let alone Arafat, to move from one location to another without risking either being killed or arrested. At my recommendation, Arafat went on public radio and asked the committee to meet directly with the Palestinian leaders. The response to his message came at dawn the next day. A meeting between an Egyptian intelligence officer—whose name I never learned—and Arafat was arranged, to take place as soon as possible at our secret PFLP headquarters in Amman. We brought the Egyptian officer to our office blindfolded so that our location would remain secret to anyone outside of our trusted group. Once he had entered the office, we removed his blindfold. When he opened his eyes, he found himself seated at a desk across from Arafat. The officer explained to Arafat that the committee members had decided to postpone their departure after hearing his radio message, and they now wanted to meet with him. The officer was to arrange Arafat's safe arrival at the Egyptian Embassy in Amman, where the committee members were waiting for him.

Getting to the embassy would be no easy task. The road to Amman was fraught with danger: Jordanian tanks were everywhere, and soldiers were patrolling the streets. Besides that, the Egyptian Embassy was also surrounded by Jordanian soldiers, as were all embassies in the capital. Arafat asked Ali Salameh (one of his officers in Fateh) to work with the Egyptian officer to determine the safest way to get to the embassy. The two men decided that it would be best for Arafat and his bodyguards to travel on foot using back roads. That way, they could climb over walls between private homes to avoid any direct confrontations with Jordanian soldiers. The two men also decided that Arafat should enter the embassy through its back entrance, which opened onto a small side road, rather than the front entrance, which was highly visible from the main street. The Egyptian officer was then escorted back to the embassy the same way he had arrived.

Arafat, his bodyguards, Ali Salameh, and I moved after sunset; we knew it would be safer to make our way through the side roads while it was dark rather than to try to get to the embassy in broad daylight. The shelling was severe everywhere. Heavy machine-gun fire exploded all around us, filling the night air with the echoes of rapid-fire and single shots. The landscape that had once been so familiar to me during the years I had grown up in Amman had changed from what I lovingly remembered into a hellish nightmare of burned-out buildings, rubble, black smoke, and gouged-out streets that had been ripped to shreds either by heavy tanks or bombs. I had grown up in this city, gone to school here, and played as a child in these streets. The city of my youth contained many of my fondest memories, but now it had become a war zone, and I was being regarded by the Jordanian government as one of its worst enemies. Familiar faces had been transformed by worry, fear, and sadness over the turmoil, danger, and destruction all around. Common citizens were trying desperately to hide from the raging battle all around them, but they could not escape the emotional one roiling within. No one dared to look out of a window for fear of being hit by a stray bullet or sniper fire. People lay on the floors of the homes they had once considered their personal sanctuaries. I found out later that some people had even hid in their bathtubs to protect themselves from bullets and shrapnel. Perhaps it was best for them not to know that the walls of a bathtub were in no way a match for missiles, shrapnel, and artillery shells.

As we proceeded through the side roads and down narrow alleys, a couple of Arafat's bodyguards would always go before us to make sure the coast was clear before we proceeded from one point to another. When we had almost reached the embassy, I left the group to return to our Amman office. Arafat wanted someone he could trust to be in the office in case anything of dire importance came up while he was in the meeting with the committee. I learned from Ali Salameh what had taken place afterward, as they made their way to the embassy. Once they had reached a small road that was opposite the location of the embassy, two of Arafat's men quickly crossed the street and took up positions within the embassy's garden, where they could provide cover for Arafat as he crossed the street. When Arafat made his move, he was completely shielded by five of his bodyguards. As Arafat waited under cover in the garden, one of his men indicated to the people inside the embassy that Arafat had arrived; the door opened as Arafat, with his bodyguards still surrounding him for protection, quickly made his way through the back door. The door was locked behind him and his guards took up defensive positions in the garden. While this was happening, the sounds of machine guns and exploding bombs never relented.

Once safely inside the embassy, Arafat was ushered immediately into the meeting room where the committee anxiously awaited his arrival. There was no time for greetings, introductions, or personal niceties. The men got down to business as soon as Arafat entered the room. The ruthless pounding of exploding shells and the endless rat-a-tat-tats of machine guns spitting out bullets all around them punctuated every idea and each plan that was being discussed in the embassy that night. The committee presented King Hussein's proposal to Arafat, which called for the following:

1. No armed presence of the PLO in any refugee camps or in any of the cities;
2. All Palestinian forces were to move out of the city into the Dbein mountains and forest in the northern part of Jordan;
3. A committee made up of Jordanians and Palestinians would be the supreme decision makers regarding any future legal problems that might arise between the two parties;
4. All movement of any Palestinians in the country had to have Jordanian permission.

Hussein made it perfectly clear he would not accept any solution that undermined absolute Jordanian control of what was taking place in his country. He was adamant that he alone was the supreme commander of his nation, responsible for its future and security, something he felt we had attempted to undermine. Arafat knew he had no room for argument and that he would have to accept his terms eventually. However, as was his usual way, he wanted to take his own concerns to a broader arena to see what other Arab leaders thought before he made any rash decisions about the future of his people in Jordan.

At the end of the discussion, Sheikh Sa'ad suggested that Arafat go with them to Cairo to join the summit, which was still in progress. Sa'ad felt it would be possible to reach an agreement there in the presence of Arab leaders, given the fact that Nasser had great influence over everyone there. Arafat agreed to make the trip.

Ali Salameh began to draw up a plan to get Arafat and some of his entourage safely to the airport. This would be the most dangerous leg of the journey, as the only route from the embassy to the airport was swarming with Jordanian soldiers and armored vehicles. Ali Salameh urged Arafat to disguise himself in some way. He then had a brilliant idea. Why not dress in the national dress of Kuwait? Unfortunately, the only person who had such clothing with him was Sheikh Sa'ad, who was a very tall and heavy-set man; Arafat was only of medium height and rather thin. If he wore Sheikh Sa'ad's clothes, he would not only be dwarfed by the clothes, but he would definitely trip himself! People in the embassy immediately went to work to shorten and minimize the size of one of Sheikh Sa'ad's robes, haphazardly basting the hem to a shorter length, while doing the same to the sleeves. Ali Salameh said that although they were all under a great deal of stress at that time, they couldn't help but laugh when Arafat donned his makeshift disguise. They were all so used to seeing Arafat in his army khakis and black-and-white *hata*. But time for laughter was cut short once they started to leave the embassy. Much against their wishes, none of the bodyguards who had traveled with Arafat to the embassy were allowed to go with him. Ali Salameh was to be responsible for guaranteeing Arafat's safety on his journey to Cairo.

Three Jordanian armored vehicles had been arranged to transport the committee and, unknown to the Jordanian soldiers driving the tanks, Arafat to the airport. Sheikh Sa'ad, Arafat, and Ali Salameh traveled together in one tank, and the other members of the committee divided up into the other two. The Jordanians had set up roadblocks and checkpoints everywhere along the way. I was told the roadblocks were randomly placed, so they might go along the road for ten minutes, then get stopped and searched; move another fifteen minutes, then get stopped and searched again. The convoy was stopped many times, but even though the vehicles were thoroughly searched several times, Arafat was never recognized by any of the soldiers along the way. His disguise had apparently worked, or at least the members of the convoy were made to feel they had duped the soldiers who had searched the tanks. Although I have no factual proof for my belief, I honestly feel that the plan to get Arafat to the plane was already known to the Jordanian authorities and orders had been given to let him pass. In my opinion, the increase in the number of roadblocks on the way to the airport was used to show that Jordanians were in complete control of the situation, a type of muscle flexing by the government that was meant to keep the passengers in the convoy under constant stress all the way to the airport. Once the convoy finally reached the airport in Marka (the only airport in Jordan at that time), President Al-Nmeiri of Sudan ordered everyone to board immediately. It was still dangerous and he wanted to get back to the summit as soon as possible. I was told that as the plane took off, there was a unanimous sigh of relief from all the men in the group. A new battle was about to begin, one that was much more important than anything we Palestinians had ever fought on the ground. Our new battle would be in the field of politics and would be aimed at stopping the bloodshed in Jordan by creating a deal between the government of Jordan and the PLO.

In Cairo, it was decided that a new joint committee of Palestinian and Jordanian representatives should be formed. It would be their responsibility to come up with a mechanism to implement the proposal that King Hussein had put forward, including the following: All weapons of the Palestinian militia were to be collected and locked up in warehouses under the supervision of the joint committee. By that time, Nasser had passed away and Arafat knew he was in a weaker position without his old ally to back him up.

The truce between the PLO and Jordan lasted for less than a year. By July 1971, the Jordanian army, in what I believe was Jordan's major move to rid itself forever of the PLO presence in Jordan, launched a devastating attack against Dbein, the area to which we had been allowed to withdraw. Part of those troops and a number of leaders, including Yasser Arafat, were forced to move farther north of Amman, to the Ajlun Mountains, near the historical city of Jerash. Arafat's locations in particular were heavily shelled. Other PLO leaders, including Dr. George Habash of the PFLP, were forced to move north toward the Syrian border. From there, the Palestinian fighters crossed from Jordan into Syria, and then into Lebanon. A new stage of our battles was about to flare up again, only this time in Lebanon.

5

WAR AND PIECES
OF THE
MIDDLE EAST

After Palestinian troops had been driven out of Jordan into Syria in July and August 1971, it became clear that Syria, like Jordan, did not want to clash with Israel over the Palestinians. Another place had to be found for our troops or we would be facing the same problems with Syria that we had with Jordan. Arafat knew that South Lebanon was the best place to resume operations, because it was the only other country, besides Jordan and Syria, that shared a border with Israel. When forced to leave Jordan, Arafat said to his men, "The mountain, the mountain, the pinnacle of the mountain," referring to the high mountains they were going to have to cross as they entered Lebanon.

In relocating his troops, Arafat focused on strategic placements that would enable them to hold their positions while launching attacks against the Israeli forces in the north of Israel. Our PLA troops took up positions in the rugged mountains of Al-Arqoub, located in the eastern part of South Lebanon. This mountain range stretches out toward the coastal cities of Tyre and Sidon and fans across the eastern, central, and western sectors of South Lebanon, all along the Lebanese-Israeli border.

Toward the end of 1971, guerrilla operations against Israeli occupation forces began from all three sectors, making the South Lebanon front a hotspot in the fighting. Israel began to launch land, sea, and air raids in return, targeting our troops and refugee camps as well as Lebanese villages, just as they had done in Jordan. It therefore became apparent to me that the Israeli strategy was to harass Lebanese civilians so that they would turn against us, holding us responsible for the attacks.

In 1972, Israeli prime minister Golda Meir decided to wage a secret war of terror against the PLO and the Palestinian leadership in retaliation for the Munich Olympics hostage crisis.* She also gave the green light to the Mossad (the Israeli Institute for Intelligence and Special Operations), Israel's national intelligence agency, to target key civilian leaders in our movement. The Mossad tried to assassinate Wadi' Haddad, the mastermind of the PFLP's special operations, by shelling his apartment in Beirut with rocket fire. He survived the attack with only minor injuries. Having failed to kill him at home, Mossad bombed Haddad's headquarters in the mountains, but he was not there at the time. They even tried mailing him an explosive package but sent it mistakenly to another man whose name was also Wadi' Haddad, and killed him instead. Mossad also started to direct their attacks against "soft" civilian targets: intellectuals, writers, and other artists who were neither involved in our military nor in any operations against Israel.

On July 8, the Israelis assassinated my dear friend Ghassan Kanafani, one of the top members in the political bureau of the PFLP and one of our most widely published authors. I had also worked closely with him for a few years on *Al-Hadaf,* our PLO magazine, of which he was the editor-in-chief. I was so saddened by his death; only thirty-six years old when he was killed, he had already published over thirty-six books, many of which had been translated into several different languages. He was a scholar of great importance to the Palestinian people and to the world. He fought with his pen, and for that he was blown up with his young niece as they were leaving for his office that fateful day in 1972.

---

* Eleven members of the Israeli delegation to the 1972 Munich Olympics were held captive by the Black September group and were killed with their captors when the German authorities' rescue operation went wrong.

Then on July 25, the Israelis attempted to assassinate me in Beirut with a bomb hidden in a book that was mailed to my office at *Al-Hadaf* in Beirut (I discuss these events in full detail in chapter 6). Dr. Anis Al-Sayeg, head of the Palestinian Research Center, was also targeted during that time.

In April 1973, members of Mossad assassinated three of our leaders at the same time: Kamal Adwan, a Central Committee member in charge of Fateh operations in the Occupied Territories, was gunned down in his own home in front of his wife and children. Kamal Nasser, a member of the PLO's Executive Committee and a famous poet in his own right, was also murdered at home as his family was forced to watch in horror. He was the only Christian among these three men. The Israelis left him dead with bullet wounds in the shape of a cross on his chest. Abu Yousef Al-Najjar, who was in charge of Fateh operations in Lebanon, was gunned down in his apartment as well.

Fateh, the PFLP, and other groups responded in kind with retaliatory operations that were planned by Wadi' Haddad. One such operation was an attack on May 30, 1972, in which three members of the Japanese Red Army, on behalf of the PFLP, killed twenty-six people and injured eighty others at Tel Aviv's Lod Airport (now called Ben Gurion International Airport). We had close relations with the Red Army mainly because they were dedicated to assisting revolutionary groups in the Third World, regardless of political affiliation. This group also believed that helping the PFLP was another way to fight capitalism in the world. Another operation took place when a Palestinian suicide bomber detonated himself in the middle of a market in Tel Aviv, leaving many dead and wounded.

At the same time, Israel carried out a widespread naval landing operation on the shores of West Beirut, reaching all the way to the Al-Fakahani neighborhood, an inland area full of PLO offices. The Israeli troops blew up several of our offices, including those of Yasser Arafat. They must have been disappointed to find out that he had not been there, but would have been even more surprised had they known he had slipped out unnoticed just days before, right under the noses of their own special forces units. Arafat was known to be a master of disguise and someone who could remain cool headed in the most dangerous situation.

In September 1973, Egyptian president Anwar Sadat issued an invitation to Arafat to visit him in Cairo. His intention was very clear: He wanted to meet personally with Arafat to discuss his plans for how he was going to take back the Egyptian territory in the Sinai Peninsula that Israel had captured during the Six Days' War. On November 22, 1967, the UN Security Council had adopted Resolution 242, which called for a Middle East peace settlement contingent upon Israel returning to the Arab states all the lands they had forcibly taken during the war, but Israel had never complied. Sadat had urged the United States to persuade Israel to implement the resolution, but all the efforts the United States had put forth had been to no avail. Israel was adamant about keeping what they had taken from Syria, Egypt, and the Palestinians. Sadat had decided the only way to get Israel to abide by the UN Resolutions was to use military force, and he wanted to know if he could count on Palestinian support. Syria was planning a similar attack in order to win back the Golan Heights.

The UN Resolution 242 also called for the withdrawal from the West Bank and Gaza, but in this regard as well, Israel had blatantly thumbed its nose at the United Nations. Arafat looked at the big picture. Palestinian forces could not wage war against Israel alone, but as a junior partner with Egypt and Syria, we stood to benefit a great deal.

Arafat headed to Cairo accompanied by a number of Fateh leaders, including Salah Khalaf (Abu Iyad, the number-two man in the PLO), Khalil Al-Wazir (Abu Jihad, the man in charge of the organizations and activities in the Occupied West Bank), and Hayel Abdel Hamid (Abu Hol, the head of the security for Fateh), to meet with President Sadat. Those of us not involved in the meetings did not know why the men were going to Cairo until much later, when Arafat spoke with George Habash. When the delegation returned to Beirut, Arafat called for a joint meeting of Fateh and PFLP leadership, and the two branches of the PLO formed an alliance. The Central Committee of Fateh and the Political Bureau of the PFLP agreed to escalate our ongoing attacks against the Israeli forces and the Mossad. This led many Palestinians to have greater confidence in the eventual success of the resistance movement now that we were united as one fist. Arafat wanted to make sure the PLFP and Fateh were united before he told them what Sadat had up his sleeve.

I was with Arafat when he spoke with George Habash at the end of the session, when he informed him that President Sadat was planning a war against Israel to get the Sinai back. Habash was skeptical, pointing out that Sadat had declared such intentions several times in the past, but he had never followed through. Arafat's view was that we had to be prepared either way. I remember him saying: "Whoever participates in the war will reap its results, whether they are good or bad. But whoever does not participate, will lose for sure."

Preparing for the eventuality of war, Arafat began visiting all of his military sites in South Lebanon. He checked their heavy-weapon capabilities, noting the range and effect of every piece of artillery while he also worked with his military commanders to draw up a plan for advancing the troops toward the higher grounds of the Occupied Palestinian lands on the West Bank. He also rallied the officers of the Palestine Liberation Army, serving in Syria under the Syrian military command, encouraging them to do their best to support the Syrian forces should the battle begin.

Arafat planned for every eventuality. Unlike most of his advisors, he never doubted Sadat. On October 6, 1973, the Egyptian army launched a major assault against the Israelis through the Suez Canal by using water pumps to blast down the Israeli-made Bar-Lev Line (see Key Terms) of dirt, clay, and concrete. Palestinian commando troops simultaneously began to carry out attacks on Israeli troops stationed in the Golan Heights, opening the way for the advancement of the Syrian forces. Other Palestinian troops advanced from the mountains of Al-Arqoub in Lebanon toward the high hills of Jabal Al-Sheikh in occupied Syria (Mount Herman) to join the Syrian army in the battle.

From our location in the Baqa'a operations room, positioned between Syria and Lebanon, Arafat received news that the Egyptian advance through the Suez Canal had been successful. We also learned that the Egyptian troops had smashed through the Bar-Lev Line and were moving toward the Sinai. In addition, the Palestine Liberation Army was in control of the Golan Heights, despite the heavy price they had paid in casualties, awaiting the arrival of the Syrian troops.

The Egyptian, Syrian, and Palestinian armies were all doing well. Israeli general Moshe Dayan had told Golda Meir that he was planning to go on television to explain to the Israeli people their "invincible" army had collapsed in the face of the surprise attack. They had lost over 2,400 soldiers and more than $5 billion in lost equipment. Not wanting to admit defeat, Meir placed a call to President Nixon demanding U.S. aid. An Israeli officer (a friend of mine whose name I cannot reveal) told me that her message to the president was simply: "Save Israel." But an American officer (another friend whose name I also cannot reveal) told me that Golda Meir's request also contained a threat: "If the United States does not intervene, I am prepared to use nuclear weapons."

On October 25, the United States moved its naval fleet of aircraft carriers near the shores of the Sinai, landing huge helicopters, transport planes, and tanks equipped with fuel and ammunition to support Israel in its ongoing battle with Egypt. With this added military support, the Israelis were able to push the Egyptian army back to the other side of the Suez Canal. President Nixon then called Sadat, warning him that the United States would intervene directly with

U.S. troops if he did not halt the advancement of his army. Sadat knew he could not withstand the full force of the U.S. military, so he ordered his troops to stop.

The end to fighting on the Egyptian front enabled Israel to send a large brigade to attack and reoccupy the Golan. U.S. intervention had radically changed the balance of power in the war. The slopes of Jabal Al-Sheikh in Syria, however, still remained under Palestinian control.

The clashes between Israeli and Arab troops in the Golan and Jabal Al-Sheikh continued for a hundred more days. The conflict became known as the October or Ramadan War. With the support of U.S. secretary of state Henry Kissinger, Sadat was hoping to engineer a disengagement agreement between Israel, Egypt, and Syria. Meanwhile the United States continued to pour military and financial aid into Israel not only, I believe, as compensation for all the equipment it had lost, but also to ensure its qualitative and technical superiority over all the Arab countries put together. In spite of this, Arafat believed that a political solution was quietly being put together that would allow Egypt and Syria to reclaim their respective territories—the Sinai Peninsula and the Golan Heights—and he wanted to make sure the solution would include Palestine. He convened the Palestinian National Council (see Key Terms) in Cairo in 1974, knowing that Sadat would open the session by speaking about the political implications of the October War. Since Arafat believed the war had opened the eyes of the United States to the fact that Israel had still not honored its agreement to withdraw from all lands occupied in 1967, he was hoping Palestine could also be included in Sadat's speech about what the United States might do to force Israel to comply.

Sadat met with the Executive Committee of the PLO, preparing them for the implications of the possible implementation of Resolution 242. Sadat knew it would not be easy to get all Palestinian factions to agree to a resolution that meant they would have to agree to relinquish the chance of getting most of Palestine back. There were still people in the PLO who hoped to get the whole of Palestine back, including the land that had been taken in 1948. Sadat knew that was a lost cause, but it would still be hard to convince the Palestinian die-hards of that fact. Following heated discussions and some tricky maneuvering, Arafat got the council to agree to his ten-point agenda, which tentatively acknowledged PLO acceptance of a political solution that would allow the PLO to impose its national authority over a small part of Palestine (i.e., the Occupied Territories of the West Bank and Gaza) following Israel's withdrawal if it would only agree to comply with UN Resolution 242.

Arafat's vision of a Palestinian state began to take form. The battle he had fought would lead, he hoped, to Israel's withdrawal from lands it had occupied in 1967, so he shifted to a political agenda the goal of which was the establishment of an independent Palestinian state on those lands. The problem was that most Palestinians strongly objected to such a compromise, feeling that they should also get back the lands taken in 1948.

The Palestinian people entered a period of deep political division. The tremors following the October War had shaken all previous concepts related to Israel and the Arab nations. For example, the Bar-Lev Line had been regarded as impenetrable until the Egyptian forces proved it could be melted down into mush by the simple application of water power. The Israeli army had also been considered invincible, but Syria, Egypt, and Palestine had proved that it could be beaten. The new reality was this: if the Arabs joined forces and planned well, they could form one powerful fist capable of bringing down Israel's Goliath. The Arab states had to reach a consensus concerning UN Resolution 242 or political extinction for the Palestinians would be inevitable. Without Israeli withdrawal from the Occupied Territories, the Palestinians would remain dust in the wind without any state to call their own.

In 1977, a new session of the Palestinian National Council was called in Cairo. Sadat opened the session and talked frankly about a possible political agreement that would unify the Palestinians in what they were willing to accept in terms of Israeli withdrawal. Israel was there to stay and Sadat knew that, and, like it or not, it was a fact we had to accept. In a private session with the Executive Committee, which I was allowed to attend even though I was not a member, Sadat appealed to the Palestinian leadership to come to a consensus before it was too late. He was very direct: "An independent Palestinian state in the West Bank and Gaza Strip is the most you can hope for. Perhaps achieving this goal requires a second war, but we will do our best to help you if you rely on God and make a decision."

The Palestinian National Council came up with a political agenda that was filled with ambiguities and avoided the question at hand: Would the Palestinians accept a state that existed on their own land that had been occupied by Israel since 1967 and forget everything that had been lost in 1948? I said that another armed struggle would effectively emphasize the need of reaching a political solution, rather than achieve a victory against the Israeli military. The balance of power was very clear and would remain so for scores of years to come: The United

States would continue its support of Israel, thereby guaranteeing its military superiority over all the Arab countries.

We had been receiving weapons from the Soviet Union, as had many of the Arab countries in the region. Our weapons, however, were not even close to the firepower and high-tech military weaponry that Israel was receiving from the United States. After the Soviet Union fell apart, it became even more apparent that the weapons that they had been supplying to the PLA and all the Arab states were ones Soviet forces were no longer using; the fighter planes were at least five generations behind the ones the Soviets had in their own arsenal. In my opinion, and based on what I saw happening militarily in our region, this arrangement must have been agreed to between the superpowers in order to maintain an imbalance of power in the region that favored Israel.

A Palestinian state in the West Bank and Gaza Strip was to be the goal for us Palestinians, even if it would be a difficult one to attain. While working to achieve this aim for his people, Arafat also had to deal with Arab regimes that were unwilling to negotiate with Israel about anything. This is why Sadat's decision in the coming months to sign a peace agreement with Israel was such a shock to us all.

6

BOOK BOMB

After the death of Ghassan in July 1972, I assumed his responsibilities as the editor-in-chief of *Al-Hadaf*. Since I had been the deputy editor under Ghassan, it was natural that I would take over. Knowing that I, too, would be a target of Mossad, I took extra care to ensure that all mail coming into our office was double-checked for explosives. We asked the Lebanese government for a bomb detector, but the minister of communications, Jamil Kubbeh, said we could have all our mail passed through the machines the government had at the main post office in Beirut before it was sent over to us. I also made sure that even after the mail had cleared the machines at the post office, it was rechecked by members of the PFLP at the *Al-Hadaf* office.

I often worked late into the night and arrived at the office each day at about 11 a.m. But on July 25, 1972, I woke up at 6 a.m. for no particular reason. I don't know why, but instead of going back to sleep, I felt a very strong urge to go to my office as soon as possible.

My driver had not yet arrived as he was under orders to pick me up each morning at 10 a.m. After what had happened to Ghassan, the PFLP leadership had decided that our cars should not be parked in the street outside our homes. They would be easy targets for anyone to plant explosives. For this reason, our cars were kept overnight with our drivers under their protection. Before they would get into the cars, they would do a thorough check for any explosives. As heartless as this might sound, it meant that if there was any sort of car bomb placed in our vehicles, our drivers would be killed, not us. By about 7 a.m., much to the dismay of my neighbor, who knew my usual routine and was worried about my safety and wanted me to wait for my driver, I threw caution to the wind and took a taxi on my own to the office.

When I arrived that morning, there was only one guard on duty in the lobby. There were usually two stationed there, and when I asked where the other guard was, I was told he had gone out for a bite to eat. We greeted each other warmly as we always did and I continued on into my office. As I sat reading the newspapers, another employee arrived with five bags full of mail. It was office procedure to record all incoming mail, so he took them into the mail room and started to make his daily log of what had arrived, from where, and from whom.

About fifteen minutes later, he called me on the phone to tell me a special package had arrived for me and that it had the Lebanese security clearance marks on it, which meant it had been cleared officially at the post office. I went to the mailroom and saw a large yellowish manila envelope on one of the tables with all the rest of the mail. On the outside, written in bright green ink was my full name, Bassam Tawfiq Abu Sharif. Since most of the mail that came to the office was addressed either to *Al-Hadaf* or to my pen name, Bassam Zeyed, I became instantly curious. The package was slightly opened, and I could see a large book, about the size of a dictionary, sticking out of it. I love books and was especially excited when I saw that this one was about Che Guevara, the Argentinian revolutionary who helped achieve freedom for Cuba and had always been one of my special heroes. Because the security stamp that stated "Clear of Explosives" was clearly showing on the envelope, I felt it was safe to open the package. I also thought that Abu Shafiq, the man responsible for double-checking our mail, had also checked everything for explosives. I pulled the book out of its opened envelope and began flipping through the pages. Suddenly, I saw what I never thought I would see in a book—a bomb. The book had been hollowed out, and I remember seeing two brownish-colored explosive charges, realizing in a split second that they were meant to explode me into pieces. All I could do was turn away, holding my hands up in front of my face to try to protect my eyes. I heard a click, and in that instant, my life changed forever.

There was a deafening sound, and then silence. I could feel my skin tearing and melting off my cheeks. Everything around me went black. I could still feel my skin shredding off my face, but I was beyond pain by then, falling into a deep, dark pit of emptiness as sharp volcanic rocks ripped and tore at my hands. I continued to fall into a bottomless chasm of darkness and silence, until I started to hear an eerie howling inside of my head. I thought, "So this is the end. But the end is too dark. No light?" I felt I had been sent to Hell. I was melting from the heat. My first thought was there was no Heaven for me after all! It was strange, but I thought about Ghassan. Since he had died, I had thought about him a great deal. I thought that if there is an afterlife, then he and I would more than likely meet up again somewhere, sometime. We were so much alike, always dancing, surrounded by beautiful women, both of us in love with life. Now both of us were dead.

Suddenly, I stopped falling. I could feel the floor beneath me and realized that I wasn't dead after all. I came to the conclusion that whoever had sent me the bomb must have meant to hurt me, not kill me, so that they could kidnap me. I had to run! But when I stood up, I couldn't see. I felt along the wall, heading for where I thought the exit would be. (I later saw photographs of those walls; my blood was smeared all along them. I also discovered that the guard and the man in the mailroom had run away when the bomb went off, never to be seen again.)

As I got nearer to the door and I could feel the outside air hitting my wounds, I was overcome with excruciating pain. I could feel that my right eye was dangling down on my check. It felt like a bulbous teardrop. Pain burned through my face, my chest, my thighs, my legs. I could feel blood pouring from my hands, down my face and from wounds all over my body. Finally, just as I was approaching the main door, I felt two very strong hands grab my shoulders. Were these the kidnappers? I had no idea at the time, but I later found out that two complete strangers, a shopkeeper and a taxi driver, had heard the explosion and came running to see what had happened. These two were the only ones who had the courage to come and help me.

"Who are you?" I asked.

There was no answer.

"Who are you?" I asked again. "What do you want?"

Still no answer.

I didn't realize it at the time, but I had been deafened by the explosion. I knew I had been blinded because I couldn't see anything at all. Both my eyes had been damaged severely. I thought for sure that I was being kidnapped; why else would no one be answering me?

I could feel myself being led down some stairs and then helped into the back seat of a car, with a person on each side of me. I later learned that one of the men who worked at *Al-Hadaf* had just arrived to work when the two men were bringing me out of the building. He drove the three of us to the hospital.

"Take me to the AUB Hospital," I remember thinking to myself. I didn't care if I was being kidnapped anymore. I was starting to have difficulty breathing; I was drowning in my own blood, suffocating with every breath I took.

I needed air. I was struggling to breathe but still conscious. I can remember the car speeding along then slowing down, going over a big bump. It was then that I realized we had arrived at another hospital, the Maquassed Hospital, which was closer than the one at the AUB.

The last thing I remember was an oxygen mask being placed put onto my face, and then I passed out.

Eight days later, after nine hours of surgery by a team of four specialists, I was wrapped up like a mummy, my lips swollen from the burns I had sustained. I woke up to a voice calling my name from what seemed like a far off mountain.

"Do you hear me?" it was saying.

"Yes," I croaked, not sure whether I was hallucinating or not.

"Do you know who I am?" the voice shouted again.

I recognized the voice as belonging to an old AUB classmate, one of my dearest friends to this day, Dr. Assad Abdul Rahman, a leader in the PFLP. I felt safe just knowing he was there. And then I passed out for another four days.

One of the most critical times of my recuperation period came many days later when I was able to remain awake for longer periods of time. I could feel that my body, hands, head, face, and eyes were all wrapped tightly with heavy bandages. My thighs, legs, and chest were so heavy I felt as if I was being weighted down with tons of dry mud.

On another day, I felt a hand on my shoulder; it was Assad again, sitting by my bed. I whispered hoarsely to him, "Assad, you know me well. You know I am a strong man with an iron will. I can face hardship and even death bravely. Please describe to me every inch of my body and tell me exactly what I look like." He was hesitant at first and kept stopping to clear his throat, holding back his tears. Finally, he began describing the brutal truth to me, shouting at the top of his lungs into my right ear so that I could hear what he was saying. He told me I had completely lost one of my eyes and the other one was so terribly damaged the doctors didn't know if they could save it or not. He went on to say that I had lost many of my fingers and part of my face. My teeth had all been blown to bits and I had burns over most of my body. He described gashes on my neck, shrapnel everywhere and both of my ear drums had been damaged terribly by the blast. I tried to imagine the horrific creature he was describing, still unable to fully comprehend the magnitude of my injuries. Once he finished telling me the terrible truth of my disfigurement, I thought, "Oh my God! Have they done all that to me?" I was so overwhelmed by what he had told me that I slept again for another four days.

Over the months, I had several operations on my remaining eye, leaving me each time wrapped up like an Egyptian mummy. One day, when the bandages were to be removed, several doctors entered my room and began discussing my situation. My friend Assad and another member of the PFLP, Sharif Al-Husseini, were also in my room to find out if the doctors had been able to save my one remaining eye. They had also told me that hundreds of our fighters were waiting outside the hospital, anxious to know my condition as well.

The doctors were speaking in Arabic about me, so I asked them in Arabic to talk to me about my condition. They switched to French, thinking I would not understand, but were surprised when I asked them the same question in French. Then they tried speaking English, but again I understood. They soon realized that they would have to speak to me openly about their prognosis. There would be no secrets from me! They told me they had tried hard to save my sight, knowing how important it was for me to read and write, but they had little hope that their efforts would be successful. I told them to go ahead and remove the bandages. I was anxious to know the outcome even if it was bad. I had to know if I could see so that I could get on with the rest of my life.

I could feel the bandages being unwrapped. I opened my eyes, and the doctor asked me, "What do you see?"

I said, "Nothing." Then he pointed a flashlight toward my eye, and I could see a hazy light. When I told him I could see some fog, he was delighted!

"Fog? Everything isn't black?" The doctors began buzzing excitedly around me. Still pointing his flashlight into my eye, the doctor kept moving farther away from me, asking me repeatedly what I could see. I told him again I could see fog. Finally, he was standing at the foot of my bed. "What do you see now?" he asked.

"I see you pointing your flashlight at me!"

Al-Husseini ran out of the room, excited to tell everyone waiting outside the hospital that I could see. The sound of hundreds of machine guns firing into the air rang out in jubilation! Women in the street began to ululate as the guns continued to fire round after round.

One day, while I was still recuperating in the hospital, I started to feel a bit stronger. I got out of bed and made my way slowly to the bathroom to have a look in the mirror. I had not yet looked at myself, and I knew I had to face the reality of what I looked like after the blast. The face that stared back at me from the mirror was not mine. I saw a gaping hole where my right eye had been; half my face was gone, ripped back, revealing my shattered teeth. I looked like a monster. My skin was charred coal black and what was left of my lips was swollen, torn, and bruised. I was overwhelmed with grief. My thoughts were so confused: What have they done to you, Bis-Bis [my nickname]? What have they done? What happened to the handsome young man who had the entire world at his fingertips? I sadly made my way back to my bed and sank into a deep depression.

For the next six months, I had to undergo more operations in order to remove all the shrapnel (wood, glass, and iron) still lodged deeply in my body. I had several plastic surgeries on my face and hands, skin grafts, and operation after operation to save the retina on my remaining eye. One of the doctors told me later that when I was first brought in, he didn't know where my face or extremities were. He said I looked like a burnt, blackened tree trunk instead of a human being. When I left the hospital, I weighed less than 45 kilograms (90 pounds). With all my teeth broken and my face ripped off in several places, I was unable to eat anything for months. I had been kept on intravenous feedings all that time.

The doctors had saved some vision in my left eye, but they told me that I would never be able to read again. I then asked my ophthalmologist if there were any specific exercises for the eye that I could do. I was willing to try anything that might restore enough of my eyesight to enable me to read. What did I have to lose, after all? He told me he wasn't sure, but he would research it and get back to me. The next time he came to see me, he brought me some good news. He told me he had found some retinal exercises that I could do, but he didn't know if they would really work or not. He told me I would have to stare at the same color for six continuous hours every day for six straight months and this was supposed to strengthen my retina. Even before I left the hospital, I started doing the exercises he had told me about. I chose to stare at light blue because it made me think of the clear blue sky and the Mediterranean Sea I loved so much. I also found the color soothing to my mind. I have to admit those exercises were nerve-wracking, but I followed his instructions to the letter, and I am happy to say they worked. At the end of the six months, I was able to read again. Not as well as before of course, but at least I could read with special glasses.

You see, I am a fighter. I know that if I set my mind to doing something, I can do it.

I am often asked if I am embittered by what happened. I was at first. I cursed myself for letting the Israelis score a hit against us. They won when I opened that book, and that angers me to this day. And yes, I wish I could hear better and that I could read for longer periods of time without getting tired. And I wish I had all of my fingers so that I could write with less difficulty, hold things without dropping them, and open packages more easily. I am not a vain person, so the disfigurement to my face is nothing compared to almost losing my sight and hearing. The plastic surgeries I had on my face changed my appearance but I don't look like a monster anymore. Even though I lost half of my face, I am still able to smile and that is very important to me. I was a very handsome young man before the bombing; some people even said I was more handsome than a young Clark Gable. But like I said before, vanity is immaterial. What happened is past, and I can't change that. Since that day, I have tried to do the best I can with what I have. The Israelis may have hurt me, they might have disfigured me, but they failed to kill me. And they will never, ever kill my spirit. In that sense, I have won.

What has kept me going all these years has been my need to achieve something for my people. I will never give up just because I was attacked. From the moment I started to recuperate from my injuries thirty-six years ago, I decided not to wallow in self-pity but, instead, to stay actively involved in my quest for peace and in my struggle to achieve freedom for my people. I continue to work at least fifteen hours a day with only one eye that is more like half an eye and one ear that can hear about as well as half an ear. I have been called a one-man "Ministry of Information" by some of my friends and journalists because I know so much about the world, its history, economics, and politics, not to mention my thirst for knowledge about philosophy and quantum physics. Despite these physical setbacks, I have been able to achieve more in my political life than many people who never experienced any hardship, and I am proud of my achievements both past and present. In my own way, I have helped create a turning point in history and that has been no small feat.

TIME magazine may have dubbed me the "Face of Terror," but I prefer the name I was given by the international press after I put forth my proposal for a two-state solution—the "Face of Peace."

7

STEADFASTNESS AND CONFRONTATION

T he December 2–5, 1977 summit held in Tripoli, Libya (which I attended) was called for by Libyan president Muammar Qaddafi. The attendees, besides Libya, were Algeria, Syria, Yemen, the PLO, and eventually Iraq, all of whom had come together in order to confront Sadat's political path of compromise with Israel (by offering a peace treaty and opening diplomatic relations between the two countries); reunite the ranks of the PLO (dissension had taken place because Fateh members did not wish to clash with Sadat while the PFLP took a much harder stand against him); and mend the rift between Syria and Iraq (which had begun long ago in 1968 when the Ba'ath party had taken over Iraq following the 1967 War). Not only did the Syrians blame the previous Iraqi regime (Communists) for allowing the defeat in 1967, but they also blamed the Syrian Ba'ath party for not being able to defend the region from Israel. The rift became wider when the Syrian Ba'athists did not step in to help the PLO in 1970 against the Jordanian forces in Jordan.

Because Sadat had taken a unilateral decision to make an official visit to Jerusalem (with the hope of securing peace in the region) the previous month, on

November 19, 1977, those at the December summit met in order to agree to suspend diplomatic relations with Egypt. The Arab League barred Egypt from attending any of its meetings, and made a strong statement of steadfast support of the Palestinian people. In order to provide a united front, the factions within the PLO had to join together. Fateh did not want to condemn Sadat (mainly because Arafat always liked to keep Egypt on his side as a strong ally), while the PFLP wanted to cut diplomatic relations with Egypt completely.

At first, all efforts failed to persuade Iraq to join with Algeria, Yemen, Syria, Libya, and the PLO in our united stand against Israel and Sadat's visit there. (We later dubbed it "Steadfastness and Confrontation," which meant we would remain steadfast in our opposition to having any diplomatic relations with Israel and we would also continue to confront Israel with our resistance movements within the Occupied Territories.) It was clear to me that Iraq, which had openly opposed Sadat's visit, was having internal problems at the time; some supported the stand against Sadat while others did not. Iraq had a minority of people in positions of power who were primarily interested in the development of the country for their own personal benefit. They believed it was important to concentrate on domestic development first before involving themselves in regional disputes. The minority in power was thinking specifically of Iraqi interests while the majority of Iraqi citizens was thinking of the good of all Arabs and was ready to join the "steadfastness and solidarity front"—but they were not in charge. Eventually, however, Iraq did send a representative to the summit, Taha Yasin Ramadan, the leader of the Iraqi Revolutionary Command Council.

Initially, there had been disagreement among the Palestinians about who should attend the summit. Arafat wanted the delegation representing the Palestinians to be made up of members of the PLO, but President Qaddafi and Algerian president Houari Boumediene, suspicious that Arafat secretly supported Sadat, were pressuring the other groups to keep Arafat from participating. To ensure that the anti-Sadat faction was in the majority at the summit, Qaddafi and Boumediene invited George Habash of the Popular Front for the Liberation of Palestine (PFLP) and Ahmad Jibril of the PFLP-Central Command (a Syrian-supported splinter group from Habash's PFLP), who were known to oppose Sadat. Arafat insisted on inviting Nayef Hawatmeh, the leader of the Democratic Front for the Liberation of Palestine (DFLP). The DFLP initially refused to attend because of the opposition to Arafat, but in the end, all the main PLO leaders, including Arafat, attended. The fuss had been about nothing.

On the floor of the conference, however, the bickering continued. Dr. George Habash gave a speech in which he calmly presented his political strategy for opposing Sadat, and Syrian president Hafez Al-Assad interrupted him, asking him what kind of doctor was he anyway, as if to say, "Stick to what you know. Sit down and shut up." Hawatmeh gave such a long-winded speech about how we should oppose Sadat that President Boumediene got impatient and interrupted him, shouting, "Just get to the point." The disagreements continued, with no one really getting any points across at all.

Behind the scenes, more efforts were being made to unite the Palestinian ranks. Salah Khalaf (Abu Iyad), deputy chief and head of intelligence for the PLO, played a prominent role in these efforts by sitting privately with each of the leaders, trying to find some sort of compromise that would be acceptable to all, and I cooperated with him as much as I could. But when he asked me to write a statement announcing the reunification of the PLO, I pointed out that this had not yet happened. "It will," was his reply.

I remember a conversation with President Qaddafi, Arafat, and Habash that took place while these issues were being debated. Arafat asked Qaddafi, "Didn't you once say to me that I must raise the flag of an independent Palestine even if it was only over a tent?" Qaddafi had implied that even if Arafat was able to secure a small patch of Palestinian land big enough to hold a single tiny tent, he should raise the flag of Palestine there. Any scrap of Palestinian land he could secure, no matter how small, was better than nothing.

"Yes," he answered, "but where are you to find this tent?"

"I will find it," Arafat promised, "and I will raise our flag."

When this conversation took place, we were standing on the balcony of the building where the summit was taking place. The balcony overlooked a crowd of reporters milling around on the street below us. We raised our interlocked hands as hundreds of cameras flashed. The following day, the headlines spoke of a united PLO and its alliance, using the name all of us in attendance had called ourselves: the Steadfastness and Confrontation Front.

In the end, the official statement of reunification of the Palestinian ranks referred neither to the PLO's approval of Resolution 242 nor to the establishment of a Palestinian state on lands occupied by Israel in 1967. It did, however, refer to the PLO's opposition to Sadat. Arafat was not pleased with this compromise, but he was forced to accept it because of both internal (Habash of the PFLP) and external Arab (Syria, Algeria, Libya) pressures.

On the surface, it appeared that Arafat had also cut ties with Egypt, but in reality, he secretly maintained communications with Sadat because he never wanted Palestine to be completely isolated without a "door" to the Egyptian, Syrian, or Jordanian governments. Since Jordan was closed to him following Black September, he had to turn to Egypt. To ensure that Palestine was never without a strong ally, he always kept his communication lines and diplomatic relations open to at least one of his "neighbors."

In July 1978, Sadat publicly invited Israel to begin negotiations for its withdrawal from the West Bank, the Gaza Strip, and East Jerusalem over a five-year period. Although Arafat continued collaborating with the Steadfastness and Confrontation Front, he in fact was ready to join Sadat should he succeed in negotiating an end to the occupation of any part of Palestine. But Arafat never released one bird from one hand until he was certain he had ten in his other hand. Although it was also true that all the Arab countries wanted Israel to withdraw from Palestine, there was disagreement among them as to how much of Palestine should be returned. Some governments wanted all the land that had been taken since 1948 returned, while others were willing to accept the compromise of getting back the land taken in 1967. Within the Palestinian groups, aside from the issue of how much of Palestine they were expecting back, there was also disagreement about who would be the eventual leader of their new state. Also, the other Arab countries did not like the idea of Sadat making this decision without the rest of the Arab world. By taking such a drastic unilateral step, he had basically thumbed his nose at the Arab League. Sadat had done something without the approval and backing of the others, which was contrary to the principles of the Arab League. Besides all of that, the Palestinians wanted to make decisions about their future themselves. What Sadat was doing was putting Palestinian decision making into his own hands alone, not those of the Palestinians, which also meant that Arafat needed to keep on Sadat's good side politically so that he could be the spokesperson for the people of Palestine as a new state emerged out of the occupation.

Sadat's offer to Israel caused great anxiety among the countries and groups that opposed him because they worried that Arafat would join with Sadat if he were to succeed. Everyone knew that Arafat relied on Egypt for strong support both politically and militarily. An emergency summit meeting was called by Algeria in August 1978 for Libya, Syria, Iraq, and the PLO. Arafat was asked to sign a pledge promising that he would not deal with Sadat, no matter how Israel responded to his offer. Arafat tried to avoid making such a commitment. He told the members of the summit: "I can give orders now for hundreds of missiles to be fired on the Galilee. Who among you is willing to deal with the consequences of that? The Arab nations will either have to fight or negotiate." He eventually signed the pledge, but he knew he would have to break it someday in order to keep his strongest ally on his side.

Three weeks after Sadat's request for Israel to comply with Resolution 242, Israeli prime minister Menachem Begin renounced the opportunity to achieve a political settlement. Arafat knew that the Palestinian people had other battles to fight before the Israelis would ever be convinced of the need to negotiate an end to their occupation and the establishment of an independent Palestinian state with Jerusalem as its capital.

On September 17, 1978, Sadat signed an agreement with Israel at the U.S. presidential retreat, Camp David, which established an autonomous self-governing authority in the West Bank and the Gaza Strip that would fully implement Resolution 242. A week later, at a summit held in Damascus, the PLO, Libya, Yemen, Algeria, and Iraq, completely rejected the Camp David Accords. It wasn't that they opposed what had been outlined in the accords; it was simply a matter of disagreeing with how Sadat had taken it upon himself to go behind everyone's back and establish ties with an enemy. If anyone was going to be making decisions about the fate of Palestine, it should have been the legitimate representatives of the Palestinians and no one else.

At the Damascus Summit, there was fierce debate over whether to sever all diplomatic and economic ties with Egypt, with some of representatives arguing that it would be enough just to suspend diplomatic relations. A tension-filled debate also took place regarding the steadfastness of the countries that stood against Israel and Sadat's visit. Syrian president Hafez Al-Assad and Libyan president Muammar Qaddafi clashed during the discussion. Assad demanded that words be turned into actions with monetary support to be made to the Palestinians from financially able countries, especially the oil-producing and -exporting countries, such as Libya. The implication was that Libya was all words and no action when it came to supporting the Palestinians, who needed financial assistance to secure arms, to support families that had lost the bread winners either through death or imprisonment, and to finance the leaders of the PLO.

Another mini-summit, again called for by President Boumediene, took place in Algeria and included Yemen, Algeria, Syria, the PLO, and Libya. The Palestinian side attempted to reconcile Assad and Qaddafi. Khaled Al-Hassan, a member of Fateh's Central Committee, told Qaddafi that credibility is lost when words are not followed by actions, again referring to the fact that if Libya wanted to show strong solidarity with the Palestinians, he should start providing them with more financial support. When the discussion became fiery, I suggested that Syria make a list of the weapons and planes they would need for military confrontation with Israel so that the countries with financial resources would know what materiel to deliver to the Syrian armed forces. Colonel Qaddafi eventually agreed to help fund the purchase of the necessary military hardware. Shortly thereafter, Qaddafi excused himself, saying that he had another engagement. Later, we learned he had a meeting with Arafat and that they were seen leaving together for Jordan.

I later found out that Colonel Qaddafi had previously contacted King Hussein, who had indicated to him that he wanted to reconcile with Arafat. The PLO and Jordan had severed ties with each other after the battles of the Ajlun Mountains in 1970. But because of his recent commitment to severing ties with Egypt following the Camp David Accords, Arafat needed another ally. He was not in a position to leave only one political "door" open to the PLO; Arafat could not afford to have Palestine completely cut off from any of his previous allies and close neighbors (i.e., Egypt and Jordan), otherwise Palestine would be left in a stranglehold by Israel. If the one "door" to Egypt was temporarily closed due to the "steadfastness and confrontation" line the Arab league had taken, then it was up to him to open another "door" to Jordan. It was all part of his strategy. However, in reopening relations with Jordan, it was better for him to go with a strong ally; this time it would be Libya. He never wanted to appear weak when he was negotiating anything for Palestine. He knew very well that whoever controlled that "door" to Palestine would also be able to influence Palestinian decision making. If he reestablished ties with Jordan, pressure on the PLO from Syria (through Jibril's splinter group, the PFLP-General Command) would ease.

News of the planned reconciliation between Jordan and Arafat spread like wildfire. The leaders of Fateh, the PFLP, and the PFLP-GC, issued a statement condemning both Arafat's visit to Jordan and its aims. Some of the leaders wanted to wait until Arafat confirmed the rumors, but they were ignored. Arafat was publicly denounced; some of the toughest criticism came from Ahmad Jibreel, the secretary general of the PFLP-GC.

When Arafat and Qaddafi returned from Jordan, various members of the PLO were in an uproar, some supporting a reconciliation with Jordan and others not. Arafat simply said to the PLO members, "How can you issue a statement in the name of the PLO while I am away? I am the head of the PLO, not any of you." He then spoke firmly to the leaders of Fateh, who had approved the statement condemning Arafat's visit with King Hussein. "Colonel Qaddafi kidnapped me, forcing me to meet with King Hussein. If you want to blame anyone, blame him. However, do you really want the PLO and Jordan to remain in a permanent state of conflict? In light of the Camp David Accords, is it not in the best interests of the Palestinian people to have normal relations with Jordan? We will face many wars in Lebanon, do you not see that? Begin rejected the idea of negotiating with us for a withdrawal from the West Bank, Gaza Strip, and East Jerusalem because he has wars lined up for us."

Arafat's words were like a bucket of cold water over a blazing flame. The summit ended with Colonel Qaddafi confirming that he had indeed "kidnapped" Arafat in order to force the meeting with Hussein because it would be good for the Steadfastness and Confrontation Front. It was a time for unity in the Arab world, not division. Staying divided as we had been would only allow Israel to become stronger. We were prime examples of the old "divide and conquer" adage. Our divisions were making all of the Arab countries weak in the face of Israeli aggression. By November 1978, the Baghdad Summit was convened by the Arab League. Now, instead of just a small number of countries attending, this time twenty Arab countries and the PLO were going to meet to discuss their response to Sadat's signing of the Camp David Accords. The Summit sent a delegation to Cairo in an attempt to convince Sadat not to make any unilateral agreements with Israel, but he did not even allow them to enter Egypt, stubbornly insisting on following his own political path.

Many possible actions were discussed at the Summit, but it was finally agreed to expel Egypt from the Arab League. The Arab League's headquarters would be moved from Cairo to Tunis, and all diplomatic, trade, and military ties with Egypt would be severed. Egypt would be isolated from the entire Arab world, except for Oman, Somalia, and Sudan, who had not agreed to the boycott for their own personal reasons. To make sure that Syria, Jordan, and the PLO remained committed to the Steadfastness and Confrontation Front, members of the summit raised over nine billion dollars in financial aid to support the two countries and the PLO, both militarily and economically. Jordan and Syria, who had the longest borders with Israel of any Arab countries, were also suspected of secretly looking favorably at Sadat's course of action, and everyone knew that Arafat would always do what was best for Palestine by keeping all his options open.

Now Arafat had the support of the Arab League, and he had made amends with Jordan, but his main goal was to get the United States on his side. Little did he know that Iran, of all places, would soon provide him with a golden opportunity to do just that.

8

REAGAN'S BROKEN PROMISE

Before the fall of the Shah of Iran on February 11, 1979, groups opposed to his regime were active both inside and outside the country. In the late 1960s, these Iranian factions had begun contacting Palestinian revolutionary groups to ask for support and protection from the agents of the Shah. It was natural for them to turn to us since we were regarded as a people who, like them, were fighting against oppression. A large number of Iranian fighters began arriving at Palestinian military training camps, primarily those run by Fateh and the PFLP. This cooperation led to strong ties between the Palestinians and the Iranians who eventually overthrew the Shah.

While the Shah was still in power, an increasingly popular religious leader, Ayatollah Ruhollah Khomeini, had openly condemned the moral corruption that was rampant in the Shah's regime. He also publicly accused the Shah of being in the pockets of the United States and Israel, and denounced him as a "wretched man." Khomeini was arrested several times until the Shah finally kicked him out of the country into Turkey. From there, he went to Basra, Iraq, where he lived for a few years until then vice president Saddam Hussein expelled him. Hussein was not supportive of any Shiite fanatics in his country. Khomeini then went to

France, where he lived in Neauphe-le-Château. Even though he was living in exile, Khomeini still had huge support from millions of Iranians at home. From France he was able to coordinate the eventual overthrow of the Shah by organizing mass demonstrations within Iran against him. Khomeini saw the Palestinian resistance movement as another way to continue the Islamic revolution from within Israel. Because of this, he was amenable to keeping communication lines open between himself, his followers, and the leaders of the PLO. The Shah had maintained cordial relations with Israel, although his government had never officially recognized it as a country, by allowing Israel to have a de facto embassy in Tehran. Following the Six Days' War, Iran supplied Israel with oil and the two countries participated in many joint business ventures. The Shah's relationship with Israel automatically put him on the wrong side with the PLO. Arafat put Ali Salameh (Abu Hassan), Fateh's chief of operations, in charge of liaising with leaders of the Iranian anti-Shah movement both inside and outside of Iran, meeting their requests to train at our camps and providing them with whatever military aid we could. Dr. Wadi' Haddad, at the same time, was the PFLP official in charge of relations with the Iranian revolutionaries.

Khomeini cherished these ties with the Palestinians. Though he had always refused to give press interviews while he was living in France, in 1978 he granted *Al-Hadaf,* the PFLP's magazine, a lengthy interview in which he spoke of a strategy to overthrow the Shah and to change Iran's constitutional monarchy to an Islamic system that would rule justly, care for the poor, and develop Iran using the huge oil revenues that were being hogged by the Shah and his corrupt entourage. Khomeini did not set a date for overturning the Shah's regime, but he made it clear that it would be soon. In fact, he was right.

Starting in January 1978, mass demonstrations against the Shah took place throughout the country. These continued for over a year, crippling the Iranian economy when thousands of Iranians closed their businesses in unified strikes across the nation. With feelings against the Shah increasing and daily demonstrations demanding his overthrow, the Shah left Iran with his family, on the pretense of going on vacation, but he never returned. Almost at the same time as the Shah's plane took off on February 1, 1979, Khomeini landed in Tehran to begin setting up a new, Islamic government, and he was welcomed by millions of cheering Iranians. The jubilant crowd carried Khomeini on their shoulders to a large school that had been turned into temporary quarters for him. The complete end of the Shah's regime, however, took place on February 11, 1979, when the Iranian army declared itself "neutral" after Khomeini's Islamic supporters had overwhelmed troops loyal to the Shah. Khomeini never forgot the support the Palestinians had continued to give him and his supporters during his exile.

As soon as news of Khomeini's return reached Arafat in Beirut, he began making arrangements to fly to Tehran to congratulate Khomeini. However, after Khomeini's arrival, the government in Tehran closed its airspace and suspended communications between air traffic control and incoming flights, making it impossible for other planes to enter or land. Arafat waited patiently in his office as attempts were made to contact the airport. Hours later, he was told that it was no use: the airport was sealed shut. But Yasser Arafat was not one to give up so easily. He told his pilot to have his private plane ready by the time he and his entourage arrived at the airport. We were met there by Lebanon's director of civil aviation, who adamantly refused to let the plane take off. He was sticking to the rules: without Iran's prior approval of a flight itinerary, no plane could enter Iranian air space. Arafat ignored him. "I assume all responsibility. Let us take off immediately." Reluctantly, the man agreed, and Arafat, accompanied by other high-ranking Palestinian officials, including myself, was soon airborne.

As soon as Arafat's plane entered Iranian airspace, it was surrounded by Iranian F–15 fighter planes indicating to us that we were to turn back. When it became clear that our plane was not turning back, the Iranian pilots fired warning shots at us.

Inside the plane, Arafat moved to a window, where he could be seen by the pilots of the fighter jets. He took off his black and white *hata* (the traditional Palestinian head dress) and waved it at them. He wanted them to see that the plane they were trying to shoot down was carrying President Yasser Arafat, the leader of the PLO.

The fighters held their positions around Arafat's plane. Apparently, they were trying to get in touch with someone who could ask Khomeini what to do. Agonizing minutes of tension and anxiety passed; then the pilots tipped their wings in a sort of salute to us, their first official guests.

Arafat and his delegation were met at the airport by a number of high-ranking officials of the revolution, who embraced the PLO leader warmly. The convoy left immediately for Khomeini's temporary quarters in the school, which was a bustling beehive of activity. People were busy on phones, running around from room to room with papers to be signed. Arafat was invited to Khomeini's private office, and the two men spent an hour discussing the Palestinian struggle against Israel's occupation and the future of Iran under an Islamic leader. Khomeini assured Arafat that Iran's Islamic revolution was more than ready to aid the Palestinian people, both with financial support and by providing weapons to the Palestinian military in order to assist us in our fight for independence. As the men parted, Arafat said to Khomeini, "God willing, the Palestinian people will be as triumphant as the Iranian people have been."

President Arafat had been the first leader to meet with the Ayatollah Khomeini in Tehran after the beginning of the Islamic revolution. Khomeini made good on his promise to support the Palestinian revolution because the PLO had backed his opposition to the Shah. Waves of Iranian revolutionaries demonstrated in the streets of Tehran, chanting in support of the Palestinian revolution and against the United States and Israel.

On November 4, 1979, just after the Ayatollah's return, a group of Iranian student revolutionaries seized the American Embassy in Tehran and declared the fifty-two employees and diplomats inside as their hostages. The United States had not only been regarded as a staunch supporter of Israel, but also as an unwavering supporter of the Shah. Everyone knew how the CIA had interfered in their government way back in 1953 when they had helped reinstate the Shah to his throne. The CIA had also helped the Shah set up SAVAK, his ruthless intelligence agency that made sure no one could voice any opinions contrary to those of the Shah. The students were angered by this because they had lived in such difficult circumstances under the Shah and in fear of his notorious SAVAK. The demands the students gave in order for the hostages to be released were the following: return the Shah to Iran so that he could be tried for his crimes against the Iranian people, and provide an agreement from the United States that it would no longer interfere in their country's internal affairs. The hostages were kept for 444 days while various governments tried to negotiate a release, but each attempt failed miserably.

On April 24, 1980, President Carter, who was desperate to secure the release of the hostages during his own term and well before elections that were only months away, approved a rescue attempt. The mission, called "Operation Eagle Claw," involved landing helicopters near Tehran, in desert areas that the U.S. forces simply referred to as Desert One and Desert Two. The mission was unsuccessful, mainly because of an unexpected sandstorm that put three of the helicopters out of action and led to the deaths of several airmen. The following day President Carter announced that he was aborting the operation. To make any other rescue operations practically impossible, the hostages in Tehran were then scattered to various locations all over the city. Following the failed rescue of the hostages, international and regional efforts continued in order to mediate the release of the diplomats, but they too were unsuccessful. What all countries were loath to admit was that the party with closest ties to the Iranian revolutionaries at the time was the PLO. No one had made a move to contact the PLO, however, until a few representatives of European countries unofficially asked President Arafat to test the waters of negotiation with Khomeini.

Arafat agreed. This was an excellent opportunity for him. If the PLO was successful in getting the hostages released, it would improve the PLO's status as a strong power in the Middle East, especially after Menachem Begin had rejected the participation of the PLO in the peace talks at Camp David that eventually led to a signed peace treaty between Egypt and Israel on September 17, 1978. Begin had not been willing to negotiate the return of the West Bank, and because he regarded Yasser Arafat as a terrorist anyway, he saw no point in his presence at the meeting.

In 1979, the final year before the 1980 U.S. presidential elections, President Carter's first term was about to end, and the Republican Party had decided to nominate California governor Ronald Reagan to run against him in the upcoming presidential elections. Carter's success with the Camp David Accords in 1978 had increased his popularity and standing with the American voters, and the Republicans knew they faced an uphill battle in November 1980, when the American presidential elections were to be held. The campaigning that year was extremely fierce.

But the hostage crisis had presented Carter with what would turn out to be the most serious challenge to his presidency. He had worked very hard with his European allies to secure the release of the hostages still held in Tehran. I had learned at the time from some of President Carter's campaign advisors that they felt if he could successfully secure the release of the hostages during his term, it would surely end any chance of Reagan winning, despite the financial support Reagan had from large interest groups, such as the commercial sectors that supported the military and major oil companies.

Reagan's advisors had come to the same conclusion. The directors of Reagan's campaign and officials in the Republican Party knew that the PLO was the only group who could wield enough influence with the Iranians to mediate the release of the hostages. Reagan assigned one of his close personal friends and campaign managers the task of negotiating a deal with the PLO to slow down in any way they could the release of the captives until after the elections. It was believed that if anyone could get the hostages released, it would be the PLO, which meant that they also were the ones who could orchestrate not only how, but also when the hostages would be released.

If Reagan wanted to persuade the PLO to postpone their mediation efforts, he would have to offer us something worthwhile in exchange. Reagan aides drew up a plan of action of how they would approach Yasser Arafat with their proposal and worked out the necessary details of how to contact him and where and when they would meet. One aide was sent to Beirut on a reconnaissance mission to test the waters with the leadership of the PLO.

The aide, who was an old friend of mine, called me at my *Al-Hadaf* office but did not say what he wanted, only that he wanted to meet with me on a matter of great importance. He knew that I had Arafat's ear, so I was the natural choice when access to the president was needed quickly. When he arrived at my office in West Beirut carrying a letter from Governor Reagan, I realized that the matter was indeed very important. The letter asked the PLO to delay the mediation efforts for the release of the American hostages, and in exchange for our help, the aide told me that the doors of the White House would be open to the PLO if Reagan won the elections.

I went directly to Arafat's office and told him of the aide's offer. He asked me to arrange a meeting with the aide at 12:30 a.m. at my house. At exactly 1 a.m., a number of Arafat's guards entered my house, and shortly thereafter, Arafat entered the room. He appeared friendly and pleased to see the aide, who embraced Arafat, obviously awed. Arafat signaled for all the guards to leave. Whatever the aide had to say would be done in private without any other ears, including mine, to hear what was going to be said.

As the aide showed him the letter from Governor Reagan and repeated his assurance that the doors of a Reagan White House would be open to the PLO, Arafat took notes in the green notebook he always used for all his meetings. When he finished, Arafat looked long and hard at him, almost as if he were trying to read his inner thoughts. Was there a hidden agenda he had failed to see? Would Reagan remain true to his promise or, once he got what he wanted, would he turn his back on the PLO, leaving Arafat without the U.S. recognition he so wanted to have? This was an opportunity of a lifetime, if Reagan meant what he said. But he couldn't help being skeptical.

"We'll see," he finally said, and got up to leave. As I accompanied the president to the door, he said quietly to me, "Ask him about obtaining an official document regarding this matter."

I asked the aide if we could get Reagan's assurances in writing, and he promised to get back to me. But, although I followed up several times with many calls to him, I was always given a new excuse for why Reagan had not been able to write up the document.

The hostages were released on January 20, 1981, minutes after Reagan was sworn in as the fortieth president of the United States. We had kept our promise to Reagan, but the president never kept his to us.

9

INVASION

The twelve years we spent in Beirut after we had been forced to leave Jordan in the early 1970s had not been easy. Even though Israelis targeted us wherever we went and nothing came of our hopes for a Palestinian state, we did not relent in our resistance to Israeli aggression. From South Lebanon, we continued to be a major thorn in Israel's side with our sporadic military operations into the north of Israel. I was kept busy with all my work as the editor-in-chief at *Al-Hadaf* following the assassination of Ghassan Kanafani.

In the beginning of March 1982, a twenty-year-old man called Fayez Saeb, whom I had never seen before, turned up at the *Al-Hadaf* offices and said he urgently needed to see me. As he entered my office, he seemed nervous and flustered, but wasted no time in getting to his point.

"I have information. Israel will invade Lebanon, reach Beirut, then surround and annihilate you," he said in a low, mumbling voice. He was shaking and beads of perspiration stood out on his forehead.

"These are serious words," I said. "How do you know this?"

Fayez glanced around the room, as if wanting to make certain no one else was there. He told me that he had seen papers and maps related to the invasion.

"Can you get me these papers?"

"I don't know. I'll try."

"Fayez, this is a very grave and important matter. If you succeed in doing this, you'll be doing your country a great service."

After a week had passed and I had not heard from him, I thought that perhaps this young man had been imagining things. Then, almost two weeks later, Fayez returned, looking even more distraught than before. Trembling, he handed me the papers.

He gave me a map of Lebanon marked with various arrows and signs, and another map of the coast of Beirut, stretching from the Karantina district to the Riviera Hotel. I placed both maps on the small table in front of me as I tried to decipher the symbols. The maps had obviously been copied in haste with a nervous hand; the lines and the curves were shaky and inaccurate.

Fayez was reluctant to tell me where he had obtained the maps. I assured him that he could trust me. But before we could take action, I told him, we needed to be certain of their veracity. Then, speaking rapidly, Fayez said he worked for one of the leaders of the Lebanese army and that he had seen these papers in his home. How someone in the Lebanese army had obtained these maps was unclear. But the possibility of an Israeli attack against us had to be taken seriously. Before leaving, Fayez told me the operation was planned for that same summer.

According to the maps, the attack was planned in South Lebanon, extending northward to Beirut and from East to West Beirut. Politically, the possibility was both likely and logical. We had received U.S. communiqués through many Arab channels advising us to withdraw our troops to forty kilometers north of South Lebanon. If we failed to do so, the United States would not be able to stop Israel from entering Lebanon in defense of the north of Israel, which had suffered PLO missile attacks every so often.

The plan I had in front of me, however, went far beyond a defensive strike. It reached the city of Sidon and the nearby Matn Mountains overlooking Beirut. It appeared that Israel was planning to surround Beirut and invade the city from all sides, including the entire area from West to East Beirut, which included the area of the American University of Beirut campus, all the way down to the coast of the Mediterranean Sea. I held in my hands a dangerous secret, which, if proven to be true, could lead to a great victory for us. With advanced knowledge and preparation, we could stave off the attack and once again bring defeat to the Israeli table. There was another possibility, however, that I could not ignore. What if this was a trap? Was someone trying to use me to trick the leadership? I was faced with a serious dilemma. If I ignored the map, we wouldn't be prepared for the invasion if it actually took place. But if I shared the information with the PLO leadership and it turned out to be a hoax, we might be placing our troops in places that would leave other avenues open for attack. What to do? I was really in a quandary. I finally made up my mind that the map had to be taken seriously. We had to be ready for a possible invasion. Better to be prepared than to do absolutely nothing at all.

The first person I thought of telling was Arafat, even though at the time the PFLP disagreed with him over his stand on Resolution 242 and I was still an official PFLP member. However, he was still the president of the PLO and had to be told. But I was unable to reach him, so I handed a copy of the plan to Khalil Al-Wazeer (Abu Jihad), who was a member of the Central Committee of Fateh, and also gave a copy to Dr. George Habash, the head of the PFLP. I also asked some of the security personnel of the PFLP to deliver a copy to the director of the Syrian intelligence service in charge of Beirut. Everyone had to know so that they could reach a consensus about what we should do.

Still, I felt I needed to do more. The more I thought about it, the more I was convinced that the invasion was going to happen. It was vital that I talk directly to the decision makers, such as Habash and Arafat, instead of just sending them messages. I had to know that all the necessary precautions were being taken. Finally, I was able to speak to Arafat. I could see that he was taking the map very seriously, weighing the ramifications of taking action or not taking any action. He asked me a few questions about Fayez, where he had found the map, did I believe he was telling the truth, and what my opinion was as well. He then ordered his high military council to draw up a plan of defense, which included General Saad Sayel and his staff officers.

The plan of defense took into consideration the borders from the Lacoura seashore between the Lebanese and Israeli borders up to the Arqoub Mountains to the west that led to Mount Hermon. Located in that line of mountains was an area simply known as the "Middle Sector," which had been under the protection of the United Nations forces since 1978, when they had been deployed to maintain a cease-fire. No armed soldiers or militia, including Lebanese, Israeli, or Palestinian, was allowed in that sector. Because it was under the jurisdiction of the United Nations, that particular section of land between Lebanon and Israel had not been factored into our defensive plan. It would have been unethical militarily for anyone to have crossed into that area forcibly. So, leaving that area out, we divided the country into three main defensive lines, which were naturally already there as mountains. Our first line of defense ended at Sidon, a city located about forty kilometers south of Beirut. Our second line of defense ended at Damour, a town about nineteen kilometers south of Beirut, and our third line of defense was to be Beirut. It took about two weeks to work out all the particulars on paper and another month to set everything into motion. Troops were moved to pivotal locations and the necessary armaments and artillery were also moved into position. By May 1982, we were ready to confront the Israeli invasion of Lebanon.

I held press conferences throughout the Arab countries warning them of the impending invasion. Some of my colleagues in the PFLP did not believe me even though they had seen the map Fayez had given me. Over time, they had come to regard me as a rightist who would back up anything Arafat supported, so they often disagreed with me just for the sake of disagreeing. Although they didn't believe that Israel would launch a full-scale assault against Lebanon, they did concede to the fact that Israel would probably make a few strikes against us, but certainly nothing as huge as an attack on Beirut. I ignored their opinions and continued to take precautionary measures along with Arafat and Sayel.

On June 5, 1982, Israeli aircraft bombed Sports City, a major sports arena in Beirut. I saw the first plumes of smoke while sitting in my office nearby. The Israelis thought that we had turned Sports City into a warehouse for rockets and ammunition, which couldn't have been further from the truth. Their bombs destroyed large sections of the complex as well as countless shacks that had been previously abandoned by refugees who fled into Beirut to escape the Israeli attacks that had regularly taken place against South Lebanon. I called for an emergency meeting, informing everyone that we had to implement the plan General Sayel and his officers had begun working on two months earlier.

Our biggest mistake was not allowing for the possibility that Israeli forces would disregard ethical military procedure when they invaded Lebanon. When Israeli troops plowed through the UN lines without a thought and the UN soldiers (who were not just observers, but armed soldiers) did absolutely nothing to stop them, we had to make some last-minute adjustments to our defensive plan.

With the bombing of the Sports City, war had begun.

10

MILITARY ETHICS BREACHED

By following the way the battles played out in June 1982, I was able to confirm that the Israeli invasion plan Fayez had brought to me was being carried out to the letter. One action taken by Israel, however, was something none of us could fathom: they had stormed right through the UN-protected area without a thought to what this meant on the international level. They had not only violated military ethics, but they had acted in direct violation of international laws by overriding the UN's jurisdiction in that area.

Although we had prepared extremely well for the invasion, we had not factored in the possibility, however remote, that Israel would resort to unethical tactics. Our defense plans had relied on high military ethics; it seemed impossible to us that any country would attack an area where the UN flag was flying. Yet that was exactly what Israel did. Then Israeli defense minister Ariel Sharon was trampling over all international laws and conventions. Another thing that confused us was that the UN troops who were stationed there were not just UN observers, but actual armed soldiers, and not one of them had fired even one bullet as the Israelis barged through the UN-protected zone. They were given an open door to pass through, something we had never expected to happen. That area had not been part of our defensive plan, so we had to scramble to get troops into new positions to meet the invading army as best we could.

At the outbreak of fighting, Arafat had cut short a visit to Saudi Arabia, where he had gone to offer his condolences for the death of the Saudi leader, King Khaled. When he returned to Beirut, I joined him in Operations Room 5, an underground room outfitted with communications equipment, maps, simple furniture, a number of military beds, and some canned foods. As part of his defense strategy, Arafat had asked the military commander of the PLO in Lebanon, General Saad Sayel, to prepare a number of operations rooms as far away as possible from his headquarters because we expected that Israel would bomb all known Palestinian headquarters in Beirut and other cities in Lebanon. Therefore, Operations Room 5 was not as crowded as operations rooms usually would be.

Arafat and Sayel went over the defense plans that had been drawn up by the high military council along with Colonel Abu Ahmad Fuad, the military commander of the PFLP. Fuad considered Sidon (a city just forty kilometers, or about twenty-five miles, to the south of Beirut and part of our first line of defense plan) to be the heart of the defense. But Arafat knew that Beirut was the primary target.

"Is fortifying Beirut possible?" Arafat wanted to know. "I think it will be the hardest city to defend."

"Nothing is impossible." Sayel answered. "Let's fortify Beirut."

"So be it. Beirut appears to be the main target."

Abu Ahmad Fuad was then sent to Sidon and Ein Al-Helwa, a refugee camp near Sidon to join the forces in the first line of defense.

Arafat and I began to pace the room together while he told me he was glad I had passed the information on to him early, because it had given him plenty of time to work out a defensive strategy with Sayel. I told him I had no choice but to take the information as solid fact because of what our source in the United States had told us: the United States had given Israel the green light to invade Lebanon. We had also learned from this American source that Begin and Sharon had been told by President Reagan that if they failed to destroy the PLO and its leadership in Beirut, they would have to deal with the consequences all on their own. Arafat agreed that we must never forget this fact. He was still angry that Reagan had used him to get the hostages in Iran released according to his own campaign needs and then reneged on his promise to recognize the PLO. Arafat was only too aware of the U.S. laissez-faire policy toward Israel and vowed never to forget it.

Arafat was also aware that ever since our rocket attacks from South Lebanon into Northern Israel, the U.S. administration had been pounded by Israeli complaints about the security of its civilians living in Northern Galilee. They kept demanding a "clean up" operation, which would push our forces forty kilometers (about twenty-five miles) back into South Lebanon, putting our rocket attacks well out of range of their settlements. To be fair, the green light from the United States did not come right away. The U.S. administration encouraged Syria to put pressure on the PLO to redeploy its troops at least forty kilometers farther into Lebanon. I remember when the Syrians conveyed this message to us, warning us that if we didn't redeploy Israel would have the go-ahead to attack us, with U.S. support. The PLO leadership refused to comply. Arafat could see no reason why Israel should be given such a vast area, free of any Palestinian fighters, when the Palestinians weren't being offered anything in return. The Israelis kept bombarding the White House with reports of our attacks against Israeli civilians—some true, some false—in order to inflame the U.S. administration into action.

Our American source in Washington, D.C. informed us that supporters of Israel in the Pentagon and the National Security Agency were in favor of allowing Israel to invade Lebanon and put an end to us once and for all. There were some people, of course, who were against the invasion entirely, but their voices were not strong enough to reach the president's ear. Reagan finally made a decision with his advisors to give Israel the go-ahead to invade Lebanon and to push our forces back into the country by the required forty kilometers. However, he told them that this was the only action they were to take, for this was not to be seen as an act of war against Lebanon, but as a defensive operation against the Palestinian fighters in South Lebanon. This meant that the Israeli forces should have pushed us back just beyond the Beaufort Castle on the Litany River. The castle had special significance to both the Israelis and to us: To the Israelis, it represented the Palestinian power over the entire valley, for it was from there that artillery could be launched at their settlements. To the Palestinians, the castle was a reminder of when Saladin had been victorious over the invading Crusaders in 1192 as well as a symbol of our ability to stand up to Israel.

As expected, Israeli planes relentlessly bombed the Fakahani District of Beirut, where most of the headquarters of the Palestinian groups were located. Arafat's quarters, Force 17, named after his personal guards, was bombed over ten times. Rubble formed hills in front of its main entrance, and the bombs dug holes as big as swimming pools into the street. Yet, despite the fact that all the buildings surrounding and immediately above it had been destroyed, Arafat's headquarters had remained intact.

During the intense air strikes on Beirut, General Callahan, the Commander of the UN forces in South Lebanon where the Israelis had violated international law, requested an urgent meeting with General Sayel. Arafat decided that the meeting should be held at the Force 17 headquarters, despite the destruction all around it. He also told Sayel to schedule the meeting for 6:30 in the evening so that there would be enough time to prepare. Arafat told Sayel, "Let him see how strong our resistance is." Arafat issued orders for Hani Al-Hassan, a leader of Fateh and a member of the Palestinian National Council, and me to accompany Sayel at the meeting.

Sayel began pumping out orders like bullets in preparation for the meeting. "I want the following to be completed by half past five: clean the place thoroughly, replace the windows, and reconnect the electricity. The air conditioning must be working. The inside of these quarters must be sparkling clean. Wash the walls and floors. When I get back, I want to see these quarters clean and cool. And don't forget that General Callahan likes fresh lemonade. He likes it cold and without sugar." Even though our headquarters had been damaged very badly by Israeli strikes, Sayel knew that Arafat wanted Callahan to believe we were untouched by anything that Israel had tried to throw at us. He also knew that Callahan would have asked Israel temporarily to cease their air raids during his visit, allowing him safe passage in and out of Beirut in order to meet with the leaders of the Palestinian forces.

When we arrived at the headquarters shortly before the scheduled meeting, we were impressed. Within two hours, our men had been able to clear the entrance of the rubble and return the room to almost its normal state. The place was pleasantly cool, in spite of the intense summer heat and humidity outside. A clean pitcher of fresh, cold lemonade, without sugar, was also on the table.

Callahan's helicopter landed on the green fields of the Sports City complex exactly at the appointed time; he was accompanied by three UN officers. PLO military cars picked him up at the stadium and escorted him to our renovated headquarters. At the entrance, he was saluted by Honor Guards in full dress uniform. Two of our officers led him into the meeting room where Hani Al-Hassan (a member of Fateh's Central Committee), General Sayel, and I were waiting. We all shook hands and headed toward the conference table. Sayel, Al-Hassan, and I stood on one side of the table, facing our guests, while General Callahan and his officers, who remained standing as well, were on the opposite side. Callahan saluted Sayel, and Sayel returned the salute, but he did not invite Callahan to sit down. Sayel was a brigadier general, a higher rank than Callahan, and according to military protocol, Callahan could not sit down until he was invited to do so by Sayel. There was an awkward silence as Sayel continued staring at Callahan. Observing the scene, Al-Hassan and I felt as if we were trying to understand a puzzle. Callahan knew that Sayel was a distinguished military man and a West Point graduate who understood the correct protocol, and yet he was ignoring it. Finally, Sayel said, in clear English, firmly, but with dignified calmness: "General Callahan, you betrayed your military honor by allowing Israeli troops to pass through your UN posts without resistance."

Callahan, still standing at attention, replied: "General, you know better than I do the situation on the ground. The size of the attack was far too large for my officers to stop."

"General, your military honor required you to fire at least one bullet. These are the military ethics we learned, are they not?"

Callahan bowed his head as Sayel continued to stare right through him. It was clear to us that Callahan knew that Israel had broken international law, and yet he had done absolutely nothing to try to stop them. After a short silence, Sayel invited him to sit. While sipping his cold lemonade, Callahan talked more about the magnitude of the attack and said that he had not expected the Israeli ground forces to reach Beirut. Sayel's facial expression gave no indication of whether he believed or disbelieved what Callahan was saying. Sayel then said: "Time is short and I need to return to the operations room. However, I wanted to tell you that I have begun to fortify Beirut."

"But General," Callahan protested, "Beirut can not be fortified."

"Let the Israelis think that."

The two men stood to salute each other and made their way out to the cars that were waiting to take Callahan back to his helicopter. Callahan walked with his baton firmly tucked under his arm, talking casually to Sayel. Just before Callahan was about to get into the car, around the corner came Yasser Arafat, strolling through the rubble, dressed in his military fatigues, also with a baton tucked firmly under his arm. He was surrounded by several journalists who were firing questions at him and desperately trying to keep up with him as he strode quickly down the street, explaining to them all about the Palestinian resistance.

"Oh," he said, feigning surprise. "General Callahan, I had no idea you were coming. How nice of you to drop by."

Callahan saluted Arafat, saying that the situation was very difficult.

Arafat responded simply by saying, "It will be difficult for *them*, General." And with that final comment, he breezed on down the street, answering questions while the reporters stumbled through the rubble after him, minimizing the importance of Callahan's visit by just walking away.

11

WALID JUMBLATT'S MESSAGE

As the Israelis tightened their grip around Beirut, Ariel Sharon settled comfortably into rooms at the Alexander Hotel in the town of Brumana, located in the mountains of Al-Matn. Israeli officials then paid a visit to Walid Jumblatt, who was at the time the most prominent leader of the Druze community (see Key Terms), at his Al-Mukhtara mansion in the Shuf Mountains outside Beirut. Following that meeting, Jumblatt was summoned to the presidential palace in Ba'abda, a city in western Lebanon, where Philip Habib, President Reagan's special envoy to the Middle East, was staying to monitor the war. Jumblatt didn't want to go to Ba'abda because the road there wasn't safe, so Habib sent him the American ambassador's car, which was bulletproof and had diplomatic immunity that would get him through the Israeli checkpoints.

When the meeting with Habib had ended, a very tense and worried Jumblatt headed back to his home in West Beirut. He had been chosen to deliver a message from the Israelis directly to Arafat. Muhsin Ibrahim of the High Council of National Lebanese Groups was to invite the joint Palestinian-Lebanese leadership to an emergency meeting so that Jumblatt could deliver the message.

Ibrahim headed immediately to a new operations room that Abu Jihad (a member of Fateh's Central Committee in charge of operations in the Occupied West Bank and Gaza) was using as his temporary headquarters because of the continuous Israeli shelling of the other operations rooms and their surroundings in Beirut. This operations room was in the basement of a building near the Lebanese Al-Helu Barracks, the headquarters for Force 16, better known as the Riot Force, one of Fateh's Special Forces units.

Abu Jihad and I were already there, discussing the possibility of Sharon storming Beirut with his ground forces, including the possible locations for that incursion. My opinions were based on the maps that Fayez had brought me before the invasion had begun. As we were discussing various strategies of how to fortify Beirut, in rushed Muhsin Ibrahim, informing us that Jumblatt needed to speak to us urgently, and that he had requested an emergency meeting of the joint PLO leadership. He believed that whatever Jumblatt had to say was going to require the joint leadership to live up to its historic responsibility to serve both Palestinian and Lebanese national interests. Abu Jihad nodded. "Where do you propose we hold this meeting?" he asked. "We need an unmarked location."

Ibrahim suggested a place close to Al-Helu Barracks, which was located in the Ajami Carpet Warehouse, owned by a friend of his. He described the layout of the building as well as its location and entrances. Abu Jihad agreed, noting the location in his message to Arafat. The meeting was scheduled to take place four hours later so that everyone could be informed, especially as they would all face complicated security risks just to get there.

By the appointed time, the place was packed. I sat next to Ibrahim, who did not say what Jumblatt was going to talk about, only that he was about to deliver a message to the leadership that he had received from the Israelis, which had been sent via Habib.

When Jumblatt arrived, he was visibly nervous. When Arafat arrived, Ibrahim asked us to wait for George Habash to arrive as well. He knew that Habash's presence was essential because the decisions we were going to have to make would have an impact on all of our PLO organizations. Arafat agreed.

Moments later, in walked Habash, leaning on his cane. He had had an operation on his leg to remove a dry vein, but the operation had gone badly, leaving him partially paralyzed for the rest of his life. Arafat rushed to help him down the stairs and once Habash was seated, the meeting began.

After some preliminary greetings, it was time for Jumblatt to talk. The room turned quiet as everyone listened expectantly. Jumblatt remained silent for what felt like an interminable length of time, until Ibrahim reminded him that everyone was eager to hear what he had to report. Finally, Jumblatt spoke. His voice was shaky. "In short, I have been asked to fire the fatal, merciful bullet." Then he broke down, weeping and laughing hysterically, unable to control himself. When he regained his composure, he explained that the Israelis, supported by the United States, wanted the Palestinians to leave Beirut, unconditionally, under the protection of the Red Cross. If we did not agree, then the Israeli aircraft, artillery, and navy would destroy Beirut.

The silence in the room was deafening. None of us could believe what Jumblatt had just said. Destroy Beirut? Impossible!

Habash was the first to speak. "I ask our brothers, the leaders of the national Lebanese groups, to allow us to die as martyrs on their lands in defense of Palestine, the Arab nation and Beirut, the first Arab capital in our region."

In the discussion that followed, most of the leaders of the Lebanese National Movement—a front of parties and organizations active during the early years of the civil war in Lebanon, founded by Walid's father, Kamal Jumblatt—stood by the Palestinian revolution, and said that they, too, were more than willing to die in defense of Beirut. The great courage and determination of the men around him, who were ready to stand up against Israel regardless of the odds against them, inspired Jumblatt and helped him to regain some of his self-confidence.

Then Arafat spoke, and his words represented the feelings of everyone there: "I thank my brothers for such a great national stance. Together we will stop Israel from occupying the first Arab capital. Our path is one and the same, and history will record this brave and dignified stand. Do not forget that we will be alone in our fight against the strongest army in the Middle East, with only light weapons at our disposal. This is the miracle of a strong will. As for my brother Walid, I want to say that we are together in fighting this diabolical invasion, but let us not forget that political work is also necessary. We will remain side-by-side."

As the meeting adjourned, everyone left for the operations room to begin formulating defensive strategies. More Israeli incursions were expected soon.

12

A CLOSE CALL

As the siege continued day and night, the nights began to seem longer as the bombings from sea, air, and land increased in both intensity and devastation. Air-raid shelters were being buried, buildings destroyed, and well-worn roads no longer existed. Israeli bombs were massacring people and obliterating concrete indiscriminately. Near Sharon's headquarters in the Alexander Hotel, Israeli artillery and tanks could accurately strike at targets in the city. Israeli aircraft could strike at locations that were hidden from the artillery by high buildings. The area of Beirut in which the leadership could move relatively freely had become increasingly smaller. Convening a meeting became a complicated security matter.

Despite the heavy bombing and destruction, our communications network remained operational, enabling Israeli collaborators access to information about the locations of our joint forces as well as those of the leaders, which they would then pass on to the Israelis. Because of the very real danger, Arafat issued orders to all high-ranking Palestinians not to travel around the city in their own cars, which would be recognized and attract unwarranted attention. We all had black Mercedes cars, and each of us would travel with two cars of bodyguards, one in front and one behind. We would also travel within the city at high speeds so that we would at least be moving targets rather than slow-moving sitting ducks. Anyone could spot us a mile away.

Because of the bombing, Arafat also forbade the leadership from meeting under the same roof. However, despite the heavy shelling and Arafat's orders, leadership members continued to travel to meetings either in their own black cars or in those of their staff, giving collaborators ample opportunity to inform Israelis in East Beirut of the location of each meeting we were having in West Beirut, where we were headquartered. Most of the leaders followed Arafat's instructions if they knew he was going to be in attendance, but when they were traveling about on their own, many of the leaders just threw caution to the wind. They felt they weren't important enough to be targeted anyway, when compared to Arafat. They weren't being defiant, just careless.

On August 10, 1982, Arafat called for an emergency meeting of the leadership to discuss the latest military and political developments in the city. He felt we needed to meet together, face to face, to make sure that all operations were well coordinated. The Israeli stranglehold around Beirut was getting tighter and tighter. The orders to attend the meeting were hand delivered to make sure that everyone who was supposed to be there had received them. There would be no excuse for missing the meeting. Also, he didn't want to call everyone on the telephone because he knew all phone lines were being monitored by the Israelis and their collaborators. The orders contained instructions that we were going to meet at a building located in Al-Ramla Al-Baida, a residential area of Beirut. When we all arrived at the specified location, we were then told that the meeting place had been moved to another site far away from Al-Ramla Al-Baida. This was another of the security precautions Arafat had in place. We would often be told to meet at a specified location, only to be told once we got there to go somewhere else. We were moved around the city like chess pieces until Arafat felt our meeting venue was a safe one. His intuition had never failed him, and we trusted in him implicitly.

Once I had arrived at the new location, I joined the others who were just getting seated. Arafat arrived soon after I did. He greeted everyone, but seemed nervous and edgy. Before the meeting got started, Arafat stood up and said, "Everyone out! Evacuate the building immediately!" Some started to complain, but Arafat was adamant. "Everyone out! This is an order!" As everyone got up and started heading for the doors, he grabbed my arm and rushed me to the nearest exit, where his car was waiting for us. We drove away at breakneck speed toward Al-Hamra Street in Beirut, a busy commercial sector of the city. As we neared the

Piccadilly Cinema, a major landmark in Beirut, Arafat ordered his driver to take us to the garage of the cinema complex, which was six floors underground. It was only then that Arafat revealed to me that he thought the meeting place we had just left was going to be bombed any minute. I asked him how he knew this and all he said was, "Analysis and hunches. As I was arriving, I noticed a crowd of people gathering on the balconies of the building across the street. They were obviously watching with great interest the arrival of many high-ranking Palestinians. Any one of them could have been an Israeli collaborator. Besides that, I realized that the location of our meeting was exposed to Israel's artillery, which as you know is based in the hills of Brumana."

Arafat got out of the car and started to pace slowly back and forth, deep in thought, as if he were waiting for something. Within seconds, the echo of heavy artillery shelling filled the air. We found out later that our meeting place had indeed been bombed by the Israelis, but thanks to Arafat's quick thinking, the Palestinian leadership had once again survived annihilation.

13

PRACTICAL SOLUTIONS TO IMPRACTICAL PROBLEMS

Although the Palestinian leadership knew that Israel intended to invade Lebanon, we did not think that Sharon would go so far as to place Beirut under siege for any length of time. We simply had not taken into account the possibility of a long-term siege, only an invasion that required defensive operations. A siege meant that there would be a depletion of such supplies as food, fuel, weapons, and medicine, and we had not built up extra stores of anything like that.

The prevailing opinion of the Palestinian, Lebanese, and Syrian leaderships had been that the Israeli incursion would extend only forty kilometers north of the Lebanese-Israeli border and that Israel would launch air and naval strikes against other locations, including our headquarters in Beirut. However, even though Menachem Begin had declared an end to the invasion once his troops had reached Beaufort Castle, saying, "The Peace of the Galilee is now achieved," Sharon continued on further into Lebanon, following the plans I had seen earlier on the map that Fayez had brought to me, disregarding the terms the United States had outlined for Israel regarding their operations in Lebanon.

As a result of our not planning for a long-term siege, our preparations did not include important practical details such as building up extra supplies. This miscalculation in our planning resulted in many problems during the invasion, some of which paralyzed the movements of the troops and their leaders since they needed fuel for their vehicles.

Gas stations in Beirut had not increased their stock in anticipation of the invasion. Just days into the siege, gasoline became a precious commodity and began selling for astronomical prices on the black market. The *tanzims* (military organizations) tried to solve the problem on their own rather than coordinating their efforts with each other, which could have resulted in better negotiations over costs. The administrative personnel of the *tanzims* rushed to buy up the inventories of gas stations in West Beirut, where we were headquartered. The stations then took on the job of managing the distribution of gas for the cars and machinery belonging to the *tanzims*. Eleven liters per vehicle per day was the standard ration, but if the individual was an active leader or member of the military, this amount would only last him half a day because he would have to move about the city several times since we could not communicate with each other by phone.

A month into the siege, the gas crisis worsened, forcing the *tanzims* to buy gas on the black market at very high prices. One hot day, I was trying to buy gas and was told that huge fuel tankers would be trying to enter Beirut through one of the Israeli checkpoints. A man from one of the gas stations told me he was paying US$1,000 to an Israeli officer at the checkpoint for every tanker he allowed through. Even at that price we would be saving a great deal of money.

I thought I would try this strategy as well, but not without making sure that what the man had told me was actually true. I wanted to be sure that the deal he had mentioned was neither a trap nor some sort of fraud to get money out of us for nothing. The first time we had arranged to pay for a tanker, we had a trusted Lebanese citizen positioned on one side of the Israeli barrier and another on our side. The Lebanese were happy to help us get more gasoline into their country because it was to their benefit as well. We couldn't have any of our people standing on either side of the Israeli barriers or we could have been killed by the Israeli soldiers. The first exchange, if it were to happen at all, would take place on our side of the barrier. Luckily, everything went smoothly, and the fuel did get to the gas stations. We let it be known to members of various *tanzims* that the Israelis at the checkpoints could be bribed with U.S. dollars.

Since diesel fuel was also needed to operate generators, tanks, and military vehicles, larger quantities of it than usual were also required. The gas stations in Beirut did not typically keep much diesel fuel on hand during the summer months because demand for it was only high in winter, when it was used for heating. Now we were facing a severe diesel shortage. When the problem was discussed at one of the leadership meetings, General Sayel announced that he had found a solution but did not wish to say what it was yet. That was his nature: he was discreet until he was successful.

A week later, we found out what Sayel had done. All apartment buildings in Beirut stored diesel fuel in underground tanks, enough to supply every apartment, even in buildings ten or twenty stories high. The heavy Israeli shelling in July had forced tens of thousands to flee their apartment buildings in the southern suburb of Beirut, the areas around the airport, and Hassan Well, Shatilla, and Al-Barajna Tower, seeking refuge in either South Lebanon or Ras Beirut, an upscale residential area in West Beirut. Sayel had purchased pumps and outfitted empty tank trucks with them, and then, despite the heavy shelling, he sent the empty tankers into all the abandoned areas. He ordered that every drop of diesel be drawn out of those tanks. It was then transferred into the tanks of gas stations that had run out of gas or diesel and had had to close down. Sayel's solution had been pure genius.

As the days rolled by, the siege conditions became worse as fuel, water, and electricity became even more scarce. And the shelling continued to increase. Just when we thought things couldn't get much worse, another problem emerged that we hadn't anticipated at all. Bakeries began selling bread to civilians at extremely inflated prices. Before long, these prices reached such high levels that poor people could no longer afford to eat bread. It appeared that the bakers were taking advantage of people who were caught in a desperate situation.

The subject came up during a meeting of the joint Palestinian-Lebanese leadership at which only a few members were present. Arafat viewed this as a serious problem and promised to do something about it. He did not say what he was planning to do, but everyone knew that if Arafat made a promise, he kept it.

The next day, he ordered all the flour that had been stored in Beirut's warehouses to be confiscated. Then he invited all the merchants in the city to a meeting and asked them only one question: "What is the price you had planned to charge for flour on the open market?"

No one said a word; they were all terrified to answer. Then Arafat spoke to the merchants about the siege, the constant fighting, the suffering of the citizens of Beirut, and the need for everyone to stick together. Then he asked the question again.

Finally, one of the merchants spoke up, naming a price that was obviously much higher than market price, and the others agreed that it was the right price. Arafat then ordered that they be paid that full amount for the confiscated flour and that the flour be distributed to all bakeries in the quantities that they usually received, on one condition—that the bakers would then distribute free bread to all the citizens. The merchants knew that Arafat could have left them with nothing since he had all the flour under his control, but he had been more than fair to them. By implication, he had made it clear to all the merchants that in the future, he would be watching them, making sure they were not taking advantage of anyone by selling any of the commodities at extraordinary rates when everyone around them was suffering. The bakers understood the message: Arafat would not allow anyone to make a profit on someone else's suffering. Arafat's generosity, compassion, and sense of fair play during those trying times were gratefully remembered by the Lebanese people long afterward.

14

THE SOVIET INVITATION

Ever since the bombing of the sports arena on June 5, 1982, the Israelis kept insisting that their invasion of Lebanon was simply a defensive military operation. They claimed that they only wanted to clear a forty-kilometer stretch along their northern border in order to prevent the joint Palestinian-Lebanese troops from shelling Israeli towns and settlements located there.

Israeli prime minister Begin even implied that the goals of the invasion had been met once they had occupied Beaufort Castle on the Litany River; nonetheless, the Israeli troops under Sharon continued to advance farther north toward Beirut. While the joint Palestinian-Lebanese forces were fiercely fighting against the Israeli army in Tyre and Sidon (cities in the south of Lebanon), the Israelis, using American-made naval ships, unloaded dozens of amphibious tanks near the Khalda Beaches south of Beirut. The Israeli plan was twofold: first, they hoped this strategy would take the leadership of the joint Palestinian-Lebanese forces by surprise, and second, they saw it as a way of breaking the morale of the fighters by making them think the Israeli forces had stormed all the areas in the south as well as Beirut. Our resistance, however, proved stronger than the Israelis had anticipated. The combined PLO and Lebanese troops managed to force the Israelis to retreat by destroying several of their tanks and capturing two.

The Syrians had not felt threatened by Israel's invasion of Lebanon. They had been assured by the United States that the Israelis were carrying out a limited operation in retaliation for a missile attack. However, the Israeli tanks had advanced deeply into the Shuf Mountains and their forces reached Bihamdoon in Jabal Lubnan, both of which are within striking distance of Damascus. These also were areas where Syria had positioned some of its troops because they considered them to be defensive lines. They never expected to have to face the Israeli onslaught, which Syria had assumed was only meant to push back the Palestinians, not to target them as well. But by June 6, the Israelis had already moved into the Shuf mountains, an area inhabited by the Druze, and were clashing with the Syrians there. The General Command in Damascus could not believe the reports they were receiving from their troops: The Syrians were suffering heavy casualties and needed help. Syrian Mig fighter planes were sent in to provide air strikes, but they also had to battle the Israeli air force. By June 10, Syria and the PLO forces were battling side by side against the Israelis. Syria called for a cease fire and Israel agreed, but only after there had been intensive Soviet-American negotiations; Syria had lost 20 planes, many tanks, and over 200 soldiers. The Israelis had also suffered high casualties, but they kept their losses undeclared until after the war. As usual, Israel did not reveal to the press any accurate figures about their losses. Syria was out of the battle while the Palestinian and Lebanese troops remained in direct confrontation with the well-equipped Israeli army.

The Palestinian and Lebanese steadfastness must have enraged Sharon so much that I believe he ordered Beirut to be bombed relentlessly from the land, sea, and air in order to punish us all for resisting his onslaught into Beirut. Israel's actions now belied their earlier assertions. It was crystal clear that their aim had never been to just clear forty kilometers along their northern border. They were evidently hell-bent on eliminating our leadership while also "cleansing" Beirut of all Palestinians, a fact they couldn't deny any longer. Sharon had promised he would only push us back those agreed-to forty kilometers, but once he had entered Lebanon, he was determined to annihilate us.

Arafat and the Lebanese government were in regular contact, either directly or indirectly, with the ambassadors of the permanent members of the UN Security Council (France, the United Kingdom, the United States, China, and the Soviet Union), trying to convince them to put pressure on Israel to stop its advancement. However, the PLO depended mainly on the Eastern Bloc (East Germany, Bulgaria, Rumania, Poland, and Czechoslovakia), led by the Soviet Union, to pressure the United States into stopping Israel's military operation. But once Syria had signed the cease-fire, the Eastern Bloc countries suddenly became incapacitated by fear of the United States and Israel, along with all the other Arab countries. Due to the U.S. and Israeli barricade that they had put up in the Mediterranean, no one had any access to Lebanon, unless they wanted to risk enraging either the United States or Israel by breaking through their sea blockade. With Syria out of the battle, nothing could even be smuggled in through Syrian borders. Now nothing could be done to help us or our Lebanese brothers. The PLO and its Lebanese partners were left to stand alone against Israel, an effort made all the more difficult thanks to the siege of Beirut. Our ammunition, food, and medical supplies had been severely depleted.

An honorable solution had to be reached. Arafat and the rest of the PLO leadership began to work on setting up some negotiations with the United States through Philip Habib. He was in contact with the PLO leadership through the Lebanese, either by way of official government representatives like Prime Minister Shafiq Al-Wazan or unofficial ones like former prime minister Saeb Salam. In the end, however, nothing came of any of these attempts.

Apparently, even the Soviets knew that the United States had okayed Israel's invasion of Lebanon. They had not officially informed us of their previous knowledge, although some of our leaders claimed they had received messages from Moscow. It turned out that they had heard it only from their representatives in Moscow, not from anyone in the Kremlin. Some of our leaders were delusional enough about Soviet support to talk at official meetings about the imminent arrival of a Soviet aircraft carrier near the shores of Beirut and of an imminent Soviet intervention. Although the Soviets had been supporting us financially and militarily since our defeat in 1967, we knew that this was their policy for revolutionary groups all over the world. Our relationship with the Soviet Union was not a unique one, for they were also supporting liberation groups in Africa, Latin America, and Cuba, as well as in the Middle East.

The discussion seemed childish to me. We all knew the Soviets would not get involved in a war that might lead to a direct confrontation with the United States just because of us. At one meeting headed by Arafat, some of the members claimed that the Soviets had confirmed directly to them in an urgent communiqué that they were going to back us up in the fighting. This only made me laugh, and Arafat was also skeptical. "And why would the Soviets contact just anyone in the leadership when they could contact me directly with such an auspicious announcement? I am the President of the PLO after all!" he asked.

The Kremlin finally did send a message directly to Arafat, at 3 a.m. on July 17. Colonel Nuscov, who was in charge of Soviet military intelligence at the Soviet Embassy in Beirut at the time, came to my home to tell me that the Soviet ambassador in Beirut wanted to deliver an urgent message from the Kremlin to Arafat.

I hurried to Arafat's secret headquarters in West Beirut to deliver the message personally. We were both curious and anxious to know what the Kremlin had to say. As Israeli flares lit up the Beirut sky, we headed to the embassy amid a steady barrage of Israeli land and naval shelling, apprehensive about reaching our destination. Even though we were nervous and in a hurry, Arafat ordered the driver to drive at a normal speed so as not to draw any unnecessary attention to our car.

We arrived at about 4 a.m. and were greeted at the gate of the Soviet embassy as official guests, even though Arafat had not informed the embassy that he was coming. Together, Arafat and I strode side by side to the staircase of the main building where the Soviet ambassador and his team welcomed us. Arafat greeted him in Russian, and then we were quickly escorted into the embassy as the impact of nearby Israeli missiles and bombs shook the building.

The ambassador began, "I have just received a communiqué from the High Soviet Council and it is addressed to you, Mr. President. The situation is dangerous for it seems that the United States considers this territory to be under its jurisdiction. Besides allowing Israel to invade Lebanon, we also have it on good authority that the U.S. government had given the thumbs up to Israel to eliminate all the leaders of the PLO while Israeli troops were still within the borders of Lebanon. The message I received from the Kremlin is very clear. Our comrades feel it would be wise for you to bend a little to save what can be saved. Soviet intervention is not possible, whether for political, military, or even humanitarian reasons. They feel that if you have been offered the chance to leave Beirut onboard a U.S. naval ship, then you should not hesitate to accept."

Arafat's response was cold as ice. "We know all this, and still, we have decided to stand firm and resist until we are able to find an honorable political solution on our own terms. We will not leave in Red Cross trucks with our hands raised in surrender, nor will we leave onboard a U.S. naval ship. We will leave eventually, but on our terms only, when we know that our revolution is intact and our future secure. We will leave with our dignity unbroken as we continue our struggle to prevent Sharon from entering Beirut personally no matter what. I hope you will relay this message to our dear comrades in Moscow." We were still under siege, but Sharon had not yet sent any of his infantry into Beirut; all of his attacks on Beirut had been from the sky and the sea so far.

Arafat then thanked the ambassador, apologizing that because time was short, he would have to leave immediately for his headquarters in Beirut. He had to prepare for the inevitable confrontation ahead: Sharon was planning on entering Beirut himself with his infantry that very same morning.

15

THE STORMING OF BEIRUT

General Sharon underestimated us. He thought that the daily and nightly shelling by land, air, and sea would wear us out, making the storming of Beirut an easy task. He also believed that the depletion of our ammunition in the siege would make difficult any defense of Beirut, either by us or our Lebanese allies.

The Museum Area (whose name is taken from the fact that the area's largest landmark is the huge Lebanese Museum), which is adjacent to a large, well-known racetrack called Al-Hursh, became the point where the city was divided into East and West Beirut. Ariel Sharon, who at that time was Israel's general minister of defense, thought that if he attacked from that point and then pushed forward with his tanks toward the sea, he would be able to tear apart West Beirut. He also planned on taking a shortcut by pushing his tanks a few kilometers along the Corniche Al-Mazra'a on his way to the sea. The Corniche is a highway that penetrates West Beirut from the east and goes along the beach. East Beirut starts at the point of the Lebanese Museum. If Sharon could make his way through the racetrack, rather than having to go around it, he would not only be able to split the city in two, but it would be easier for his troops to strangle the PLO forces.

But what he failed to reckon with was the sheer determination of a people who were willing to defend the city at all costs. Every few feet throughout the city, there was a barricade manned by armed fighters who were prepared to give their lives in defense of the first Arab capital city and its people. Sharon did not think for a minute that on the confrontation line would there be young men who would soon be boasting about having destroyed his tanks.

The Israelis had stronger armaments than we had and far more destructive weapons such as tanks, ships, and aircraft. Sharon had thought that the storming of Beirut would take no more than an hour or two, at most; he had forgotten to factor in a very crucial piece of information: during the civil war in Beirut that had begun in 1975, the city had been transformed into a war zone of trenches and guns.

Although collaborators were helping him from the inside, Sharon relied fully on his arsenal of weapons. He gathered his machinery and soldiers behind the Lebanese Museum, where he planned to penetrate the walls of the racetrack from the eastern side before advancing toward the city. He would then have his troops break through the western walls of the racetrack, eventually aiming the cannons of his tanks at the Corniche Al-Mazra'a, where the people of Beirut were innocently buying their sandwiches.

I believe that Sharon thought his plan was foolproof and guaranteed to take us all completely by surprise.

The Czech Embassy was in a tall building on the opposite side of the racetrack, which overlooked the Lebanese Museum, the Corniche Al-Mazra'a, and neighboring areas. General Sayel and Abu Jihad notified Arafat that Sharon did indeed plan to storm Beirut because their scout could see what was developing on the other side of the racetrack. Unknown to the Israelis, Abu Jihad had sent a young man named Samir up to the roof of the embassy with long-range binoculars and told him report any movement of the Israeli troops.

In no time, the operations room became a beehive of activity; orders were being delivered to all of our military positions, most of which were not in permanent locations, and were ready to move at a moment's notice. Sayel, who never smiled, wore mixed emotions on his face: seriousness, anger, determination, and defiance. Because he wanted to know the appropriate coordinates for every cannon and rocket launcher as well as the exact amount of ammunition he had, he summoned the military officers of the *tanzims* to an immediate meeting to report on what weaponry and ammunition was on hand. Within three hours, Abu Jihad and Sayel knew they had enough firepower and ammunition to stop the incursion.

Officers gathered around a detailed map of the site to receive their individual missions, which involved pinpointing the location of cannons and reconfirming the coordinates of each. The men were also told not to fire on the enemy unless the order came directly from the Central Command room. Arafat gave Abu Jihad, who was heading the main operation, the go-ahead to proceed to the racetrack to check on the readiness of the fighters.

The indiscriminate shelling from land, air, and sea continued relentlessly, resulting in untold civilian death and destruction of property. That day was a hellish one. Though military experts differ on the exact number of explosives Sharon dropped on Beirut that day, there is a general consensus that it was at least equal to the amount that was dropped on Dresden, Germany during World War II, when the city was completely destroyed. Sharon bombed high-rise apartment buildings using concussion bombs, often killing up to 480 civilians in one go. One such example of this was the Israeli bombing of the Acre Building in an area called Samayeh. Only one person survived that bombing. He lost his wife and all eight of his children when the building crushed them all. The poor man went mad.

Samir's voice crackled over the receiver in Sayel's hand. "They are moving slowly toward the wall of the racetrack. The tanks are advancing slowly. Behind them are hundreds of soldiers ready to move."

The battle was beginning.

Sayel reiterated his orders: no one was to fire until ordered to do so.

Then Samir informed us that ten tanks were already inside the racetrack walls, advancing toward the western wall. When he reported that dozens of soldiers behind the tanks were halfway between the eastern and western walls, Sayel signaled his officers to prepare to fire. Three minutes later, he gave the order to open fire.

Instantly, our field guns, automatic sub-machine guns, grenades, and inertia rifles rained down on the infiltrating Israeli force. Above the sound of howling missiles and pounding cannons, Samir gave a blow-by-blow description of the Israeli tanks being torn apart by our heavy artillery that was blasting them from the mountains, as well as by our Katyusha rockets and mortars from closer range. The Israeli soldiers were unable to retreat through the surrounding wall of flames we had created with our resistance.

When General Sayel again ordered his men to fire, the second stage of missiles and cannons poured down on Sharon's troops. After a short time, Sayel ordered a ceasefire. Samir reported that there was a lull in the fighting and that Israeli soldiers were advancing to pick up those who had fallen. Sayel ordered the men to open fire again.

The shooting continued until nightfall, leaving Sharon bewildered by his inability to storm the city as easily as he had thought. He stopped thinking about his victory celebrations and concentrated on picking up the pieces of his damaged tanks and wounded soldiers. The taking of Beirut had not at all gone as I am sure he had pictured it would. On that day alone, Sharon lost over a hundred soldiers and thirteen tanks. That day ended Sharon's plan to enter Beirut on land, although he kept up the shelling from the air and the sea.

Although we had taught Sharon a huge lesson that day, he never seemed to learn anything from it because he never stopped targeting Palestinian civilians. It was as if he thought we would stop resisting him out of fear that he would retaliate if we stood up to Israeli aggression. We were determined that he would never fulfill his promise to kill the leadership of the PLO, nor would he ever succeed in putting any of them on trial. We were stalwart in our decision to back up the Lebanese and fight back. We took defending Beirut very seriously; it was, after all, the first Arab capital in the Middle East. Sharon never did succeed in entering Beirut while we were still there.

But like I said before: Sharon never learned anything about us nor did he ever appreciate just how stubborn we could be.

16

A TERRORIST
AT BUCKINGHAM
PALACE

E ven though Arafat and his forces were eventually driven from Beirut in the fall of 1982, Arafat still believed that Sharon had not been victorious. This was because Sharon had failed to achieve his main objectives: to enter Beirut and eliminate Arafat, or at least have him tried for terrorism. Arafat was very worried about the civilians who were going to be left behind in the refugee camps in Beirut. He trusted neither the Israelis nor the Lebanese Phalangists (Christian militia). Even though the United States had given written guarantees to the Palestinians that they would protect the Muslims in West Beirut with deployments of multinational forces to defend the camps, Arafat believed that Sharon would not respect this agreement. He had already proven he was not to be trusted when he had his troops carry on into Beirut when he was supposed to have stopped at the Litany River, only forty kilometers (about twenty-five miles) into Lebanon. Sharon had also proven that UN troops were not a deterrent to his aggression when he stormed through Callahan's encampment. What was to stop him from doing the same thing this time? Many of the families of the PLO fighters lived in those camps, making up, in fact, the majority of the population. Arafat had been worried that either Christian militia groups, Israeli soldiers, or pro-Syrian groups within Lebanon would seek vengeance on those who were related to Palestinian fighters. Arafat had not been mistaken to worry about the safety of those Palestinian families who would be completely defenseless once we had left.

Two days after we left Beirut, on September 3, Israel deployed its forces around the camps. Sharon claimed that over 2,000 PLO fighters had remained, which was categorically denied by the PLO leadership. On September 15, following the assassination of Bachir Gemayel, the president-elect of Lebanon, by a member of the Syrian Social Nationalist party, Sharon had his troops reoccupy West Beirut, killing almost one hundred people in the process. Israel's occupation of Beirut violated all the peace agreements that had been made with Syria and Lebanon as well. Ariel Sharon and Rafael Eitan, a general in the Israeli army, allowed Lebanese Phalangists to enter the Sabra and Shatilla Palestinian refugee camps, giving them carte blanche to do whatever they felt was needed to capture or kill all the PLO fighters suspected of living there.

The Israeli army completely surrounded the camps so that no one could escape. They also set up observation posts on tall buildings nearby so that they could observe what was happening inside the camps. Sharon, Eitan, and top Phalangist leaders met the day before the massacre to work out their plans. Late at night on September 16, Phalangists, led by Elie Hobeika, stormed the camps. For the next two days, they massacred civilians while the Israeli army sent flares into the night sky to provide light for the slaughter. One unit of Phalangists was sent into the camps with guns, knives, and hatchets. Any Palestinians who tried to flee from the camps were turned back by the Israeli soldiers.

When the Phalangists reported to the Israelis about what they had accomplished, they were told to "mop up" operations and were given another day to continue the carnage. Under U.S. pressure to stop the massacre, Israeli leaders gave the Phalangists only a few more hours to finish their mission. Some survivors were lined up and randomly shot, while others were sent to the Sports City arena to be interrogated. By the time foreign journalists had been allowed into the camps, they found hundreds and hundreds of mutilated bodies of men, women, and children strewn throughout the camps. A bulldozer had also been used to try to cover up just how many people had been slaughtered. The majority of the victims, as I said, were relatives of the fighters who had left Beirut to their new assigned posts.

As Israeli military involvement in Lebanon increased and word of the massacres that took place in Sabra and Shattila reached the world, Begin withdrew more and more from the world of politics, eventually resigning in October 1983. In my personal opinion, I believe that Begin was not only tired of Sharon's deceptions, but he also wanted to atone for the mistake he had made by believing in his own defense minister Sharon, who had continually acted unethically when it came to all pledges, promises, and agreements.

The eyes of the world were again focused on the Palestinians who were leaving Beirut. Sharon thought that this would be the end of the PLO. The world had been shocked by the magnitude of the crimes committed by Sharon in Lebanon, at the enormity of the destruction caused by his air and artillery shelling of Beirut, but mostly by the massacres that had been committed. What Sharon did not expect was the negative public opinion that his insolence and disregard for human life had generated.

International reaction had been so negative that it put pressure on President Reagan to do something to help resolve the conflict in the Middle East. Immediately after the Palestinian troops and leadership left Beirut, he proposed his "Land for Peace" initiative. Naturally, this repositioned the media spotlight on the Palestinian issue once again.

We left Beirut for Syria on September 1, 1982, and arrived at 3 a.m. at Tartoos Port, off the coast of Syria, only to discover that no one had made any living arrangements for us. The arrival of thousands of Palestinians over the previous months had caused the rents and hotel room prices to skyrocket, making it difficult to find affordable places to live. We parted ways and at 5 a.m., after much searching, the night concierge in a hotel in the Al-Midan neighborhood in Damascus finally took pity on me, letting me have one of the rooms. It had been a harder day than even the worst days of shelling. I slept like the dead.

In the following weeks I spent most of my time in one meeting after another: political evaluation sessions; appraisals of the leadership's performance in battle; and sessions to make administrative military and political arrangements after most of the leadership of the PFLP moved to Damascus. Only a few Palestinian leaders had been allowed to stay in Lebanon because they were Palestinian refugees who had fled in 1948.

As we familiarized ourselves with Damascus, local politicians and reporters began to find their way to us. One morning when I was at the political bureau office, some foreign reporters arrived. At first, their questions were all about the fighting in Beirut. At the end of the session, one of them informed me that he had received a telegram from American journalist David Brinkley asking if I would appear on a live television broadcast dedicated to the Palestinian issue, entitled "What after Beirut?," with others participating in the show. I agreed immediately.

The following day, I met with Brinkley's crew in a suite at the Sheraton Hotel in Damascus that had been transformed into a studio for the live broadcast. I still did not know who the other participants would be. David Brinkley began the show by directing the first question to me: "The PLO and its troops have left Beirut and are displaced in many countries. Their path is very difficult now so why does the PLO not agree that the Palestinians should become citizens in either Jordan or Israel?"

My answer was brief. "A long time ago, the Palestinians had proposed the idea of a democratic country in which Arabs and Jews could live with equal rights and equal duties under a democratic secular system. Israel rejected the idea because they still wanted the state of Israel to be a Jewish state, rather than a secular one. They fear that Jews would soon become a minority in a democratic secular state that includes the Palestinians. Therefore, we decided to struggle to establish our Palestinian state, and despite this, the Israeli army hunts down the Palestinians, wanting to annex what remains of our lands. What Sharon did is the biggest proof of what I am saying. He wanted to eliminate the Palestinian leadership and troops so he could annex the West Bank and Gaza Strip." On the subject of Jordan, I reminded him of the events of Black September in 1970, when we had faced forces who wanted to eliminate us there, too. For that reason, I told him, Palestinians wanted their independence. Unbeknownst to me, the other two participants in the program were none other than Sharon and King Hussein.

King Hussein immediately objected, protesting: "Mr. Abu Sharif is mistaken. What happened in September was a family dispute; we consider the Palestinians our brothers." Sharon, not surprisingly, insisted that the PLO was a terrorist organization that should be hunted down and eliminated.

As a result of this interview, my name was added to the blacklist files in Jordan, which effectively closed the door to any positive relations with King Hussein. One of the people who had been with His Majesty in the Jordan TV studio later told me that he had been angered deeply by the way I had answered the questions.

Five years later, I was in London and the British protocol officer, whose first name was Simon, told me that King Hussein was coming. I told him that I wanted to meet with His Majesty and asked him to inform me of a way to contact him. Two days later, he told me that I could contact the King through his PR manager, Elizabeth Cork, who agreed to try to arrange a meeting.

The following morning I was awakened in my hotel room by a ringing phone. Still a little groggy, I picked up the receiver and heard a deep, resonant voice saying, "Good morning. This is Hussein. Is Bassam there?"

It was King Hussein himself! He had called me personally to set up the meeting. As soon as I hung up, I phoned Arafat.

The next day, I was in His Majesty's residence, drinking coffee and smoking with him. I apologized about my remarks on the David Brinkley show, admitting that I had not been objective at the time and that what I had said was, perhaps, even hurtful.

He smiled. "I was surprised by your reply because I felt you could have used that opportunity to corner Sharon more than you did. In any case, consider the matter closed. Let us talk about the present and the future."

We talked for a whole hour, finding points of agreement and compatibility in political analyses and predictions. This pleased me because a common political language is one of the shortest paths to making a strong friendship and a closer relationship.

As our meeting ended and His Majesty accompanied me to the door, I expressed the hope that we would be able to meet more often. He responded, "Gladly. I would like to exchange opinions. What we are facing is complicated, and a collective mind is more effective in handling the situation." That was when His Majesty had begun treatment for his cancer. He had mentioned to me that he was getting ready to leave for a clinic outside of London for more medical tests and that he would return in five days.

Six days later, I was invited to lunch with His Majesty. I was his only guest. Since His Majesty appeared reluctant to begin the conversation, I decided to apologize once more for the David Brinkley interview, telling him that I had never meant to offend him.

"Let's let bygones be bygones," he repeated. "I like the way you think, Bassam, as well as the courage you show when you express what's in your heart. Your clarity of vision regarding the Middle East, including solutions to our problems, is exactly what we need."

I was very thankful for his praise, as well as for his graciousness in forgiving my inappropriate responses on TV. His Majesty went on to say, "I hope you'll always be close to me so that I can benefit from your advice."

He looked a bit saddened when he said, "I lost; you should have been with me all the time." I knew he was referring to the difficult days in 1970. When lunch was over, he said, with all sincerity, "Bassam, stay close. I need your advice. Don't hesitate to call me or come to Amman any time you feel it is necessary." I promised him that I would.

I left for Tunisia the following day.

Two months after my visit with Hussein in London, the British ambassador to Tunisia, Thomas Day, informed me that William Waldgrave, Britain's minister for foreign affairs, had invited me to London to discuss the dimensions of the peace process in the Middle East. I relayed the news to Arafat immediately. This was the first time Britain had agreed to such a meeting at the cabinet level. Arafat enthusiastically urged me to use the opportunity for the benefit of the Palestinian people.

The following day, I headed for London. The meeting with Waldgrave went very well, resulting in a new chapter in the relations between Britain and the PLO. Since this had been the government's first high-level meeting with the PLO, it was covered by all the British media. Not unexpectedly, some Zionist extremist reporters denounced it.

Arafat was pleased with the results and called to congratulate me on this achievement. He was also happy when he learned that I had invited Minister Waldgrave to Tunisia to meet with him and other officials.

The late Sheikh Zayed Bin Sultan, who was then the leader of the United Arab Emirates (UAE), was making an official visit to Britain at the Queen's invitation. After consulting Arafat, I called the delegation accompanying Sheikh Zayed to request a meeting for us to discuss the latest political and field developments.

Later on that evening, I was with a number of influential Lords of England's Conservative Party when Simon informed me that Sheikh Zayed's protocol officer had phoned to say my meeting with him would be at Buckingham Palace, where Zayed was staying as a guest of Queen Elizabeth II. The meeting was to take place in just thirty minutes. I had to leave immediately if I were to make it before the gates of the palace closed. My host, Lord Palumbo, graciously understood the great importance of the meeting, and insisted that I leave posthaste and that we would get together another time.

Simon and I arrived at the massive outer gates of the palace exactly on time. Our car entered the palace grounds and headed toward the building occupied by Sheikh Zayed bin Sultan. A red carpet stretched from the entrance of the palace to where our car had stopped; I was received by the Master of Ceremonies and others wearing their traditional Eastern dress. The press was also there.

I waited in the lobby, which reminded me very much of a museum. I summarized developments, explaining to His Highness the difficult circumstances of occupation under which our people were living. He would interrupt me once in a while to ask for more details, but I could see he was deeply moved by what I was telling him. Sheikh Zayed was an Arab who remained true in his national stands; Palestine had a very special place in his heart.

Due to His Highness's busy schedule, I was granted only a twenty-minute meeting. When my allotted time was up, I stood to leave, apologizing for having taken up so much of his valuable time. He motioned for me to remain seated, saying firmly, "Palestine is more important." We continued talking for a whole hour, which both amazed and confused his staff. Before I left, Sheikh Zayed pledged to aid the Palestinian people and encouraged us to remain firmly committed to freeing Jerusalem.

The following morning, I was surprised to learn that my visit to Buckingham Palace had caused a huge uproar in London. A rightist newspaper had run the headline: "A Terrorist in Buckingham Palace."

The palace responded that, as the Queen's guest, Sheikh Zayed bin Sultan had the right to receive whomever he wished in his guest quarters.

It was obvious that my visit had annoyed the extremist right as well as Zionist groups, but it had also become a political gift for the Palestinian people. I was the first Palestinian ever to enter Buckingham Palace.

The news of my meeting reached Arafat before I had had a chance to call him. When I did get him on the phone, he jokingly remarked, "Buckingham Palace, Bassam?" He was pleased with the outcome, saying, "Our people are in desperate need of aid."

When I returned to Tunisia, I had much more work ahead of me.

17

TENSION
WITH SYRIA

To better understand the developments that eventually led to
the tension that existed between the PLO and the Syrian
government by the 1980s, it is necessary to explain some of
the events that took place in Lebanon back in 1975. A civil
war broke out in Lebanon around that time, due to an accumulation of resent-
ment by the poor (mostly Muslims) against those who monopolized the wealth
in the country (mostly Christians, known there as Maronites). It was not by
chance that certain religious communities became richer than others. Economic
privileges had been established for the Lebanese Maronites long ago by the
French colonialists, who made sure the political system they engineered for the
country would protect those privileges by law. Maronites were given key political and security positions, with the requirement that the president of the country and the commander of the army must be Maronites. This allowed Maronites
to be in positions where they could make decisions that would guarantee certain
rights for some, while denying the rights of others.

The poor grew in number through the decades, whether from influxes of
refugees or just from natural population growth, and as their numbers increased,
they started to feel that they had been victims of the system, made poor by the

system itself. Political parties started to develop (Christians on the right and Druze, Shiites, and Sunnis on the left), each striving either to maintain the status quo or to change it. The private sectors within Beirut exemplified these divisions, depending on what the majority was who had settled there (East Beirut was predominately Christian and West Beirut predominately Muslim, for example).

Attitudes of superiority and segregation in Lebanese society were deeply rooted in all levels, whether they were social, religious, or political. From the time the French had first set up the system that guaranteed the Christians special privileges until the end of the 1960s, the dynamics had changed radically. The majority were no longer the Christians, but the non-privileged Muslims. For half a century, the French colonialists had made sure that the Maronites could develop into a wealthy, ruling class with its own armed militias to make sure their rights were protected. The bulk of the population was now poor, however, and they were demanding their rights to share in the political and economic benefits of their country. They too had established their own armed militias. Each of these parties depended on external financial support as well: The Maronites depended on the French, the Greek Orthodox on Greece, the Protestants on the United States, the Druze on the United Kingdom, and the Sunnis on Syria. The Shiites remained "orphans," without any outside help until they found their "godfather" in Iran. The Maronites were against establishing a secular government, which would mean their days of privileges would end. This is what brought the various sides into confrontation. Basically, it was a case of one side trying to maintain the status quo while the other was fighting for change.

While all of this turmoil was developing in Lebanon, Israel was secretly monitoring all of our (i.e., the PLO's) movements within the entire country in order to pinpoint the perfect time and location to destroy the PLO and its leadership. By eliminating the PLO, it could then concentrate on negotiating with a Lebanese government that would sign a peace treaty with them and remain loyal to Israel, not allowing any more attacks to be launched from Lebanese borders. Israel's calculations took into consideration all regional ties, such as those with Egypt and Jordan, seeking to achieve at least a minimum number of regional alliances with countries who would support the establishment of a Lebanese government that would prevent any power, especially Syria and Palestine, from using its lands to launch any attacks against Israel.

Regional tensions were already running high, and during this period the conflict between the Palestinians and Syria reached confrontational levels. Syria was trying to control both the Lebanese and the Palestinians so that it could become the Arab regional power that would negotiate with Israel to end its occupation of the Golan, the West Bank, and the Gaza Strip. For Syria to insist on deciding the fate of all the Palestinians in the Occupied Territories was simply unacceptable to Arafat. He had fought long and hard for the Palestinians to be in charge of their own destiny. Sadat had tried to appropriate that right and now Assad was doing the same. It was simply unacceptable for anyone except the rightful representative of the Palestinian people to make decisions regarding their homeland, and the rightful representative of all the Palestinians at that time was the president of the PLO.

Yasser Arafat rejected all attempts to place authority over Palestine in the hands of the Syrians. If Syria were to start making decisions about the Palestinians, this would mean that Palestine as an independent entity simply would not be able to exist. It would have been under the direction of Hafez Al-Assad, an autocratic leader who would have destroyed any chance for the Palestinians to have enjoyed a democratic country. Anyway, even if another country with a more benevolent leader had wanted to decide everything about Palestine, it would not have been acceptable either. It would be like the Mexican government deciding policies for the United States. Each country should be responsible for its own decisions, including Palestine. Arafat also worked hard to prevent the PLO from becoming militarily involved in the internal Lebanese conflict. At the same time, he continued to support the National Lebanese Movement (see Key Terms), which was not only working to end the injustice that prevailed in Lebanese society as described earlier, but also was trying to create a balanced government based on the new demographics in which the Christians were no longer a majority.

Arafat feared, as did Syria, that the rightist Christian groups in Lebanon who wanted to maintain Christian control within the country, such as the Christian Lebanese Front (i.e., Phalangists, National Liberal Party, and Maronites) would seek aid from Israel, which also regarded the Palestinians as a common enemy. Arafat tried to prevent this by rejecting the pressures that some PLO groups and the National Lebanese Movement were exerting on his troops to enter the ongoing conflict on the side of those working to change the status quo in Lebanon. Arafat did not want to get involved in Lebanon's internal struggles. He wanted his troops focused on one thing and one thing only: resistance against Israel.

Syria, on the other hand, decided to provide military support to the rightist Christian groups in the hope that this would stop them from turning to Israel for help. Syria was part of the Steadfastness and Confrontation Front against

Israel, so Syria was trying to keep Israel out of the equation completely. This increased the pressure on Arafat to get more involved militarily, but he continued to oppose taking sides in the civil war.

At that time, Syria did not know about the ties between the rightist Lebanese groups and Israel, in terms of military training and arms, which had already been established for some time. In order to serve the strategic interests of the rightists, Israeli intelligence circles tried to provoke the Palestinian troops onto the battlefield with the Syrian forces to induce the Christian rightists to strengthen their ties with Israel on the one hand while dragging the Syrians into a confrontation with the Palestinians on the other.

For the tens of thousands of armed men fighting on the battlefield as well as for many leaders, these maneuverings were neither clear nor conceivable. Each party involved in the civil war was out for its own interests; the Christian right was fighting to maintain the obsolete status quo in support of the Christian minority, while those Muslims in the majority were working haphazardly to change it without a clear plan in mind.

In other words, the great tension in Syrian-Palestinian relations can be traced directly back to the Lebanese Civil War, which began in 1975. Syria insisted on dominating Palestinian decision making so as to strengthen its negotiating position. But now Syria was in no position to negotiate for itself, let alone for the Palestinians.

But in spite of the Syrian-Palestinian enmity, Syria began to secretly establish ties with powers inside Fateh. It had a dual agenda: it wanted to undermine Arafat's leadership and persuade Fateh to join with them in a strategic alliance against Arafat. This was clear when the Palestinian National Council (the PLO Parliament) convened in Damascus in 1979 for the main purpose of electing the leadership for the coming term. The coalition of the leftists (the PFLP and DFLP, for example) as well as some of the power centers in Fateh's Central Committee had been able to paralyze the voting process of the National Council by continually arguing about who should be their leader, leaving the possibility of a terrible void in the leadership. It was time for us to elect our leaders, but if this in-fighting and vying for positions of power continued, it was obvious we would be left without anyone as a recognized leader. It was at that moment, when it appeared that no one could agree whose name should be put forward and voted on, that Arafat began to mobilize the Fateh members in his favor. He persuaded large numbers of them to leave the session so that the PNC would lose its quorum and a vote could not take place. When they returned, they were to chant: "I am the son of Fateh. I follow no other." Because Arafat was also the head of Fateh, it was clear for whom they were campaigning. He also had them do this to inspire others to join in and vote for him while also slowing down the voting process. He wanted to prove that there was unity, not disparity, within the ranks of Fateh. The PFLP was a larger voting group within the PNC, and Arafat could have lost his position as president of the PLO if he did not play his cards right during that session.

This fighting within the ranks of the various groups under the umbrella of the PLO went on until a totally unanticipated event occurred. On his way to the troops stationed in the Baqa'a Valley between Lebanon and Syria, Ali Salameh—who was Arafat's personal guard and head of military operations for Fateh, as well as being the head of Force 17—was assassinated by Israeli soldiers. Salameh was very dear to Arafat; he was so deeply saddened by his loss that the members of the National Council decided to pay their condolences directly to Arafat. Arafat also used this opportunity to receive their promises to remain loyal by voting for him as their president once again.

Not long after he had received condolences for Ali Salameh, Arafat returned to the hall of the National Council, announcing to everyone that enough was enough; it was time to vote for their leaders and it should be done without any further delay. He went on to propose that the leadership remain unchanged, reelecting the previous Executive Committee members, keeping him as their president. He wanted to prove to the Syrians that Palestinian governance would remain independent of any outside influence or control, even if Syria did manage to form coalitions with some members from Fateh. Even though I was still a member of the political bureau (we were the decision makers) of the PFLP, I stood by Arafat during his battles with the conference members. I saw the wisdom in what he was doing at the PNC; our cause could not afford any rift whatsoever within our ranks. The squabbling and in-fighting among us was weakening our stance and making us look indecisive and divided in our purpose.

The majority of the National Council voted to accept Arafat's proposal, making him once again the president of the PLO. The next day, Arafat left for our headquarters in Beirut, taking me with him because he valued my advice.

The attempts to mend Syrian-Palestinian relations continued after Arafat and I had left. The Syrian government invited a delegation of Fateh Central Committee members, headed by Abu Iyad, to discuss relations on an unofficial level, which meant that Assad and Arafat would not be attending. The result of the discussion was a draft document titled "Palestinian-Syrian Strategic Cooperation," which basically stated that we would remain allies in our resistance against Israel. Both sides agreed, however, that this document would not go into effect until the two absent leaders had approved it.

"What does Hafez Assad want?" Arafat asked me after reading the draft of the strategic cooperation document that had been sent to him for his approval. President Assad had already added his addendums to the document before it had been sent to Arafat. It was just before midnight, and we were in his office in the Beirut headquarters of the Palestinian Liberation Army. He had asked me to read it too and to give him my feedback. I told Arafat that I thought that it was clear that Assad wanted to be the one who decided the future of Palestine. Arafat was particularly concerned about whether implementation of the agreement would mean losing the independent nature of Palestinian decision making. I told him it was very likely the case. In order to prevent this from happening, we would need to add our own stipulations so that the document maintained the Palestinian vision.

The following morning, at about 3 a.m., I was discussing the situation with dear friend and respected Palestinian poet Mahmoud Darwish when we heard a loud knock on the door. There stood Fathi, Abu Ammar's most senior bodyguard, carrying his weapon. "The president is coming," he announced. Such late-night meetings with Arafat were common.

A few moments later Arafat came in, acting as if he were shocked that we were meeting without him. With a devilish smile on his face, he joked, "I caught you," laughingly implying that his two most trusted men might be plotting behind his back. He liked to joke with us like this whenever he walked in on a private meeting.

Again he asked me, "What does Hafez Assad want?" And again I gave him the same answer.

"Then we must keep the decision making in our hands, no matter what we have to do." He realized that this might put the Palestinian leadership in direct confrontation with Assad, not a person who accepted defiance very easily.

When Arafat sent back the documents with his conditions, it soon became clear to the Syrian government that the attempts to restrain the PLO and dominate it had failed. It was clear that the leadership of the PLO would not be bullied into rescinding their right to act in the best interests of the Palestinians. By the end of the 1970s, Israel had already sent, via the United States and some European countries (such as France and the United Kingdom), more than one threatening message to Syria that could not have been clearer: "If you do not restrain the PLO and stop them from their constant resistance against us, their continual attacks against Northern Israel, we will have to take care of them ourselves."

The Israelis put pressure on Syria to force the PLO to redeploy its troops forty kilometers away from the Israeli-Lebanese border, so that the Palestinian missiles were out of range of Israel. Israel conducted a limited incursion into Lebanon against our troops in 1980, but Israeli officials continued to urge the United States to give them the green light to clear forty kilometers in South Lebanon of any Palestinian presence. In the spring of 1982, President Reagan did exactly that (details of the storming of Beirut can be found in chapter 15), setting off a conflict that came to be known as the Lebanon War.

The tensions between the PLO and Syria had reached a breaking point by June 10, 1982, when Syria signed a cease-fire agreement with Israel after battling its invading army for only five days when they invaded South Lebanon. In doing this, the Syrians had left the Palestinian and Lebanese national troops exposed. Palestinian defense plans had relied on Syrian troops to protect their flanks in the mountains between Syria and Lebanon. Syrian troops had done well in Bihamdoon (a summer resort located in the mountains on the road to Damascus) and the eastern mountains, stopping the progress of the Israeli army there, but the cease-fire agreement took them out of the battle. At the same time, the Syrian troops deployed in Beirut, which were small in number, were rendered ineffective because of depleted ammunition. The Palestinian troops had to take on the responsibility of looking after them with regard to ammunition and food. It was an added burden we could have done without.

The accumulation of all these actions led Arafat to reject the idea of going into Syria after it was agreed that the Palestinian troops and their leadership would leave Beirut under international protection according to an agreement made with Philip Habib, the U.S. presidential envoy to Lebanon. Syria was a natural choice for the Palestinians to go to since it shared a border with Lebanon. But Arafat did not want his Fateh troops to go there, because he and Assad were not on good terms with regard to who had the right to decide the future of Palestine. He also felt the Syrian government had let the Palestinians down when they were fighting the Israeli forces. The PLO could not go back into Jordan since they had been evicted in 1971. The only way he could leave with his fighters would be by sea, to Cyprus. Multinational troops were also to replace the Palestinians who had been protecting the refugee camps.

No one had any doubt that Arafat's decision to head first to Cyprus was a form of censure of the Syrian stand. Arafat, however, had not been successful in dissuading the leaders of the leftist Palestinian groups (i.e., PLFP and DFLP) or the leaders of the left wing of Fateh (the General Command under Ahmad Jibril) against going to Syria. Three days before we left for Tartoos, a Syrian port city on the Mediterranean, the political bureau of the PFLP held an emergency meeting to finalize their arrangements to leave Lebanon. They also discussed how they wanted to continue working from Syria.

The meeting was headed by George Habash, and was held in my office at *Al-Hadaf.* While we were discussing the arrangements, in strode Yasser Arafat accompanied by armed men. Once again he said, "I caught you." Joking and laughing, he hugged Habash before sitting down. He then said:

> Consider me a member of your political office; I am not speaking as your president. Let's continue our discussion.
>
> Please allow me to say a word before leaving you to carry on with your business. Despite the paucity of our capabilities, we beat Sharon . . . alone. He was not able to set foot himself in Beirut as he had planned. We pushed back his ground troops and forced him to rely on long-range artillery. This in itself is a victory for us. Do you know what that means? Israel thinks once we leave Beirut, we will collapse and disappear into oblivion, but we will not. I *will* return to Jerusalem, as I am sure you would like to do, but the road to Jerusalem does not pass through Damascus. We must make our own way. For this reason, I ask you, George, my brother, to come with me first to Greece, then on to other places, but not to Damascus. Our battles in the field must now be followed by political ones.

With the utmost politeness, George Habash replied that his destination had been decided for him by the PFLP political bureau; it was not his decision alone. Since the bureau had decided that he and his members were to go to Syria, he had no choice but to go there.

"In that case, I have come to say goodbye. We will definitely meet again." I walked with Arafat until he had reached his car. Before driving off, he said, "We stood firm and were victorious. Our departure from Beirut is part of our journey to Jerusalem. I don't know where or when, but you and I shall meet again."

"Won't you be coming to Damascus eventually?" I asked.

"Of course."

Then he drove off to board a Cypriot ship on August 30, 1982. Going to Cyprus first was Arafat's way of telling Syria that he would return to his headquarters located there on his own terms, according to his own timeline, and not with his tail between his legs after being expelled from Lebanon. When he returned, it would be *his* decision, another message to the Syrians that Palestinian rule would never be in their hands.

The tension in Syrian-Palestinian relations escalated with the first visit Arafat made to Damascus in September 1982. The Syrian authorities had increased their measures to restrict Palestinian activity. In the Baqa'a region, the movement of Palestinians was highly restricted. They were not allowed to move from one place to another without receiving official permission from the Syrian authorities.

Arafat was supposed to go to Lebanon to join our troops for the celebration of the Muslim holiday Eid Al-Fitr in September 1982, but he canceled his trip based on warnings he had received from his own intelligence officers that he was being targeted. After leaving Beirut, the Palestinian leadership had been forbidden to return to Lebanon, so Arafat had warned all high-ranking Palestinians against traveling there. However, Saad Sayel, the commander of the Palestinian troops in the Baqa'a Valley (an area located between Syria and Lebanon), had insisted on going, hoping to raise Palestinian morale after their leadership had been forced out of Beirut. Sayel was assassinated on September 29 in an ambush en route. His car was surrounded by armed men who then proceeded to unload their machine guns into his car. Rumors were rife with accusations of Syrian involvement, while others placed the blame on Israeli agents. One thing was absolutely clear, though: The Syrian government had failed to send a helicopter to move Sayel to a hospital, leaving him there on the road to bleed to death.

The Syrian government would not allow the media to enter Damascus to interview Arafat. In a small inner room in Arafat's office, he asked me if I thought he should go to the airport and meet with reporters there. I warned him against being too hasty. The shock of the Sabra and Shatilla massacre (see Key Terms) was still eating away at us all. During that period, Arafat, contrary to his usual way of being selective about who would be allowed to interview him, agreed to conduct a series of interviews in order to focus on the slaughter. But he couldn't do this in Damascus with the media being banned from entering the city.

Arafat's visit to Syria created even more tension when the Syrian authorities noticed a wide redeployment of Palestinian troops in the valleys of Baqa'a and

Harmel. The Syrian government issued orders to deport Arafat because he was moving his troops without Syrian permission. Both George Habash and Nayef Hawatmeh accompanied him to the airport in the same car, fearing possible attacks or arrests he might encounter on the way.

At the airport, procedures were anything but courteous. A low-ranking officer, rather than a high-ranking one, as would be standard protocol for someone of Arafat's position, told Arafat that he had to leave Syria. They were under orders to put him on the first flight out of Damascus, regardless of its destination. This kind of treatment was totally unacceptable to Arafat, who was not one to be told where he was to go. Arafat's companions, all carrying machine guns because they wanted to make sure he made it to the airport safely without any incidents, immediately began looking for a plane Arafat could board that would take him to a safe destination of his choice. They found a Tunisian pilot who had his own plane. He was given official clearance from the Tunisian government to bring Arafat to Tunisia.

The following year, in 1983, the government of Czechoslovakia called for an international peace conference on the Middle East to take place in Prague, which was to give the PLO and Syria a chance to try to resolve our differences, but we did not know whether Arafat would be able to accept the invitation. I was part of the PLO delegation that was to represent Palestine at this conference, so I left for Prague. The delegation included many high-ranking Palestinians. Early in the day of the opening session, the Palestinian ambassador in Czechoslovakia, Atef Abu Bakr, informed us that Arafat would be coming and that anyone who wanted to welcome him should head for the airport without delay. Needless to say, I left immediately.

It was a cold day, but despite the chill, I stood on the tarmac waiting for him, as was the custom in those days when official guests arrived at an airport. As Arafat and his entourage walked down the red carpet, he shook everyone's hands and embraced each one of us in turn. When he hugged me, he squeezed my shoulder tightly without saying a word. When the greetings were finished, everyone rushed toward the waiting cars to take them to their hotels. I walked slowly, deep in thought and deeply moved. It had been months since I had last seen Arafat in Damascus. I had missed our discussions and his wisdom. He and I would often discuss philosophy, history, and art. We were always so engrossed in our political lives that we rarely had time to think of other things. But when we could, Arafat and I would escape the pressures of our work by talking about what interested us, rather than what drove us.

I had been so lost in my own thoughts, so engrossed in my own nostalgic feelings that I soon realized I was standing all by myself in the pouring rain. It must have started raining while I had been standing there but I hadn't noticed. I was soaked already. All the cars had left, and there wasn't a taxi to be found anywhere. I was going to have to walk about a kilometer in that stormy weather to reach the nearest taxi stand. As I began walking, I suddenly heard cars coming up behind me. It was President Arafat's convoy. He opened the door and indicated for me to get in next to him. He squeezed my hand tightly without saying a word. We had missed each other and were so happy to be together again, working on a peaceful solution for our country that we didn't need any words to describe our feelings. We both knew each other so well, our silence spoke volumes.

The conference was like all other conferences, a great deal of talk and little to no plans for positive action. But it was after the conference when we were able to talk about what we should do about Syria and its continual pressure to control our leadership and our fate as a people. Since the Syrians were also represented at the conference and we had not been able to come to any friendly agreements there, we avoided any chances of clashing with their representatives by meeting in the residence of our Palestinian ambassador to Prague, Atef Abu Bakr. Arafat talked with those present about the dangerous situation in the region and about the attempts of the Syrian authorities both to split up Fateh and to cause division among our troops. He also informed all of us of how the Syrians had used some of the dissenting leaders of Fateh to stand with Syria against their own people. He explained that such behavior was a continuation of the Syrian conspiracy against the PLO and their attempt to eliminate our leadership, something even Israel had not been able to do.

After the meeting had ended, Arafat took me to one side, asking if I was going back to Damascus, to which I replied that I was.

"Be careful. As for me I am going to Tripoli soon."

"Tripoli, Libya?"

"No. Tripoli, Lebanon."

18

A DANGEROUS JOURNEY

I could not believe what I had just heard Arafat say. Aside from the fact that Israel wanted to eliminate him in any way possible—either by arresting him or killing him on sight—and that Syrian authorities did not want him in Lebanon at all, Arafat knew that Tripoli was surrounded by the Israeli military on all sides, including the sea. I felt that he was making a dangerous, almost suicidal, decision, but I remained silent. It often appeared that Arafat disregarded dangerous risks to himself when he had a goal in his sights, but in reality he took only calculated risks. He always took into consideration all the potential problems that might arise, and did as much as anyone could to eliminate any surprises.

I knew I could not change his mind. It was obvious that he wanted to send a message to the Syrian authorities that they could not decide Palestine's future and that the Palestinians who had dissented and joined the Syrian side represented the official positions of neither Fateh nor the PLO. He was also making it clear that he was willing to die a martyr in defense of an independent Palestine. In addition to all that, he wasn't a man to be told what he could or could not do. By going to Tripoli to join his troops, he was making a huge statement to Syria: No one would decide what he was going to do, either personally or in regard to the fate of Palestine.

But how was he going to reach Tripoli? Syria and Lebanon were closed from the land by military personnel and by sea, which was swarming with Israeli naval ships.

To avoid potential security breaches, Arafat's trip to Tripoli was arranged without using phones, faxes, or electronic mail. Instead, the trip organizers met directly with the persons involved. The men chosen to make the trip with Arafat were known for their loyalty and devotion. Those who accompanied Arafat that day were the finest, bravest men, all officers in his group of bodyguards.

The Palestinian ambassador in Cyprus, Fuad Bitar, played a key role in arranging the trip. It was decided that, for the first time, Arafat would not carry a gun nor wear his military uniform or his trademark black and white *hata*.

On the morning of September 16, 1983, two days before Eid Al-Adha, Arafat's headquarters in Tunisia phoned Bitar to tell him that a group of the president's very dear friends would be arriving in Larnaca and that Arafat was requesting that they be treated well. Three hours later, Arafat's office phoned Bitar again and made the same request, this time telling him that when the group reached Larnaca, he was to arrange not only a hotel but also a visit to Tripoli, where they would meet with Abu Jihad. His arrangements also included hiring a speedboat capable of covering the distance between Larnaca and Tripoli in three hours.

The ambassador knew that this was no usual request. Even though he had asked about the details, he was not told the group's flight number, arrival time, or date of departure for Tripoli. Bitar realized that these friends must be on a special mission. But the less he knew, the better, so he didn't ask.

The following day, Arafat himself phoned Bitar. "Fuad, these are important friends of mine and they carry a message to Abu Jihad. I want you to take care of them personally." The ambassador assured him that he would take extra care of his guests, but privately he was even more puzzled. He had wondered at first whether Arafat might be accompanying the group, but after this last phone call, he dismissed the idea. After midnight on September 18, Bitar received another phone call from Arafat's office telling him that the passengers would be arriving that morning on a private plane. About an hour later, Arafat called again, reiterating the need for Bitar to take care of his friends himself, not to send anyone from his office. Then Arafat explained that he was heading for Algeria, and then heading for Yemen to spend the Eid with the Palestinian troops based there, and thus would not be able to call again for several hours. Bitar promised to do his best and assured Arafat that everything would go smoothly.

Bitar received word early that morning that the private plane would soon be landing at the airport. By 9 a.m., he was entering the aircraft to greet his mystery guests. Bitar told me later that he was certain that Arafat would not be on that flight. In fact, he did not recognize the president at first because he was clean shaven, except for a small and neat black moustache, and he was wearing civilian clothes. When Bitar finally realized who was onboard, he was stunned, realizing the enormity of the responsibility that had been placed upon him at that moment.

"I cannot accept this responsibility, Mr. President."

"This is a military order," Arafat replied. "Let's move quickly and not waste time."

Bitar told Arafat that it would be best to move immediately to the official residence so that their secret would not be discovered.

Everything went smoothly, but despite the careful organization and planning, at the last minute, the unexpected happened. The owner of the speedboat had apologetically informed the deputy ambassador that he would not be able to make the trip. I can't be sure, but I have a feeling that he suspected he might be involved in some sort of clandestine meeting and wanted nothing to do with it. Bitar made several calls to try to secure another boat, but the only one available was not a speedboat, but a smaller, slower boat. This meant that the journey would take nine hours instead of three, putting the boat at greater risk of being discovered by a coastguard patrol or by Israeli naval vessels patrolling the area. Nonetheless, Arafat insisted that the trip should continue.

Arafat and his party returned to Larnaca in a car with curtained windows. At the port, Bitar completed the arrangements with the owner of the small boat. He handed Arafat a Greek newspaper and asked him to pretend to read it as part of his disguise.

Within minutes, everything was ready. At 11:30 a.m., Arafat and his entourage boarded the boat. Not wanting to attract unnecessary attention, Bitar did not go onboard to see Arafat and the other men off. He bade them farewell with tears in his eyes, and it was agreed that they would call him as soon as they had safely arrived in Tripoli.

Back in his office, Bitar called together all the people who had participated in arranging this trip and told them that they were to remain with him until Arafat arrived in Tripoli. He wanted to make sure no one called anyone or leaked the fact that Arafat was on the boat. He kept all of his staff in his office until he received the call from Tripoli that they had arrived safely.

The boat's slow speed made everyone in Arafat's party anxious; in addition to that, and against the better judgment of his companions, Arafat went on deck so that he could see the shores of Lebanon and Palestine. The captain, who was of Syrian origin, had suspected there was something unusual about his passengers, but when he saw Arafat on deck, he ran to hug him. I was later told by one of Arafat's guards that the man was so overwhelmed, he said through his tears, "You are our leader and our symbol. Your safety is in my charge." From that point on, Arafat knew that he could enjoy the rest of his journey. He was in safe hands.

When they reached Lebanese regional waters, the captain informed Arafat that the shore near the Al-Bared River was not deep enough for his boat; he would have to anchor further off-shore. The captain negotiated with a nearby fishing boat to take the group ashore for a handsome sum. The fishing boat also had to stop meters away from the sand because it could not go any further. One of Arafat's body guards did not want Arafat to have to walk through the water, so he insisted on carrying Arafat on his shoulders, and crossed the stretch of waist-high water with the rest of the men following closely behind.

Having made it to the shore, they walked a short distance to the main road. They flagged down a car and asked the driver to take them to where the Palestinian troops were encamped at the Naher Al-Bared (Cold River). The driver kept looking in his rearview mirror, trying to figure out who these men were. Suddenly he shouted out Arafat's nickname, "Abu Ammar, our leader! All our lives are at your command." He wanted to stop the car immediately and embrace his hero, but Arafat told him that it would be too dangerous. Once they had reached the entrance to the camp, the driver rushed around to open the door. He hugged Arafat and told him that everyone was praying for his victory.

As they moved toward the camp, relief washed over Arafat's face; his tension seemed to ease with each step. He walked briskly toward the officers' headquarters, where Abu Jihad was waiting for him.

The dangerous leg of Arafat's journey had ended, but a treacherous battle would soon begin.

19

GETTING THE TRUTH OUT

On the eve of his visit to Tripoli in 1983, while attending the International Peace Conference in Prague, Arafat had urged all the *tanzims* to send their troops to join his in Tripoli. He wanted to make it clear that the Palestinians were unified in their rejection of anyone who would try to take away their right to self-determination.

At the same time, Arafat asked Bilal Al-Qasem, a member of the PFLP leadership and a member of the Palestinian delegation at the conference, to carry a letter from him to Abu Abbas (see Principal Characters) that outlined the sensitive and dangerous nature of the situation the Palestinian leadership was facing regarding Syria and asked him to move his forces to Tripoli. Arafat did the same with the DFLP, which was helping Abu Jihad to move his troops and to transfer officers with DFLP ID cards to Tripoli. Troops were being moved from many locations within Lebanon and Syria.

Just as Arafat was mobilizing his troops in Tripoli, Syria was mobilizing the *tanzims*, such as those of Jibril's PFLP-General Command, in addition to Abu Musa's and Abu Khaled's Fateh groups against Arafat. Syria had signed a cease-fire agreement with Israel and it was determined that no one, especially Arafat, would do anything to bring the wrath of the Israelis down on them.

All sides were worried about what might happen next. The PFLP did not want to get involved with this internal conflict of Fateh, yet they condemned Arafat's move to Tripoli and demanded his immediate departure.

Mamdouh Nofal, the commander of the DFLP military, played an important role in helping Abu Jihad and his officers move troops from the Baqa'a and Al-Harmel in Lebanon to Tripoli in order to support Arafat, much to the annoyance of the Syrians.

Ahmad Jibril, the secretary general of the PFLP-GC, led forces equipped with Syrian weapons and machinery into Tripoli where they attacked the positions of Fateh and Arafat in the north of Lebanon. Large media facilities were placed at Jibril's disposal, from which he could broadcast his pledge to annihilate Yasser Arafat.

I was in Damascus when the shelling of Fateh and the DFLP began on November 6, 1983. In addition to my work as editor-in-chief of *Al-Hadaf,* I was in charge of all PFLP media relations.

The Palestinians in Damascus were focused on what was happening in Tripoli. All the Palestinians who had left Beirut for Syria at the end of 1982 recalled the shelling that they had suffered in the three-month war with Sharon's army.

I felt trapped while I was in Damascus. I wanted to get the truth out in *Al-Hadaf* about what the Syrians and the splinter groups were doing to Arafat's troops in Tripoli, but I knew that I wouldn't be free to report exactly what was happening. The Syrian government did not allow for freedom of the press. What was I to do? Staying in Damascus meant that I would have to abide by Syrian rules: I would have to keep my mouth shut about the atrocities the Syrian troops were committing against Arafat's troops. The Palestinian soldiers who had headed to Tripoli to join Arafat had taken a clear stand favoring the Palestinians, and those who headed to Tripoli under the banner of Ahmed Jibril had taken a position supporting the Syrian government. Those who remained neutral stayed silent at best or voiced criticism of Arafat's actions, also pushing for his departure from Tripoli; being neutral simply meant not taking any action, only talking about what they felt Arafat should do.

War drums sounded and the shelling began on November 6. The area of conflict stretched from the Palestinian camps in the north of Tripoli by Al-Barid and Al-Bdawi Rivers to Tripoli and the port of Tripoli. All Palestinians who watched what was taking place in Tripoli, regardless of which side we supported, were saddened by what we saw. Palestinian fighting Palestinian, some on Syria's side, others supporting Arafat, but all against each other. We all hurt deeply inside: It was a case of brother fighting brother, and it was wrong.

The fighting in Tripoli was major news. I had to cover these bloody events while also preparing the weekly issue of the magazine for print. Writing up the stories, working on the layout, choosing the pictures and articles that were to be included as well as printing and distributing *Al-Hadaf* all took place in Damascus. Our printing presses in Damascus were (and perhaps still are to this very day) under constant surveillance by government intelligence and censorship departments in order to prevent anyone from printing material that criticized the Syrian government.

How, then, were we going to report the bloody clashes in Tripoli without making waves? Our magazine represented the views of the Palestinians; Syria and Syrian-supported splinter groups from Fateh were bombing Fateh and DFLP forces. It was my duty to report the truth, but that truth was not going to be kind to the Syrians, nor would it be kind to the Palestinian splinter groups they supported. The editors of the various sections of the magazine and the art editor worked on the layout and content of the magazine. We had official permission from the Syrian government to print the magazine, but what about the content I was going to publish this time? I had never published anything directly critical of the Syrian government, so we had always been allowed to print without any problems. And there was another issue: I was still a member of the PFLP and the magazine was under the PFLP, yet I was going to be publishing articles supporting Arafat and condemning the Syrian onslaught. I would be publishing material that was in direct contradiction to my party. I had included articles that condemned the attacks against the refugee camps in Tripoli, where people had taken refuge since 1948 when they had been forced out of Palestine by the Israelis. Arafat had initially been in the camps, but when Jibril's troops, along with the Syrian troops, started to shell the camps using heavy artillery, Arafat left so that the people would be safe.

How would I get it past the censors and out to the public without getting my presses shut down? And if I did manage to get it printed, how was I going to distribute it without getting arrested? Besides that, how would PFLP members take what I was going to publish?

I decided to not worry about the logistics: I would just throw caution to the wind and get the truth out to the public any way I could, regardless of the consequences. Worrying about what might or might not happen wasn't getting the magazine anywhere. The time for action had arrived.

It was late at night when I told the manager of the printing press to prepare all the equipment for immediate printing. I called the art director of the magazine and explained my idea for the cover. It would be solid black with the word "crime" written in blood-red letters dripping down the front of the page, symbolizing the Palestinian blood that had been spilled in Tripoli.

At 10:30 p.m. that same night, the master copy of the magazine arrived at the printing press. The Syrian sergeant responsible for monitoring everything we published had left the building due to family commitments, and the manager of the printing press, also a Syrian government official, wanted to go home early and did not bother to check the magazine's content. If he had simply taken a look at the cover, I am positive he would have stopped us from publishing it right then and there. We were good to go.

I sighed with relief once the first bundle of *Al-Hadaf* was finished and ready for distribution. I gave orders to begin distribution immediately for fear that the issues might be confiscated. I knew that this issue was going to cause a huge commotion, but I would not have reported the story any other way. The truth had to be told.

I didn't have a chance to hear any reactions to that issue because I had to leave the next day for New Delhi to attend the NAMEDIA (nonaligned media) conference. Before I left, I called Arafat in Tripoli for any last-minute orders. He wanted me to take a message to the Indian prime minister, Indira Gandhi. "Remember to tell her of my position, not that of the Syrians." This was Arafat's way of making an indirect reference once again to Palestinian decision making remaining in the hands of the Palestinians, not the Syrians. Since Arafat also presumed the phones were being tapped from both sides, he wanted to make sure that whoever was listening to us would know he was adamant about his stance.

When I had returned to Damascus from India, I came back to face two raging storms—one that took place behind closed doors and the other out in the public. The public storm was led by those Syrians and Palestinians who stood against Arafat and were angry that *Al-Hadaf* had described the fighting in Tripoli as "a bloody crime." My colleagues at the PLFP political bureau opposed my comments both behind the scenes and behind my back. They feared showing any open animosity to what I had published because the general population of Palestinians and Syrians were clearly opposed to the attack on Arafat and the Palestinian forces in Tripoli. Even though I had upset my colleagues in the PFLP, I remained deeply convinced that I had done the right thing. As I had mentioned before, for Palestinians to be fighting each other was indeed a crime. The other crime was the Syrian army using its heavy artillery against the refugee camps that had nothing more than light weaponry with which to fight back. How anyone in his right mind could not see that was beyond me. That particular issue of our PFLP magazine was so popular that we had to print extra copies to meet the demand. Because the government was busy with its war on Arafat in Tripoli, we got away with that first issue without any problems. Our presses were not closed down and no one was arrested. I was excited to get our next issue out the following month and include even more articles about the war.

The shelling had intensified on Arafat's location in Tripoli, the Palestinian troops in the camps, the city, and the port. In addition to the Syrians and Jibril's Syrian-supported Palestinian forces fighting against Arafat's troops and the DFLP, another clash took place that was completely unexpected, and ridiculous. Some of Fateh's allies who were Islamic extremists in the north of Lebanon had clashed with the Lebanese Communist Party (this event is explained in full detail in chapter 16), who were also allies of the Palestinian revolution. The Islamists killed a number of the Communist group members because they considered an alliance with Communists against their religious beliefs.

Days passed with the Syrian shelling intensifying from the land and then starting from the sea, an indication that the Israeli navy was now involved because they were the only ones, aside from the United States, who had naval fleets in the Mediterranean. There was no confirmed information about the source of the shelling, but accusing Israel served a purpose for Arafat. By spreading the word that Israel was now attacking them all, it was further proof that the attack was all part of Sharon's plan to eliminate Arafat along with the entire Palestinian leadership, thus putting an end to the Palestinian resistance movement. If Sharon ended the Palestinian resistance movement, then Israel would then have complete control over Palestinian decision making through the Palestinian groups and parties that had sided with Syria, including some Fateh leaders and part of its troops. Arafat was attempting to reunite all Palestinians under one banner again by giving them the common enemy of Israel. Unfortunately, he was unsuccessful at that time.

One month had passed and it was time to start preparing for the next issue of *Al-Hadaf,* which had already become famous in Syria after the publication of the previous issue. This time, I sent our two best editors to Tripoli to interview Arafat. Although some of my PFLP colleagues accused me of being insane, I defended our right to both freedom of speech and press. I was a journalist and the truth had to be told. That was my motto. If I got arrested then so be it, but at least I had told the truth. Others insisted that it would never be allowed to be published. My response was simply, "We won't know unless we try." I knew of many people who had been arrested and thrown in prison simply for questioning the Syrian government (to this day, there are people imprisoned in Syria for criticizing the government back in the 1980s).

When the editors returned from Tripoli, I listened to their tapes before they were transcribed. Although Arafat had been dubious that the interview would ever reach the presses, knowing the strict controls the Syrian government had over its newspapers, radio, and TV programs, he answered all their questions. They asked him why he thought the battle was taking place, to which he answered that it was Syria's way of controlling the Palestinians. Arafat also criticized the Syrians for accepting a cease-fire with Israel in 1978, which had left the Palestinians open to attack when the Syrians withdrew. He went on to say that the Syrians had done their best to split the Palestinian leadership. The editors then asked Arafat what he thought about the splinter groups, to which he responded that he felt they were Syrian agents. He didn't hold anything back; he was brutally honest and scathing about the Syrians and their attacks on the Palestinians in Tripoli. Arafat was direct and sharp in each of his responses, calling things as he saw them. In short, his interview was a time bomb set to explode. It would cause crashing waves of anger from the Syrian government and jubilation from all the Syrian and Palestinian citizens living in Syria who were hungry for the right to question their government openly with regard to its bombing of the Palestinians in Tripoli. With the distribution of this issue of *Al-Hadaf*, I was about to cause a political tsunami in Damascus and all across the Arab world—if we succeeded in printing and distributing it.

News of Arafat's interview leaked to the political bureau, and George Habash asked that the publication of the interview be postponed until he had a chance to read it. Naturally, we agreed out of respect for his wishes—it was only right that he should read the issue, since it was the magazine of the PFLP and he was our leader. While he reviewed the interview, we continued working on other articles for that issue, documenting the storming of the camps at Al-Bdawi and Al-Bared Rivers by pro-Syrian Palestinian parties. I will never forget what he said to me.

"Bassam, how do you expect to get this past the Syrian authorities?"

"It's an interview. Those are Arafat's words, not mine. I am simply printing his words. The one to be blamed should be the one who said them, not the person who printed them."

Habash just smiled at me and shook his head, giving me the go-ahead. I think he also knew I was planning to publish it anyway, but was just being polite by giving him the chance to read the issue first. He knew me so well.

Once we had Habash's approval, we set out to publish the interview.

As usual, I worked with the art director of the magazine on the cover. I had acquired a photograph of a Syrian soldier who had put his weapon aside and was resting his head on the trunk of a tree at Al-Bdawi camp. We agreed this would be the cover photo with the title, "The Defeat of the Victorious." I used that title to imply that even if the Syrians were victorious in this battle against Arafat, they should never consider it a victory over Arafat, but a defeat of the Arabs by themselves. The Syrians were fighting their own people, Arab versus Arab. They might have pushed Arafat out of Tripoli, but they had weakened the Arab confrontation front against Israel.

By some miracle we were able to print and distribute the issue. Again, no one stopped us and no one checked our issue before it went to press. And, once again, the demand for the magazine was huge. People distributed the issue all over the city as well as across the Middle East. It was also circulated to Arabs living outside the Middle East, in countries like the United States and the United Kingdom. In fact, we had to print three times our usual weekly number of copies to meet the heavy demand, mostly from Syrian revolutionary and fighter groups that were against the Syrian government. The issue even attracted international attention, and calls intensified from the Arab communities living abroad in other Arab countries, Europe, and the United States. At the same time, I was in daily contact with Arafat to learn of any further developments as to where he was while I kept him informed of what was happening outside of the siege.

Naturally, the overwhelming firepower of the Syrian army was too much for Arafat and his troops to withstand. Both sides had suffered great casualties, but Arafat's side received the bulk of the damage. He had not planned on staying in Tripoli; his motive for going there was purely to make a statement that he was in charge of what the Palestinians would do, not Syria. Once the fighting came to an end, it was agreed that Arafat and those with him would leave by sea once again. At the time, everyone assumed his destination would be Tunisia, where one of his headquarters was located.

Arafat knew that leaving Tripoli after he had already been forced to leave Beirut would mean that Lebanon would be closed to him and the Palestinian forces forever. In addition, Syria could no longer be considered part of any coalition with the PLO. He also knew that a move to Jordan after the Lebanese and Syrian fronts were closed as locations from which he could launch attacks against Israel meant that he would be in a position of weakness. As our relations with Cairo, the traditional ally of the PLO, had been severed after Camp David, Arafat could not even seek Egyptian help to ensure that the PLO would receive fair treatment in Jordan. As I had mentioned earlier, Arafat never liked to keep Palestine in a stranglehold with no ally to whom he could turn.

Arafat had always known that the Palestinian revolutionary efforts would inevitably lead to tensions in the relations between the PLO and the Arab countries surrounding Israel. In order to make sure the PLO was never alone, he had managed a balance by allying with Syria while differing with Jordan; then allying with Jordan while differing with Syria. He always felt it was necessary to form an alliance with a country that shared a border with Israel. That way he would always have a base from which he could continue staging his resistance operations, either by smuggling in arms to his fighters inside the occupied territories, or by launching military operations from across the borders of whichever country he was in at the time.

Now, even though Arafat felt he was being forced into an alliance with Jordan, given that Lebanon, Syria, and Egypt were all closed to him, he still felt compelled to turn to Egypt, his customary ally. He and King Hussein had reconciled on a personal level after 1970, but they had not yet reconciled on a political level. No strong alliance had been made since he had been expelled from Jordan. He wanted to form another alliance with Jordan, but he wanted to do so from a position of strength, not weakness. He was hoping his longtime friend Egypt would be able to help. He knew his action would cause tremors among both Palestinians and in other Arab nations, but he felt it was necessary to prevent the tightening of the siege on the PLO. Since Sadat's assassination in 1981, Arafat had kept his secret communication lines open with the new president, Husni Mubarak. He planned to meet with President Mubarak by passing through the Suez Canal from the Mediterranean Sea.

When his ship docked at the Port of Ismailia, at the end of the Canal, the ice had already been broken between the two leaders. Arafat had taken a step that no other Arab leader had even dared to attempt at the time.

Once he had realigned with Egypt, the atmosphere soon became ripe for balanced discussions with Jordan. Arafat would be able to talk to King Hussein with a strong ally backing him up.

Meanwhile, some of my colleagues in the political bureau were trying to get me excluded from media work because of the two issues I had published about the war in Tripoli. What I had done was not in compliance with the PFLP's party line, so they wanted me out of that job. Because of what was happening in the Middle East regarding the Palestinians, the tasks of the PFLP had changed from military and security operations to largely political media tasks, which required us to make our ideas and political stance known to the rest of the world. Since the Palestinian forces had been forbidden to work militarily not only by Lebanon, but by all other frontiers, our forces had been distributed throughout many Arab countries in an operation very similar to exile and deportation. Therefore, the work of the media became much more important.

I was informed by George Habash that there had been a change in my responsibilities, which meant I was no longer to be editor-in-chief of *Al-Hadaf*. My job had grown from being in charge of a monthly magazine to being responsible for PFLP's communications with the entire world outside of the Middle East. My office moved from Damascus to Al-Yarmouk Camp in Syria.

(above) *Abu Sharif (with megaphone) giving press conference at Revolution Airport (Dawson's Field), September 1970, when planes were hijacked to Jordan*

(right) *Abu Sharif in the* Al-Hadaf *office, Beirut, 1971*

Sheikh Khalifeh ibn Zayad, leader of United Arab Emirates, with Arafat and Abu Sharif, July 30, 1978

Abu Sharif at Beirut Airport during Israeli invasion, 1982

Arafat and Abu Sharif at tomb of assassinated Prime Minister Indira Gandhi following her state funeral, 1984

Abu Sharif, Arafat, and George Habash at the Palestinian National Council (PNC) in Algiers when the PLO was reunited

Yasser Abed Rabbo (PNC member and one of Arafat's advisors), with Arafat and Abu Sharif at the United Nations in Geneva, 1989

Abu Sharif giving a speech, Moscow, 1989

Arafat shaking hands with Frederik Willem de Klerk, President of South Africa, in Namibia, February 15, 1990

Dr. Nabil Sha'ath, Abu Sharif, and Arafat in an airplane en route to India for official visit

(left) *Arafat and Abu Sharif on an airplane, en route to Turkey for official visit*

(below) *Sultan Qaboos bin Said, King of Oman, greeting Abu Sharif and Arafat*

*Arafat, Abu
Sharif, and
then
President
Sam Nujoma
of Namibia*

Official visit to Indonesia

Arafat saluting the flag of Palestine

Arafat and Abu Sharif

20

INDIA LOVES YOU

n between the publication of our two controversial issues of *Al-Hadaf* in Damascus, on December 9, 1983 I traveled to the NAMEDIA conference in New Delhi, to present to the other Third World countries in attendance my plan for a collaborative program among the media services of the nonaligned countries. The news was so negatively biased when it was presented from a Western viewpoint. I proposed that we break from the Western news agencies that had a monopoly on reporting the news, such as Reuters and the Associated Press, and that we unite together so our one voice could be heard by forming our own news agency that would better represent our perspective and our take on what was happening in our part of the world. And, while there, I would also follow through on Arafat's request that I meet with Prime Minister Indira Gandhi. If anyone could help Yasser Arafat get out of his predicament in Tripoli, it would be Mrs. Gandhi.

Indira Gandhi's friendship with Yasser Arafat went back many years, starting with his respect for both Mahatma Gandhi and her father, Jawaharlal Nehru, who had been India's first prime minister following its independence from Britain, as well as its longest-serving one. When Indira Gandhi accepted the position of prime minister following the death of her father in 1966, it was clear to Arafat that she stood for all her father's ideas and policies. Since the 1970s, she and Arafat had shared a strong bond based on clear political principles, including freedom, development, and the growth of nations. They had always treated each other like family. In fact, I had often noticed how well they complemented each other. She was a person of great wisdom, strength, and independence, who carried upon her shoulders the responsibility of millions, while Arafat was a man who was struggling for the freedom and independence of his people.

After I had met with the news services and the representatives of the non-aligned countries, I was informed that Mrs. Gandhi would receive me at 4:45 p.m. in her office at the Prime Ministry. When I entered her office, I was amazed by its similarity to a huge reception hall. Her desk was a three-foot-wide circular wooden slab that stretched from one end of the room to the other. In front of the desk were very practical chairs. Mrs. Gandhi also had a simple chair on wheels that she used to move from one person to another.

Mrs. Gandhi had agreed to meet with all twelve people who had requested an appointment with her that day. I was to be the last one she saw, so I was seated last in line with everyone else ahead of me. I watched her as she listened to each person and spoke briefly about the topic of concern. She took copious notes then wheeled her chair to the next person. She never stood up to see each person off, but stuck to a strict, fair schedule, giving each person equal time. She wasted no time on small talk or niceties such as offering coffee to her guests; she was all business. When it was my turn, she asked me, "Mr. Abu-Sharif, what is the news of President Arafat?" There was sadness in her voice, and I felt as if she were asking for news of one of her own children. I explained the situation, telling her that Arafat faced grave danger in Tripoli, and asked her for help in getting him out. Sighing deeply, she answered, "The problem with President Arafat is that he relies too much on the countries of the Arab peninsula and the Gulf. He must be wary of them and be wise for they do not like him."

She summoned her office manager to place a call to President Hafez Al-Assad. The Syrian president had recently suffered a heart attack, and she first asked me if he had recovered from his illness enough to speak over the phone. I said that he had, so she placed the call. I asked if I should leave the room so that she could speak in privacy, but she signaled for me to remain seated.

As Mrs. Gandhi spoke with Assad, she first asked after his health, and then sweetly asked him to stop the bombing of Arafat's troops in Tripoli by reaching some sort of a cease-fire. She went on to say that Assad should allow Arafat and his men to leave through Syria, because it would be too dangerous for them to leave by sea, which was controlled by the Israeli navy. When the call ended, she turned to me and said, "Give my greetings to President Arafat and tell him that

India loves and respects him very much. Tell him that we know that he is facing a difficult situation, but that it will be impossible for him to leave through Syria. He must make contact with Europe. I hope that he remains in contact with us."

Since I had been the last guest to be received that day, Mrs. Gandhi walked me to the outer side gate of the ministry, where her modest car was waiting to take her home. Much to my surprise, she had no bodyguards and no official escort. I had often warned her of the dangers of refusing military protection, but she had always replied that she was not afraid of death, adding, "My people elected me to this office by a great majority. This in itself gives me great self-confidence."

As we walked side by side, the prime minister spoke with me calmly while on her shoulders rested burdens that would bring down the toughest of men. Before getting into her car, she bade me goodbye, saying, "Go in peace. Do not forget to tell President Arafat to take precautions, to be wary of everyone and to protect himself. Many people want to get rid of him."

But before leaving, she added, "Do not forget to tell him that India loves him." As she drove away, I was left in awe; what a great, brave leader she was.

That night, I returned to Damascus, knowing that I had to get word as soon as possible to Arafat about what Indira Gandhi had told me, but I did not want to speak to him on the phone. I was sure the Syrians were tapping our lines. I knew I would have to get as close to Tripoli as possible, so I smuggled myself into Lebanon, leaving through Syria and entering by way of the Baqa'a Valley between the two countries. Just trying to get into Beirut was very risky business as the shelling was dreadfully intensive. I was driven into Beirut by some of my Islamic friends (some Sheikhs), who drove me in one of their small cars right into the capital. I then had to get my message to Arafat, but there was no way I would be able to get through the Israeli lines without being captured. My first wife, Amal, with some of her friends, bravely made the drive, getting through the Israeli lines and hand-delivering Mrs. Gandhi's message to Arafat.

He then knew that the only way out of Tripoli alive would be to accept the French initiative of leaving by sea. Syria was a closed passage for him.

21

THE HANDSHAKE

n March 1987, the Palestine National Council met in Prague (under the auspices of the Czech Communist Party) to make a formal agreement stating that all parties of the PLO would promise to attend the National Unity Session, a meeting that was going to be held from April 20 to 25 in Algeria. There was only one item on the agenda: reuniting the ranks of the PLO. After Arafat had signed the Amman Agreement with King Hussein on February 23, 1984 (see Key Terms for details), the PLO had been boycotted by many of its own political factions, including the PFLP and the DFLP. I set up meetings in Prague between Abu Jihad of Fateh and Habash of the PFLP before they headed for Tripoli, coordinating arrangements with Abu Hisham, the Palestinian ambassador in Czechoslovakia.

The first meeting in Prague took place at Abu Hisham's house. Naturally, Fateh was supportive of the Amman Agreement, but Habash felt the agreement had taken the decision-making power out of the hands of the Palestinians and put the PLO in a weakened position by sharing it with the government of Jordan. He also was unhappy with Arafat's tendency to support the leadership in Egypt since Sadat's recognition of Israel. Other points of agreement and disagreement were noted so that follow-up discussions could resume later. Immediately following that meeting, Habash and I left for Moscow to have direct discussions with the party's central committee to discuss with them any other ideas they might have that could resolve the split in our factions. Habash and I were surprised when Abu Jihad, Abu Hisham, and the rest of the Fateh leaders we had seen in Prague also showed up in Moscow. They wanted to continue the discussion we had started in Czechoslovakia. In the meantime, however, the PFLP had released a statement in Damascus stating that any agreement between Abu Jihad and Habash did not represent the position of the party.

I couldn't believe they would do this, but Abu Hisham showed me a copy of the actual statement carrying the official stamp of PFLP, so we ended our discussions with Abu Jihad and turned our attention instead to our meetings with the party Central Committee in Moscow in order to get their ideas before attending the conference in Algiers.

Following the general meeting in Prague, Abu Jihad convinced Libyan president Muammar Qaddafi that all of the PLO factions should meet in Tripoli, Libya, before the PNC meeting in Algiers in order to get all of their differences out in the open and resolved before the April meeting of the PNC. Naturally everyone attended because Libya was a big financial backer of all of the groups, and no one wanted to get on Qaddafi's bad side by refusing to attend, a fact that had encouraged Abu Jihad to suggest Libya in the first place. There was lengthy dialogue among all the Palestinian factions in Libya about ways to reunite the Palestinian ranks. I accompanied Dr. George Habash to Libya, which aggravated some members of the PFLP political bureau, who accused me of having an "Arafat-like" political viewpoint.

I spoke to Habash of the importance of reuniting the Palestinian groups before the U.S. president Ronald Reagan and the secretary general of the Soviet Communist Party, Mikhail Gorbachev, met in Moscow on May 29, 1987. It was obvious they were taking steps toward ending the Cold War, and if that were to happen, the superpowers could very well start to pay attention once again to the various hot-button issues in the rest of the world, such as Palestine, the Berlin Wall and German unity, the Cuban situation, and the Soviet presence in Afghanistan. Once the Cold War ended, I felt the superpowers might begin to work harder at solving all of these pressing issues that required them to talk face to face. Habash, however, did not agree with me. When I suggested there could be an imminent end to the Cold War, he simply said, "No way! Not in the next twenty-five years will such a thing take place!"

Quite by accident, I had already set the foundations for this meeting in Libya, even before I knew we were going there. The DFLP and the Palestinian Communist Party had quit the coalition that they had formed earlier that same year with the PFLP, and then made an agreement with Fateh, with whom I had arranged for them to meet in March at Prague. Wanting to rejoin all their ranks again with the other PLO factions, the same parties agreed to attend the National Council meeting to be held in Algiers.

I was certain that reuniting the Palestinian groups would positively impact the political standing of the PLO, which in turn would lead to an improvement of our people's situation. It was of paramount importance that we all join together in one united front for the sake of the future of Palestine. I dedicated all my efforts to finding ways of joining us all together. Those opposed to our reunifying our ranks believed that the Algerians would not allow the National Council to convene before an agreement in Libya had been reached that would reunite the PLO. Contrary to these beliefs, Algeria announced well before any agreement had been reached in Tripoli that they would host the Palestinian National Council on April 20–25, 1987. Frankly, I was not surprised by this in the least. The Algerian government had always been supportive of the Palestinian cause and knew that what we needed was to continue to hash out our differences, regardless of the venue, until a solution could be reached.

I confirmed the news of the meeting to Habash while we were still in Tripoli. Habash was still dubious that the meeting was really going to take place, but high-ranking Algerian officials called from Algiers and told us bluntly, "The continuation of discussions within the PLO is a luxury that your cause cannot afford because your people are suffering. It is time to resolve your differences and come to a consensus for the sake of the Palestinian people. We have invited everyone to Algiers to resolve all differences once and for all."

In order to ensure that Habash would attend the meeting in Algiers, I called and asked the Algerians to deliver an official invitation personally to Habash while he was in Libya and then to send one of their private planes to Tripoli fly him directly to the meeting. I also suggested that they discuss with him the necessity of national unity in light of the current international situation, hinting at the importance of our coming to terms with our grievances well before the upcoming meeting between the United States and the Soviets in Moscow, which was just a month away.

Before Habash left for Algeria, he was informed by members of the PFLP's political bureau in Damascus who opposed negotiating with Fateh that I was to return to Damascus immediately. They were not at all happy that I had been with Habash in Libya, and they wanted to make doubly sure I would not be involved in any dialogues that would take place in Algeria. In their minds, I was more like Arafat in my thinking, more moderate with regard to my views on achieving a peaceful solution to the Palestinian question. Habash told me I was needed back in Damascus and took his deputy instead of me. When I returned to Damascus, I learned that Habash's deputy had agreed to go to Algeria only on the condition that I leave Libya first and return to Damascus.

An amusing aspect of this conference was that the Algerians had decided to have all the members of the PLO stay in one large hotel that was located in the center of a zoo! It was as if they were implying that the disagreeing factions were a bunch of wild animals that needed to be caged in one place until they reached an agreement. There was only one way in and one way out, so it almost appeared as if they wanted to guarantee that no one would be able to leave until an agreement had been reached. All participants had to travel together in buses from the hotel in the zoo to the conference hall, which was located in another part of the city. All bickering factions were forced to be in close contact with one another at all times on the way to and from the conference.

I remained behind in Damascus for two days only. How could I stay away from such an historic meeting? Since I was a member of the National Council, which is a democratically elected body, and I had not been appointed to attend the meeting in Algiers as a member of the PFLP, I decided to go to Algeria on my own no matter what. Needless to say, when I arrived, many of the PFLP members were not only surprised, but also greatly displeased to see me.

While I was at the meeting, and even before I had arrived, the conference was filled with heated debates about what our united stand should be, if we were to take one at all. On April 25, the last night of the conference, I was both surprised and pleased to hear the deputy secretary general of the council, who only a month earlier had considered it a treasonous act to shake hands with a Fateh member, make a statement that was very much like what I had been fighting for all along. The PNC had taken a united stand, and the PLO, including the disagreeing factions of DFLP, Fateh, and PFLP, called for a development of relations with the democratic forces within Israel. It was also proposed and accepted by all that there be an international peace conference in which the Palestinians would be "on a footing of equality" under the umbrella of the UN with participation of the permanent members of the Security Council, Syria, and Israel. It was also put forward and agreed to that there was indeed a special relationship between the Palestinian and Jordanian people, which meant they should continue to work together toward establishing an independent Palestinian state. The door had been left open for future links to be made once again with Jordan, even though the Amman Agreement had been nullified the year before by King Hussein. The way to national unity had finally been opened wide. The PLO had been reunited.

At the end of the conference, I decided to stay behind in Algeria. I needed some time to contemplate the paradox I was living between my personal beliefs and my organizational commitment. I found myself torn between being a member of the PFLP—which had stood so strongly against Arafat's moderate stand with regard to a Palestinian state—and supporting Arafat's views and methods. I remembered the meetings of the political bureau of the PFLP and of the Central Committee in Damascus. I remembered my statements before the Central Committee regarding the attacks that were to be launched against our camps in Lebanon between 1985 and 1986.

I remembered how many times my proposals to open a dialogue between PFLP and Fateh to accomplish national unity had failed. In the last session of the Central Committee my proposal to accept a two-state solution with Israel had finally won by a majority of one vote—that of George Habash. During earlier sessions my vote had been the only one in favor of my proposal. Naturally, I felt both a national and a personal satisfaction for the eventual results because I knew that the PLO was now able to accomplish Palestinian national goals.

But why had it taken so long for anyone to listen to me? It was then that I experienced my political catharsis. I realized that I had been exhausting myself by silencing my real beliefs in favor of my party commitment to the PFLP. All those times when I had wanted to openly support Arafat's position with regard to Resolutions 242 and 338 (see Key Terms), but then silenced my own voice because it did not reflect that of the PFLP, were situations I never wanted to repeat again. I had always fought for individual freedom; now it was my turn to free myself in order to stand up for what I believed, something I had devoted myself to doing since graduating from the American University in Beirut in 1967. The more I thought about it, the more I realized that returning to Damascus would be dangerous, so I stayed in Algeria to plan my future. I had to decide what path my life in politics was going to take, which path best exemplified my own beliefs and allowed for me to express myself openly without being labeled negatively for having an opinion contrary to that of the party.

In May 1987, just one month after the PNC meeting in Algiers, Arafat invited me to his headquarters in Tunisia. Someone had informed him that I was living in seclusion in Algeria. Arafat encouraged me to return to my work. "You should not be a recluse for there is national work to be done. I would like you to be part of my delegation to the African Summit in Addis Ababa."

Although I was still ambivalent about what path I should take, I agreed to go with Arafat to the Ethiopian city, even though I did not have the proper clothes with me for such a formal occasion. It was my first trip with Arafat on board his private plane. As we talked over pressing political issues, he noticed that I was preoccupied with other thoughts. He spoke to me like a father: "You have work ahead of you upon which our national cause depends. We have all devoted ourselves to it so you must not let anything either distract or discourage you from achieving our aim. Nothing must weaken your will."

"Nothing will ever discourage me or keep me from thinking of how I can double my efforts to serve our cause and that of our people," I told him.

In Addis Ababa, Arafat and all the other presidents were taken to their lodgings in private villas; the rest of us were put up in hotels. The other men with Arafat and I agreed to meet at Arafat's villa half an hour after we arrived.

At the meeting, Arafat was cheerful and energetic, saying that we had to do the usual round before the summit sessions began. "The usual round" to Arafat meant a visit to each individual president to discuss what the proposals were that he planned to put forth at the summit.

We began with a brief visit to President Kenneth Kaunda of Kenya, and then moved on to the quarters of President Mubarak of Egypt. Not surprisingly, dozens of reporters and television crews were on hand, bombarding Arafat with questions, snapping pictures, and filming as we neared the entrance to Mubarak's villa. Cameramen followed us inside. As Mubarak and I shook hands, we were blinded by the explosion of flashbulbs. It was the first time a leading member of the PFLP had shaken hands with an Egyptian president since the signing of the Camp David Accords, and it was major news. In Damascus, reporters began grilling the PFLP about it.

The question they all were asking was: Did my handshake mean a fundamental change in the policy of the PFLP? The PFLP officials were taken by surprise and refused to comment until the news had been confirmed. There could be no question once they saw the photographs for themselves.

The following day, the political bureau of the PFLP issued a brusque and angry statement declaring my dismissal from the PFLP, something they did not even have the authority to do. A dismissal can only take place after a decision has been made by the National Conference of the PFLP, which is the democratic body that not only elects its leaders but also decides laws and policy, the same body that had elected me to both the Central Committee and the political bureau. In response to their denunciation, I issued a brief, yet polite statement confirming my pride in my long history of struggle, in my comrades who had fought and died along the way, and in those who were still fighting. Although I was considering leaving, the decision on whether I was still a member of the PFLP was my choice to make, not theirs. I had been democratically elected and that would also be the only way I could be officially dismissed.

After the African summit, Arafat and I headed for Abu Dhabi, the capital of the UAE. Arafat reported to Sheikh Zayed bin Sultan on what had been accomplished, both in Algeria and at the African Summit. He explained that there had been great support for the Palestinian people's right to self-determination and also highlighted the explosive situation in the Occupied Palestinian Territories. Palestinians were being treated as unwanted strangers in their own land, paying high taxes but not getting any benefits, and their land was still being occupied by illegal settlers on a daily basis. Palestinians could not carry arms, yet Jewish settlers were allowed to carry arms and harass the Palestinians who lived near the settlements. The living conditions were becoming increasingly more unbearable by the day. Sheikh Zayed again pledged his support for the Palestinian people, confirming that the UAE stood without hesitation by the Palestinian struggle to free Jerusalem. He pledged continued financial support to help with our armed struggle and to help finance families who were becoming destitute by the Israeli occupation.

Two weeks after that meeting with Sheikh Zayed, Arafat and I headed for Cairo to meet with President Mubarak and other Egyptian leaders to discuss a plan of political movement after the Amman Agreement had been canceled.

After President Arafat and President Mubarak had shaken hands, President Mubarak extended his hand to me, and when we shook hands, the press and all the other people present looked shocked, thinking I was officially representing the PFLP. "They dismissed you from the PFLP because you shook hands with me in Addis Ababa, so maybe I should kiss you this time so they will accept you back in." We all laughed.

Arafat and Mubarak then had a private meeting together, and half an hour later, the delegations were called in for a general discussion to draw up a political plan that would lead to the implementation of UN Security Council Resolutions 242 and 338 as well as all others that had been put forward by the United Nations that were related to the Palestinian people's right to self-determination, such as Resolution 194, which gives Palestinian refugees the right to return to their homeland, and Resolution 181, which called for a two-state partition of Palestine way back in 1947.

Egypt has always been a strong supporter of the Palestinian people's movement to gain freedom and independence, providing protection and refuge for the Palestinian people and their leaders when the situation became difficult within other Arab countries or the differences in the Middle East escalated. Mubarak stepped in when the PLO was in desperate need of a strong ally. The cancellation of the Amman Agreement had put a huge strain on Palestinian-Jordanian ties, Syria had severed its relationship with the PLO, and Lebanon was closed to the PLO.

The Egyptian support had much more weight at that particular time than it had ever carried before. Arafat was mindful of the fact that he had the Arab triangle of Egypt, Iraq, and Yemen, whose political support he could count on for some time—or at least until circumstances changed once again.

22

ALMOST DEPORTED

From November 8 to 11, 1987, when Jordanian-Palestinian tensions were still running high and battles between Iraq and Iran were raging, the Arab League held a summit in Amman, Jordan, in order to reconcile differences with Egypt following Sadat's recognition of Israel in 1977. The summit was also called to show solidarity with Iraq in its ongoing eight-year war with Iran.

Arafat flew to Jordan in an Arab military plane. I accompanied him at his request, the only high-ranking Palestinian on the flight, as the rest of the Palestinian delegation had traveled to Jordan earlier.

During the two-hour flight, Arafat spoke little, which indicated that he was worried about something, but he listened intently to everything I said in reply to the questions he would occasionally ask me. Our conversation revolved around the aim of this summit. Iraq did not expect to receive any military help in its ongoing war against Iran. The most it hoped for was a statement of political support. But what would the other members of the Arab League expect in return? This was what worried him. He wanted to make sure that whatever statements were issued at the conference, the Palestinian people would not lose their right to determine their own future in establishing and running their nation. He also hoped for a consensus regarding Egypt. It was time to accept Egypt, his long-term ally, back into the League.

The plane's captain informed Arafat that we would be landing in Amman in twenty minutes. Arafat looked at me and said: "We need to give you an official designation so you can attend the summit." I was still a PLFP member, and since 1970 I had been blacklisted in Jordan. The Jordanian authorities would have had every right to refuse me entrance if I did not have diplomatic standing at the conference. On his presidential stationery, he wrote a decree appointing me as his advisor and asked the members of his entourage to witness and sign the document immediately. He wanted to make sure that whoever saw the document would know it had been ratified democratically by the other representatives in the PLO delegation.

Moments later, we touched down at Marka Airport in East Amman. The plane taxied up to the terminal, stopping near the reception hall, which was a separate building set aside only for VIP guests. From the window of the plane, we could see the red carpet that had been laid out to receive the conference guests and the officials who were approaching to greet us.

Arafat noticed immediately that King Hussein was not at the head of the welcoming delegation, as was his custom when visiting heads of state arrived in Jordan. In his place was Jordanian prime minister Zaid Al-Rifaai. The president ordered the flight crew not to open the doors.

"What do you think, Bassam?" he asked, "Should I order the crew to take off in protest?"

I considered my answer carefully. This was a serious breach of protocol that could lead to an escalation in the already tense Jordanian-Palestinian relations. I looked out through the window and saw Zaid Al-Rifaai, other Jordanian ministers, and army officers standing on the first step of the stairs waiting for the doors of the plane to open.

"King Hussein's absence is no coincidence of course. This was deliberate. The question is, what is the aim of such a move? Is it to provoke you so you will take off without attending the summit? Something is going on, and we will find out what it is soon. But my opinion is that you should ignore the slight and attend the summit." Arafat thought about my answer, and then unbuckled his seatbelt. "You're right. Let's see what they have in store for us."

The Jordanian protocol officer and the Palestinian ambassador to Jordan, Atayeb Abdullahrahim, were also there to welcome the president, who was smiling as he exited the plane, in spite of his concerns. Arafat warmly shook hands with Prime Minister Rifaai and the others. Then I shook hands with the prime minister, whom I have known since childhood. My father's house in the Lweibdeh district of Amman was across the street from the house of Samir Rifaai, the prime minister's father, who had also been an important political figure in Jordan. Our parents had not only been neighbors, but close friends as well.

When I shook hands with Rifai, he winced. "Don't press too hard on my hand, Bassam. Your people wounded it when you tried to assassinate me in London."

"We didn't try to assassinate you; that was a different group. The important thing is that you don't try to assassinate the Palestinian cause."

Rifai was known to be anti-Palestinian, especially after 1970, and I wanted to make sure he knew that I hoped he wouldn't do anything at the summit that would stand in the way of our plans for Palestine.

As our motorcade moved through the city, I noticed how much Amman had changed since the last time I had been there. It had been seventeen years since I had been banned from ever entering Jordan again because of my involvement in the events of September 1970.

We reached the Plaza Hotel, where the kings, presidents, and official delegations attending the summit were staying. Arafat went directly to his suite, accompanied by the welcoming committee, while I headed for the room where identification tags for delegation members were being issued.

The room was packed with ministers and delegation members. I spoke to many of them while we waited to receive our identification tags. The room soon emptied, leaving me conspicuously on my own, feeling that something was wrong. I went up to one of the officials in charge of issuing the tags and asked what the delay was. He then answered with exaggerated politeness that he was awaiting instructions.

I understood then that even after seventeen years my official banishment from Jordan was causing a problem. I also understood why the president had insisted on officially appointing me as his advisor before we left the plane. I went back to my chair and closed my eyes, trying to relax. I do not know how long I waited, but I was jolted to attention by a voice asking: "Where is Bassam Abu Sharif?" I just looked at him. I was the only person in the room, so why was he bothering to ask? The officer walked closer to me and asked: "Are you Bassam Abu Sharif?" I replied: "Why do you ask when you know very well that I am?" The officer was Mustafa Al-Qaisi, the director of the Jordanian General Intelligence Department. He apologized for the inconvenience, but informed me that I had to leave the country without delay because of my lifelong ban from entering Jordan. I was to be escorted to the airport to ensure that I left Amman immediately.

"I have not come to Jordan," I replied. "I have come to the Arab Summit. This spot now belongs to the Arab League, and I am a member of my country's delegation. No one has the right to prevent me from attending the Summit."

"These are our orders, and we will follow them," he answered.

Remaining calm despite my outrage, I told him: "I only take orders from President Yasser Arafat. If he orders me to leave, I will leave immediately. Otherwise, I'm not leaving."

Al-Qaisi left the room. Minutes later, Abdel Razeq Al-Yehya, the former head of the PLA, entered. He was smiling. "The problem has been resolved. Trouble always follows you, Bassam." I replied that I always seek my rights, not problems.

He took my arm, and we walked together into the lobby of the hotel, which was packed with Arab ministers and delegation members. He led me toward a group of Jordanian officers that included Mustafa Al-Qaisi. In an attempt to lighten the atmosphere, Al-Yehya said, "Thank God, the misunderstanding has been resolved and everything is ending well." I just looked at Al-Qaisi with a raised eyebrow, but he was not fazed in the least. He was obviously only following orders.

I shook hands with one of the other officers who said, "You spoke against His Majesty in your interviews, especially on Syrian television."

"That's not true. I didn't even hold any interviews with Syrian television. But if you mean other television stations, especially international ones, then I was merely defending the point of view of the PLO and our position."

Al-Yehya, wanting to avoid more confrontation, suggested that I go to my room to rest. Before I left, one of the officers handed me my identification tag and informed me that it had been issued on King Hussein's orders.

What a day that had been!

Moments later, I was taking the elevator up to my room, when it suddenly stopped on a floor before mine. I braced myself, not knowing what to expect next. The elevator doors opened to reveal none other than King Hussein himself, accompanied by two men. The second he saw me he smiled. "Welcome, Bassam! Welcome to your country."

"Thank you, Your Majesty. That is indeed how I feel."

"I heard that there was a slight misunderstanding. Again, I tell you that this is your country, and you are welcome here."

23

LOST IN TRANSLATION

fter relaxing in my room for a while, I headed for President Arafat's suite. It was packed with members of the delegation and the embassy staff. "You've finally made it," he smiled. When I tried to explain what had happened, he said that he knew all the details. Later I learned that on hearing about my problem, Arafat had made it clear to the Jordanian authorities that since we had come together on the same plane, we would leave on the same plane. If I was to be forced to leave, the leadership of the PLO would also leave.

We quickly got down to the business at hand. Farouq Al-Qadoumi, the minister of foreign affairs for the PLO, explained the details of the proposed political statement that was to be released by the Summit. It pledged to support Iraq in its fight against Iran as well as to work on creating international pressure to liberate the Iraqi lands that Iran had occupied from 1980 up till that time of the war. What most attracted our attention, however, was the fact that the proposed statement did not, as similar statements had in the past, refer to the PLO as the sole legitimate representative of the Palestinian people.

It appeared that this was not a slip but an intentional omission. Certain parties, such as Syria and Lebanon, wanted to use the emergency summit to marginalize the PLO's position with the Palestinian people, thus paving the way for other countries, such as Syria, to step in and take over Palestinian decision making. When everyone had left the room, I stayed by the president's side. He called the head of his security group and asked how the matter of searching the suitcases was coming along. The Jordanian security services had insisted on searching Arafat's suitcases, and Arafat had given orders to refuse. He did this not because the luggage contained anything illegal, but because searching it was a breach of protocol and a direct insult to Arafat. He was told by his men that there had been no change.

Later, I decided to find out what was going on. I headed to one of the suites in the hotel where Jordanian security forces had set up electronic scanning devices specifically for checking the suitcases. There I met Colonel Misbah, one of our PLO officers, who was standing guard to make sure the president's suitcases, which were onboard a military truck, were not touched.

I heard him tell the Jordanian colonel in charge that no one was allowed to touch the president's luggage. I went back to Arafat's suite and told him that the situation looked complicated. He smiled and said, "The men are dealing with it. Don't worry." Just before the opening session, Arafat's suitcases were moved to his suite without having been searched. As always, Arafat was on top of the situation. When he wanted something to happen, it did.

During the summit, thousands of Palestinians demonstrated in the streets of the West Bank and Gaza Strip in protest over Arafat not being personally received at the airport by King Hussein. The welcoming of presidents and kings was shown live on television and the Palestinians saw that their leader had not received a proper welcome according to official protocol. The news channels had shown how each head of state had been met at the airport, with King Hussein greeting them officially, as per protocol. To see their leader snubbed on television was a huge sign of disrespect to the Palestinians, and they made their displeasure known loudly in the streets of the Occupied Territories. It was a huge coup for Arafat, for it was a clear sign to all members of the Arab League that he was indeed the chosen representative of the Palestinian people. No one else except Palestinians would ever be able to decide their fate.

The opening session of the summit was like the opening session of all Arab summits—elegant words were spoken in elegant speeches, meaning absolutely nothing and suggesting nothing practical at all. Verbal and moral support was given to Iraq on a superficial level only, but critical issues were not discussed in depth and no practical solutions were ever proposed. Nothing was suggested as to how we could help resolve the war between Iraq and Iran. Words were offered as support, but nothing more. King Hussein suggested allowing Egypt back into the Arab League, but Syria refused. The collapse in oil prices had meant that some of the richer countries felt they could not continue to support Syria, Jordan, and the PLO (as they had promised before in the Steadfastness and Confrontation conference). Issues were not sidestepped, but they were talked about and left hanging without any resolution.

Finally, the sensitive matter of the PLO's status as the sole representative of the Palestinian people came before the delegates, moving the disagreement from behind closed doors and turning it into a public confrontation in front of the local and international press agencies.

Press reports shifted from the topic of supporting Iraq in its war against Iran to the political matter of changing the official Arab position, which had previously been decided by the Rabat Summit. It was there that the PLO had been confirmed as the sole legitimate representative of the Palestinian people. Plans at the Amman Summit, however, were to draw up a proposal that would allow one or more states, such as Syria and Jordan (possibly in conjunction with the PLO) to represent the Palestinians.

The discussion became heated between the foreign ministers and the delegation members, but Jordan's position remained adamant. They refused to allow the phrase "The sole legitimate representative of the Palestinian People" to follow the name of the PLO.

As Jordan was the only country that had agreed to hold a summit in support of Iraq in its war against Iran, the Jordanian position carried significant weight, especially with Iraq, which traditionally had been a strong ally of the PLO. With Jordan holding a conference to publicly support Iraq, it was obvious that Iraq felt obligated to support the Jordanian stand as well. It was a long night of haggling and debating before the morning of the closing session.

As far as we knew at that time, the statement was going to be printed without the all-important phrase we wanted to have included.

The atmosphere was tense at the Plaza Hotel in Amman, especially in Arafat's suite. Arafat called the Palestinian delegation together to find out whether they had been more successful in any of the side debates that had taken place. They assured him that they had tried everything, but that the majority of the delegations had decided to turn a blind eye to their concern because the Iraq-Iran War was far more important.

The delegation left Arafat's suite a little before midnight, but he was not ready for sleep. He paced back and forth across the room, deep in thought. He told me the members of the Arab League were trying to use the Iraq-Iran War to take away the Palestinians' right to autonomy. Those same countries were trying to put the control back into the hands of the Arab League, where it had been before 1967, which had been a disaster for the Palestinians.

I suggested that Arafat talk to Taher Al-Masri. He was not only the Jordanian foreign minister and Jordan's representative in the meetings of foreign ministers, but he was also on the ministerial committee for phrasing the final statement issued by the summit.

Arafat went along with my idea, but he was not convinced that such a discussion would change anything. At his meeting with Arafat, Al-Masri tried to downplay the significance of the phrase, saying it didn't really signify anything if the phrase were omitted or not. Arafat disagreed, saying it needed to be officially stated again and again so that all the members of the Arab League would stop trying to control the fate of the Palestinians for their own benefit. Arafat had been right: the discussion had changed nothing.

The situation was critical for Arafat. The closing session was only hours away.

In the morning on November 11, the members of the Palestinian delegation gathered in Arafat's suite. It was his responsibility to maintain the independence of Palestinian decision making and to defend the right of the PLO to represent the Palestinian people. He was looking at the matter from a strategic perspective.

He sat at the meeting table in the suite, holding a folder in his hand, speaking calmly to all who sat around him. "All our attempts to confirm the status of the PLO as the sole legitimate representative of the Palestinian people in the closing statement have failed. Therefore, the only choice we have is to take a clear and direct stand by boycotting the closing session." All of us sitting at the table nodded in agreement. If we stayed, it would infer that we accepted the omission and what it implied. He then told all of us to go to the conference room to await further instructions. When Arafat and I were alone, he said, "Prepare yourself. If my last attempt fails, we will have to declare a firm stand regarding this matter and leave immediately."

At the front of the conference room heads of state and other delegation members were standing in groups and talking informally, waiting for the closing session to start. Arafat joined a group that included Iraqi president Saddam Hussein; Yemeni president Ali Abdallah Saleh; Moroccan prime minister Azzeddine

Laraki, who headed the Moroccan delegation; and King Hussein of Jordan and his chief advisor, Adnan Abu Odeh.

After greeting them all, the president removed from his folder the text of the closing statement and reminded Saddam Hussein about the lack of an official declaration that the PLO was the sole legitimate representative of the Palestinian people. As everyone in the group listened intently, the Moroccan prime minister said, "It must be a mistake or an oversight." Saddam Hussein, however, tried to downplay the situation by suggesting that it really wasn't very important whether the statement contained the provision or not. Adnan Abu Odeh remarked that the Palestinians were just wild mobs anyway, to which Arafat firmly replied that he should respect himself in front of His Majesty and not make such insensitive comments.

Arafat then dropped his political bomb, saying that if the closing statement did not contain the phrase he requested, he would have no choice but to boycott the closing session, refusing to attend any of the official final speeches. He knew that by not attending the closing session, he would be making a strong statement of protest about everything the members of the conference had discussed. In addition, he promised them he would then hold a press conference to explain the serious implications of the omitted phrase. By this, he meant he would reveal to all journalists, both international and local, the hidden agendas of the Arab countries who were trying to control Palestine's future. This would have caused protests to erupt all across the Middle East by Palestinians who believed in Arafat's vision for Palestine. Such protests would not have been anything any of the leaders would want to have happen.

Saddam Hussein then agreed that the phrase should be added, and Ali Abdallah Saleh seconded him. Then King Hussein, too, reluctantly agreed to add it.

A new statement, which included the text Arafat had insisted on, was drafted and approved by a majority of delegates, thus ending the session. King Hussein, as leader of the host country, then held a press conference to explain the statement and answer reporters' questions.

I had received a copy of the closing statement in both Arabic and English at the same time as the reporters had. To my surprise, the English language version did not include the provision, while the Arabic one did. I rushed to the president's suite to inform him of this flagrant omission. He was just as surprised as I was. He asked how we could correct this with the foreign reporters. I said I could arrange for another press conference, but he pointed out that all the reporters would be attending a press conference with King Hussein. I promised to do my best to rectify the problem.

I called the summit's media center and asked them to deliver an urgent message to Thomas Friedman, a *New York Times* columnist, requesting that he call me at the Plaza Hotel. Minutes later, I was on the phone with him. I told him that something important was up and asked him to come to Arafat's suite. I asked him to bring with him reporters from Reuters, the AP (Associated Press), and the AFP (Associated Foreign Press).

Fifteen minutes later, we were all gathered in Arafat's suite. Arafat held up the Arabic version of the statement as well as the English one and asked the reporters if they had read the English text. Some of them nodded, others said no. He told them which phrase was missing in the English version and gave the reporters who knew both Arabic and English a chance to compare both versions. The reports they filed that day focused, not on the other provisions in the closing statement, but on the omission. Thomas Friedman made sure the *New York Times* headline the following day was about this significant omission.

Arafat decided to hold an official press conference a little after midnight that same night. It was late for a press conference, and most people thought few reporters would attend. But by 12 a.m., the conference room was packed with reporters, as President Arafat repeated his message that he had given earlier in the day.

The next day, we left for Sana, Yemen, to one of his other headquarters, but only after Arafat had made his point crystal clear to everyone. Although we never found out the real reason why the phrase had been lost in translation, we took advantage of the opportunity to get the word out to Arab and international news agencies that the PLO represented the Palestinians and no one else could. Arafat had managed to put the spotlight once again on the Palestinian issue of representation and autonomy. He had also been able to make a very strong statement to the Arab League: He was the sole and legitimate representative of the Palestinian people, and the future of their country would always be in their own hands.

24

CHILDREN OF
THE STONES

Less than a month after the Amman summit, on November 29, 1987, the Israeli government held a meeting headed by Prime Minister Yitzhak Shamir. Israel's Labor Party was then part of the coalition government and Labor Party leader Yitzhak Rabin was the Israeli minister of defense. The agenda of this cabinet meeting contained only one item: the appropriate Israeli response to the worsening situation in the Occupied Palestinian Territories on the West Bank and the Gaza Strip. The oppression of the Palestinians and their deteriorating economic conditions had resulted in daily protest demonstrations, strikes, and confrontations with the occupation soldiers throughout the territories. As far as the Israeli government was concerned, a serious threat was developing.

At the meeting, two methods of dealing with the situation were proposed. One was the iron-fist approach, which basically meant that the Israeli soldiers would have free rein to deal with the Palestinians in any way they saw fit, including defending themselves against children throwing stones. The other method proposed was a military withdrawal from the heavily populated Palestinian areas such as Gaza and the West Bank, while maintaining a tight defensive ring around them. On the night of the Israeli meeting, I was with Arafat in

Yemen at one of his headquarters. While he went through his mail in his hotel room, I was sitting with him watching the meeting on television. Shimon Peres, a minister in Shamir's government, had suggested a policy of withdrawal, while Shamir and the other Likud (right-wing Israeli political party) ministers favored the iron-fist policy.

At midnight, the official announcement was made: the Israeli government had decided to go with the iron-fist policy, and the minister of defense was to be in charge of all operations.

I told Arafat the news, adding, "This means total confrontation. Don't you think that coordinating mass demonstrations everywhere simultaneously would make matters more difficult for Shamir's government?" I was suggesting that strikes across the nation and protests happening at the same time all across the Occupied Territories would make it more difficult for the Israelis to implement their iron-fist policy. At that time, strikes were sporadic and demonstrations would pop up here and there, but never at the same time. It was easy for the Israeli soldiers to arrest protesters, beat them up, and torture them once they were imprisoned. Palestinian children were also being beaten, arrested, and tortured on a regular basis.

Arafat was concerned that our people would not be able to bear the consequences of such fighting. They would be unable to go to work; they would not have money to buy food if merchants closed their businesses and all unskilled and skilled laborers went on strike. He wanted us to consider all options carefully for the sake of the people. Arafat contacted some of our people in the Gaza Strip and the West Bank, asking what means of self-defense they had. He then instructed his pilot to be ready to fly out the next morning. He had one of his closest aides inform the members of the PLO's Executive Committee that they would be traveling the next day to attend an emergency meeting of the Palestinian leadership. As usual, the destination was not to be revealed until we were en route.

I understood that these were serious developments that could present an opportunity for a new national resurgence following the Israeli invasion of Lebanon in 1982, the 1983 battles in Tripoli in Lebanon, as well as the battles in the camps of Beirut in 1985 and 1986. In 1985, the Syrian-backed Shiite-dominated Amal militia attacked Sabra and Shatilla camps as well as Bourj Al-Barajna, all Palestinian refugee camps in East Beirut. May 1985 marked the beginning of the "Camp Wars," in which the Amal militia (allowed by the Lebanese government)

attacked the camps in order to keep the Palestinians weak and powerless. They did not want them to become a strong force within the community as they had under Arafat before. The Palestinians were outnumbered by the Amal militia eight to one. In addition, Amal had tanks, mortars, and cannons, while the Palestinians only had light weapons. The Palestinians' resistance to the Amal onslaught was seen as perhaps one of the bravest resistance stands ever recorded in modern times. Just one year later, the camps were struck again and kept under a six-month siege. People were starving, and mothers trying to get water for their children were gunned down by snipers. Eventually a cease-fire was enforced by the Lebanese government.

The Camp Wars were terrible tests of Palestinian resistance and fortitude. I knew our people had been tested before and remained steadfast during the worst of times. What was about to happen in the West Bank was going to test Palestinian resolve once again, but I knew our people were up to the challenge. They had proved themselves over and over again, generation after generation.

Although Arafat was worried about what sort of reprisals the Israelis would unleash against his people once they rose up in one united force, he believed in their indomitable will to survive. Arafat was convinced, as was I, that a united stand had to be taken. I knew we were on the verge of war as our plane landed in Baghdad.

Before the committee convened, I told everyone who had arrived for the emergency meeting what Israel was planning. I briefly explained to them the possible consequences of the Israeli decision to follow an iron-fist policy in the Occupied Territories.

The Executive Committee convened that night at 9 p.m. Arafat began the meeting by summarizing the latest political developments, asking the committee to look into what could be done to deal with the dangers that were bound to arise once our people started to rebel. They looked into various strategies that involved stockpiling food, making sure people had enough money for emergency supplies like medications and water, and how we would help the families left behind if anyone in their family were either killed or imprisoned.

As usual a long discussion ensued, with each member sharing thoughts and analyses. After midnight, Arafat suggested forming a committee to set up a political, media, and field agenda to deal with the situation. He wanted to be ready for any possibilities should Israel seek a compromise with us. He wanted to make sure all avenues of the media would be covering our uprising so that pressure would be put on Israel to stop the occupation and inhumane treatment of our people, and he also wanted to be prepared to help the families in any way he could.

The Israeli government did not wait long to implement its decision. It began its aggression against the Palestinian people the following day, on December 9, 1987. Four Palestinian civilians were killed at an Israeli checkpoint in Gaza. Israelis stopped a bus that was carrying Palestinian laborers who were coming from Gaza to work in Israel. They ordered the workers to get out of the bus and then shot them in cold blood. When this happened, I told Arafat he was going to have to put the PLO on alert and notify his leaders in the Occupied Territories of what had happened. Shortly after that, a seventeen-year-old boy was killed when Israeli soldiers fired live ammunition into a crowd of Palestinian protestors. These acts of aggression were the final straws that caused the Palestinians to rise up in a united protest. Enough was enough! The Palestinians had lived under ruthless occupation for the past twenty years. Being treated like second-class citizens in their own country, being paid less than an Israeli for the same work, having to pay higher taxes than an Israeli, and having to sit by and watch the illegal settlement by foreigners of their own lands was just too much to bear. The Israelis escalated their aggression gradually after they had sent huge military reinforcements of tanks, armored vehicles, and soldiers into the West Bank and Gaza Strip.

We decided that confrontation was the only response as long as these attacks, authorized by the Israeli government, continued to take place. This was the starting point of the all-out national Intifada. Arafat instructed all the committees in the West Bank and Gaza Strip to coordinate with each other so that the protests and demonstrations would be continuous all across the Occupied Territories. At the same time, he issued a daily memo to be distributed to the various locations of the PLO around the world that contained a summary of the situation in the Occupied Territories. He gave detailed instructions regarding the political, diplomatic, and media efforts that would be needed. He also issued orders to those in leadership positions who lived outside of the Occupied Territories to rally international support for the Palestinian people against the Israeli iron-fist policy. Arafat wanted to make sure this confrontation received full media and political attention. The media covered the Israeli aggression, thereby increasing international support for the Palestinian people. The media began to see a new David and Goliath story unfolding each day, as young Palestinian children threw stones at the Israeli Goliath safely sitting in tanks and armored vehicles.

Reports, sometimes only minutes apart, came in to us of stone-throwing civilians, many of whom were children, being shot down unmercifully by the Israelis. Arafat was still worried about his people's ability to withstand a battle like this, especially an open-ended one that could go on indefinitely.

During this time, Arafat was engrossed in keeping communication lines open with leaders within the Occupied Territories, making sure that they coordinated their uprising in a simultaneous effort so as to make it more difficult for the Israeli forces to bring order to any one part of the Occupied Territories. He also kept in contact with many of our members stationed outside the Occupied Territories who were operating from Europe or other Arab nations. Much went on that I cannot disclose, but the most important aspect of his position was that he never let anyone feel that any city or village was acting alone. The Palestinians were fighting this battle together, not acting independently. The Palestinian Intifada became one united force, standing against the iron first of Israel.

In the meantime, I had started going over a special report that had been written by Lord Winchelsea for British prime minister Margaret Thatcher. He and his family had been visiting Gaza when the Intifada began. He witnessed the Israeli use of massive force against unarmed civilians who were protesting by throwing stones, and he wanted his prime minister to know exactly what the Israeli response had been to the resistance of stone-throwing Palestinians youths. He warned her of the Israeli government's plans to commit more massacres against the Palestinian civilians, especially in the Gaza Strip, and asked the prime minister to prevent them using all possible means at her disposal. The report was detailed and serious, so I outlined it for Arafat, suggesting that he call Lord Winchelsea both to thank him and to obtain any additional information that may not have been included in the report.

A month later, in January, Arafat began to propose political stands in newspaper and television interviews with the aim of showing the PLO's pragmatic way of thinking. He announced countless times that the PLO accepted UN Security Council Resolution 242, and that the solution to the Palestinian-Israeli conflict should be a political one. He made it clear that the PLO sought such a solution. His statements caught the attention of many countries in Europe, including France and the United Kingdom, as well as the United States. It was clear that the steadfastness and courage of the Palestinians in the West Bank and Gaza Strip had given the PLO and its leadership unlimited support abroad. Seeing pictures of small children bravely standing up to an Israeli tank or Israeli soldiers aiming their machine guns at women and children who were armed only with stones allowed the world the chance to feel more compassion for the plight of occupation under which the Palestinians had been suffering for so long.

Some people in the media and political circles, however, tried to separate the PLO from the Intifada, promoting instead the idea of a "spontaneous Intifada," while others implied that Palestinians were acting under a new leadership in Palestine. These attempts to undermine the movement failed as it remained clear to all that the PLO was leading the Intifada. The political, financial, and moral support provided by the PLO to the Palestinians in the West Bank and Gaza Strip no doubt played a crucial role in confirming this. This Intifada was not a military action, for the Palestinians did not fight back with guns, only stones. This Intifada was a demonstration of the solidarity of the Palestinians in their fight to overthrow the tyranny under which they had lived since the first occupation of their homeland.

Two months had passed since the bloody confrontations had begun in the Occupied Territories. The Palestinians' courage grew as they fought back against Israeli belligerence. Children throwing stones not only at armed soldiers but at armored tanks were scenes people all around the world were seeing on the evening news. International support was definitely on our side.

By March 1988, direct and indirect political communiqués from various European countries began to arrive to Arafat, asking for the formation of a political agenda from the PLO as well as for a practical political stand that would implement Arafat's announcement to accept Resolutions 242 and 338 while also finding a just political solution in the Occupied Territories. It was understood that there was a need for the PLO to propose a comprehensive political solution to the Palestinian-Israeli conflict and to work with all international parties to gain support for this vision. I saw this as the best weapon in the face of the Israeli policy of aggression, expansion, and occupation, and Arafat agreed.

25

A POLITICAL BOMB

I t was obvious to me that Arafat had become more confident in our people's ability to endure hardship in the pursuit of freedom. Even though they were under constant siege by Israeli forces, Palestinians did not stop their resistance. In spite of all the mass arrests, beatings, and torture, the Palestinians did not stop. Neither did the Israeli practice of mass punishment frighten people in any of the neighborhoods into stopping their resistance just because the Israelis threatened to blow up their homes or rip out their olive trees. The struggle went on; our people grew stronger with each stone they threw. This encouraged Arafat to propose a political move that would not only be analogous with our people's fortitude, but also something that would give the Intifada a tangible goal. Arafat did not want the sacrifices of an entire people to go to waste without any political accomplishment that must be attainable within the balance of regional and international powers. He had to get the world to force Israel to accept Resolutions 242 and 338 as well as get them to recognize the need to honor the Oslo Accords and the Camp David Agreement.

Arafat wanted to be sure of the reward the Palestinians would get in exchange for full flexibility and a realistic policy that would take into consideration the status quo while also gaining international acceptance. He knew only too well that Israel was not going away; it was here to stay. He knew only too painfully that the Palestinians would have to accept a smaller Palestine, not the Palestine of their forefathers. Whatever the PLO agreed to would have to be acceptable to Israel as well; that too was perfectly clear to Arafat. He was unsure, however, as to how much the Israelis would be willing to accept in order to reach a peaceful solution. All Arafat had ever wanted was for Israel to accept Resolutions 242 and 338. He knew that he could never get them to agree to UN Resolution 194, the right of return for all displaced Palestinians to reclaim their homes, but he wanted to have a place for that "tent" he and Qaddafi had discussed not so long ago. A small Palestine was better than no Palestine at all.

I told Arafat that I felt it was time to launch a comprehensive political peace initiative that would make Israel and the West look bad if they did not accept our proposal. We were in a strong position because the whole world was supporting our people; even countries loyal to Israel considered what Israel was doing to the civilian population to be a crime against humanity. Children throwing stones did not deserve to be threatened with tanks and machine guns. The so-called harmless rubber bullets the Israelis were using caused permanent brain damage and death in countless young people. The massive amounts of gas attacks they used led to deaths among the elderly Palestinians who just happened to be in the wrong place at the wrong time. I reminded Arafat of what he had said when we left Beirut. "You said we would head for Jerusalem." Jerusalem had always been the center of the dispute between us and Israel. As in Christianity and Judaism, Jerusalem is considered one of the holiest cities in the Arab world. He wanted Jerusalem to be the capital of the new Palestine.

I convinced Arafat to put the political ideas he had expressed in the past two months into a comprehensive peace proposal for resolving the conflict between the Palestinians and Israel. I told him I would help write up a draft. His proposal was to put forward, for the first time, the establishment of a lasting peace based on "two states on the historic land of Palestine." I suggested that we publish the peace proposal in U.S. and European newspapers under his name. This way the Western public would have a chance to see that Arafat was a man of peace who wanted an independent state for his people. I told him we would be able to put the ball back in the West's court, and the PLO would finally be a key player on the Middle East peace map, rather than just labeled as an organization run by terrorists. Even though this conversation took place just after four in the morning in Arafat's room, he told me to start writing it up. He went to bed while I went to work.

Coming up with the right words was no easy task. The fact that this document would be attributed to Arafat, a person terribly misunderstood by the West, made writing it all the more difficult. The choice of words had to be absolutely precise in order to serve the following two goals: The proposal had to show his willingness to work toward the establishment of a permanent peace while preserving our national aims of independence, with the decision making of the Palestinian people remaining firmly in their own hands.

It took me over a week to complete a first draft. During this time I consulted with some of my colleagues who shared my views, getting their feedback and making revisions. These consultations involved a great deal of time both on the phone and the fax machine.

By the beginning of April 1988 the proposal had been formulated. I sent a copy for a final review to Fawaz Najiya, the manager of the *Mideast Mirror,* a periodical published in London, who also provided valuable feedback. As a final step, Arafat would have to approve it, but he told me there was no time for that. He wanted me to prepare for the African Summit in Ethiopia, which was to be held from May 26 to 28.

In Addis Ababa we were so busy that there was no chance for Arafat to read the proposal there, either. Then, at the end of the summit, as we were getting ready to head for our headquarters in Tunisia, Arafat told me to show the document to Jamal Al-Sourani in order to get his opinion. He was a member of the PLO's Executive Committee and was highly respected by one and all. His opinion was important to us because we knew he would give us an honest evaluation of the document.

Sourani's comments were blunt: "This is a bomb; it will cause an uproar." I told him this was our aim, but he went on to add, "If you want to publish this, you have to be very careful. Many people within the PLO will consider these ideas dangerous, perhaps even treasonable. Some might even see this as an offensive action." He also told Arafat that if he insisted on publishing it, then not to do so under his own name, just in case the reaction was negative within his own organization.

Arafat told me to publish it under my name. When I asked if he wanted to see what I had drafted first, he replied that there was no need, repeating it was to be published under my name. I knew that Arafat was using me to test the waters. I was to be his scapegoat. If there were any negative reactions to the peace proposal, Arafat could honestly say that he had not read it and that it reflected my personal opinions only.

On May 30, 1988, there was to be a summit in Moscow in which President Reagan and President Mikhail Gorbachev of the Soviet Union were to meet.

The two superpowers were going to have follow-up discussions after the meeting they had had in October the previous year. It was then that they had signed the Intermediate-Range Nuclear Forces Treaty, which eliminated certain weapons in Europe. They were meeting again to discuss how these weapons would be destroyed. We saw this treaty as the beginning of the end to the Cold War. It was widely assumed that the two leaders would be discussing other hot issues, such as the Middle East crisis and the Soviet presence in Afghanistan, to name but a few.

The plan had been for Arafat to publish the announcement before this summit so it could be included on the agendas of both leaders. Arafat's decision not to have the document come out under his name, however, made this far less likely to happen. Still convinced of its importance, I began to work on getting the statement published in influential newspapers, where it could affect public opinion while also getting noticed by the White House.

My first choice of newspapers was the *Washington Post*, not only because it has a large circulation, but also because it is published out of the U.S. capital, Washington, D.C. In addition, it was the newspaper of choice for people who were in influential positions, some of whom were in the highest political circles. Another reason for choosing the *Washington Post* was that its executive editor, Ben Bradley, as well as one of its Middle East reporters, John Randall, were both friends of mine. Since getting through to Bradley was more difficult than trying to reach the president of the United States, I called Randall, who was in Paris at the time. He was coming to Tunisia the following day, so we agreed to meet in my office there.

I explained to him the importance of having the article published before May 29 so that Reagan and Gorbachev could have a chance to read it before they met, but he said he was not authorized to interfere with editorials. The chief editor at that time was a strong supporter of Israel, so Randall suggested I send Bradley a fax asking him to intervene, because he was the only one who had the authority. Despite Bradley's favorable reply to our message, the chief editor refused to publish the document. In my opinion, he was refusing because he felt it wouldn't serve the best interests of Israel. This was a setback for us, admittedly, but I did not give up. I was determined to get the peace proposal published in major U.S. newspapers.

I remembered that Arab kings and presidents were to meet on June 5 that same year at an important Arab League summit in Algeria, which was to concentrate on issues related to the Intifada. Naturally a large Palestinian delegation would be attending the summit, for in addition to there being a large Palestinian political presence in Algeria, Tunisia was the temporary headquarters of the PLO, just a stone's throw away from Algiers, the Algerian capital. I called one of the Algerian officials to ask how many reporters would be allowed to enter Algeria to cover the summit, and he told me that more than five hundred would be there. This was my chance! Distributing the peace proposal to such a large gathering would make it highly visible.

Fawaz Najiya promised me he would publish it in a special edition of the *Mideast Mirror* on June 5 to coincide with the opening of the conference. He was doing this as a special favor to me. Several days before the conference, he sent me hundreds of copies of a small booklet that bore the official PLO emblem (the Palestinian flag flying over the map of Palestine). In it were the UN resolutions related to the Palestinian cause and several articles, including mine, entitled: "The Possibilities of Peace in the Middle East" (which later came to be known as the "Abu Sharif Document").

A group of my aides had gone ahead of me to the summit to distribute the booklets so that when I arrived in Algiers the day before the summit many of the reporters would already have had the chance to read it. The first reaction came from one of the reporters who was there to represent the *New York Times* in the Middle East, who said, "This is too hot to handle. It's explosive."

Geraldine Brooks, a reporter for the *Wall Street Journal*, wrote a front-page article on the Palestinian peace project that I had written. The rest of the press picked up on her story, and reporters who had either not received a copy of the booklet or had not paid attention to it before were now trying to get hold of it. Tony Lewis of the *New York Times* had been told by the other reporter at the conference about the peace initiative. He called me from his New York office and asked me to fax him the peace plan immediately because he wanted to publish it in full in the editorial section. I also received calls from the editors of the *Washington Times* and many of the British newspapers, requesting the same thing.

The following day, I received the first comment from an Arab leader, Ibrahim Ezzideen, the Jordanian media minister at that time. He told me King Hussein wanted me to explain some of the phrases in the article. He said this was a political revolution, but I told him it was a test of the intentions of the United States and the West. He gave me His Majesty's queries, which included such concerns as: What would Jordan's involvement be? And what exactly did we mean by a "two-state" solution? I told Ibrahim that Jordan would be seen as a supporter of our cause, but not as a direct negotiator with Israel on our behalf. That would be done by the PLO, the legitimate representative of the Palestinian people. I also explained that the two-state solution simply meant that Palestine would be an independent country existing side by side with Israel and that Palestine would be run by Palestinians, not anyone else.

Talk and press reports about the document went on during the days of the summit. Israeli newspapers wrote many analytical articles about it, including articles written by Amnon Kapleliouk, a French-Israeli journalist who praised the document in *Le Monde Diplomatique*.

The summit in Algiers (which I like to call the "Summit of the Intifada" because that was the main subject of discussion) ended, but the document I had written caused a tsunami of shock waves all across the world. The "Abu Sharif Document" was even compared to a nuclear bomb in some of the newspapers.

26

THE ABU SHARIF
DOCUMENT

n a few days, Israel weighed in with its own reaction. Israeli prime minister Yitzhak Shamir accused me of misleading world opinion by making it
appear as if the PLO actually wanted a peaceful solution, adding that the
peace proposal was a Palestinian ploy. Shamir rejected every single provision contained in the document, especially the two-state solution, on the grounds
that the PLO was a "terrorist organization" and that no one should negotiate
with terrorists. In the proposal, I had not only included the two-state solution,
with Israel and Palestine existing side by side, but I also had included the following: Palestine would include the West Bank and the Gaza Strip; Israel would
withdraw from all the land it had occupied since 1967 and from which the UN
Security Council Resolution 242 had called for its immediate withdrawal.

At first the Likud Party, which was part of the Likud-led coalition government, marched to the same tune as Shamir. Its leadership remained silent for a
while until Yossi Sarid, the head of the Likud, took an opposing stand to that
of Shamir by welcoming the document, saying that peace should be given a
chance, proposing that the document I had published be looked at in a positive
light. Various Israeli peace groups welcomed the solution for it realistically went
along with the international UN Resolutions 242 and 338, which had already set

a ceiling for any possible political solution. The conflicting government viewpoints resulted in a flood of articles and editorials in Israeli newspapers and on television. Opinions ranged from absolute refusal to consider negotiations to reserved acceptance. Our peace proposal seriously called into question Shamir's continuance of his iron-fist policy against Palestine. It was clear that the Palestinians wanted a peaceful settlement and that there was no need for Israel's tough policy of military aggression against a people who simply wanted to be independent from them.

Opinions varied on the Palestinian side, too. One of the first Palestinian leaders to comment was Abu Iyad, the deputy chief and head of intelligence for the PLO, who was in charge of security. Iyad publicly attacked the peace proposal, describing it as "political tomfoolery." The rest of the Fateh leadership remained silent, perhaps concerned that it really was Arafat's opinion, and not wanting to object to it before meeting with him in person. Arafat was both pleased and surprised when the officials of some of the other organizations within the PLO enthusiastically welcomed it as the foundation for a peace initiative.

Added to all this, the different leaders of the various PLO organizations used the document to launch a political public relations campaign aimed not only at the Israeli leadership, but at public opinion as well, which still tended to support the premise that the PLO was a terrorist organization, highlighting the peaceful intentions of the PLO. The peace proposal refuted categorically the line of official Israeli propaganda, which claimed that the PLO was a terrorist organization, that the Intifada was a terrorist movement rather than a popular resistance, and that the Israeli occupation was legitimate. Abu Iyad and I were close friends and colleagues, so I called him into my office to reprimand him for his inflammatory statements. He quickly replied: "Bassam, I'm not a spectator in this revolution. Conjuring up politics behind my back is something I will not tolerate." He felt left out because he had not been included in the formulation of the proposal. I told him there was no sleight of hand going on and that the document was merely a point of view that I had published to see what reactions it would get. Although I firmly believed in what I had written, I could not yet tell him that Arafat also supported it and was using me to see what the general reaction would be. I went on to tell him that it was also meant to show the Americans and the Europeans that the solution to our situation could only come from the international resolutions that had already been set down by the United Nations. I ended by saying that if the PLO accepted the international resolutions and the two-state solution, then the West would more than likely impose what we wanted, since it had been the UN that had put forward the resolutions in the first place.

Our conversation was friendly but firm.

"How could this happen without my knowledge, Bassam?" Abu Iyad was not only the head of PLO intelligence, but he was also the most senior Fateh official after Arafat. What Iyad said was regarded as an official stand within Fateh and the PLO.

"Nothing happened. An opinion was published, that's all." I wanted to assure him that no action had been taken. It was just a publication to see what people all over the world would think.

He was persistent, asking if any American promises had been made in exchange for these stands. I told him that no Western leaders had been contacted personally so far, but he remained skeptical, thinking that we must have spoken to someone with influence in the West to be able to get the news out into the media. "This document has become the main topic of discussion for everyone from Tel Aviv to Washington. I know how the media operates; if they hadn't been given the green light to highlight this issue, they would have dropped it like a hot piece of coal." He remained doubtful about what I had told him, thinking we must have had clearance from someone in a powerful position in the West to have not only had the document published, but for it to have received so much media attention all over the world. I could also tell that he was still upset that the formulation of the document had taken place without his knowledge or input. "In most cases, yes, that's true, but this time the media were taken completely by surprise, so they were unable to give it a low profile."

"Perhaps. But tell me in all honesty, off the record. What does Abu Ammar [Arafat] *really* want?" he asked again.

"You know exactly what he wants: an independent sovereign state in the West Bank and Gaza Strip, as do you."

He smiled. "That's true. Let's stay in touch with each other."

Before he left, I told him, "I suggest that you change your position. Don't refer to this document as 'political tomfoolery.' It's a serious and practical political stand, one that is internationally acceptable." It was important that Abu Iyad change his original statement because his opinion was regarded as an official one within the PLO.

The following day, Abu Iyad made a public statement supporting the document, adding that the PLO was willing to announce mutual recognition between the states of Israel and Palestine. After that, the discussion about our peace proposal became more serious; people began to view it as the general stand of the PLO, although Arafat had not yet put his official stamp of approval on it, as far as the media were concerned. But with Abu Iyad's statement supporting the proposal, it was starting to look like an official stand after all.

Inside the Occupied Territories, Faisal Husseini, a senior official in the Palestinian National Council, who also served as the spokesperson for the Palestinians; Sari Nusseibeh, an organizer of this Intifada; and other Palestinian leaders used the document to achieve the political breakthrough they needed in both the Israeli and Palestinian arenas. Heated debates and in-depth discussions over the peace initiative continued on all levels, both on the Palestinian and the Israeli sides. The leaders inside Palestine had always tried to create an atmosphere that would enable a political solution that would end in peace. The document undoubtedly gave them a push in their dialogue with their Israeli pro-peace counterparts, such as the Israeli Council for Israeli-Palestinian Peace (ICIPP). It was more difficult, however, dealing with those who could not forget the original 1964 PLO charter and agenda, which had called for the complete destruction of Israel.

Some Israelis insisted that the document only represented the opinion of its author rather than that of the PLO, and without Arafat's byline, other countries wanted assurance: Did the article express the official opinion of the PLO or not? Although Abu Iyad had endorsed it, what about Arafat?

The United States asked the Saudis to investigate. Khaled Al-Hassan, a member of the Central Committee of Fateh, called me while he was on a visit to Saudi Arabia. He informed me that the U.S. State Department's Middle East representative was in Riyadh, asking the government of Saudi Arabia to find out whether the article did or did not express the official opinion of the PLO.

I told him I was not at liberty to answer that question.

"Bassam, I can give an official stand if you assure me that Abu Ammar has approved what you published."

"The truth is that Abu Ammar never set eyes on the article, but I know that it expresses his point of view. I suggest that you call him."

The Soviet Union also showed great interest and activated both its diplomatic and non-diplomatic channels to find out whether the document was official or not. We were contacted by diplomats in official capacities as well as by friends who asked me, unofficially, whose opinion the document represented. I always told them it was mine and mine alone, but that I knew Arafat supported it. The governments of Germany, Britain, and France also showed great interest, making inquiries to me at high diplomatic levels. Soon after, other European countries followed their lead.

Amid all this turmoil, Arafat remained silent. Such was his way. Had he decided to throw the bait, just waiting to see who would take it? Knowing Arafat as I did, I knew he wanted a peaceful solution to our crisis in the long run. It had not been a ploy to fool anyone, but just his usual way of testing the waters without getting wet himself. Arafat wanted one thing only: a sovereign independent Palestinian state with Jerusalem as its capital.

Arafat knew that given the international, regional, and Arab realities, it would not be possible for the Palestinian people to reclaim all their land. Keeping this painful fact in mind, he had begun to think of a possible solution that could preserve what was possible of the Palestinian people's interests while also providing them with a refuge that would restore their dignity and humanity, giving them room to grow and develop. He was willing to make this historic bargain on the condition that it would guarantee the Palestinian people's best interests, which would be an independent state, existing side by side with Israel, but not including all the land that had been lost since 1948.

Arafat was pleased with the international interest the document had generated. The PLO's position had been strengthened. The Intifada had focused the eyes of the world on Palestine. In conjunction, the PLO had given the Intifada a political stand, not just a stand of resistance, but one that strengthened its position, its influence, and its ability to corner Shamir's government. It was now clear to the world that the Palestinian people were not terrorists, but a people who were in need of and seeking the peaceful solution to the illegal occupation of their lands, which had been mapped out years earlier by the United Nations in Resolutions 242 and 338. The controversial relationship between the struggle on the ground and the practical political stands that had been accepted by international society came close to being perfect. I cannot emphasize enough the contradiction people saw between children throwing stones at armored Israeli vehicles. Leaders and the general public alike were starting to question Israel's claim of being the victim. This new view of Israel would hopefully put pressure on Israel to respond positively to international peacekeeping efforts, even if only as a tactical move, to get them to accept and adhere to Resolutions 242 and 338. That was all we wanted.

But Arafat was still waiting for the most important result: U.S. acceptance of the two-state solution. If the United States accepted our proposal, we had a better chance of getting our wishes met. U.S. support of Israel was known to everyone, but we also knew that if pressure could be put on Israel to do anything, it would come from the U.S. government.

In light of Arafat's continued silence about whether the peace proposal reflected his opinion or not, the discussion among Palestinians became even more heated. In the meantime, the official government representatives as well as institutions located in Germany, Britain, France, Norway, Sweden, and Finland started to invite me to visit them to discuss what I had published.

It was then that Arafat decided that we should make a quick tour of some of the Eastern European countries. He knew that Romania and Yugoslavia had close ties to both the West and to Israel. He believed he could get a better sense of their leaders' opinions about the proposal by meeting with them in person and that this would help him determine what he would do next (i.e., remain silent and listen to world reactions or declare his open endorsement of the two-state peace initiative with an official PLO stamp of approval).

Arafat realized that the proposal had made an impact as soon as he landed at Belgrade Airport, where Yugoslav president Dobrica Ćosić welcomed him and asked almost immediately about whether the peace proposal expressed the PLO's official position.

Arafat told him that it had been written by me, not him, so he should ask me about the proposal. Arafat then whispered to me, "They are asking about your article. They're very impressed with what you wrote."

I shook hands with President Ćosić, who said: "What you published was very good; it opens the way to peace. Continue writing this way."

"Thank you, I will, but I must say that although I wrote the proposal, it contains the ideas of President Arafat." Arafat grinned as he headed to the guest house. He was pleased with what I had said.

Minutes later, Arafat was told that the Soviet foreign minister Eduard Shevardnadze was on the phone wanting to speak to him about the Israeli aggression against our people. Arafat asked him to help stop the violence against his people. It was apparent that Shevardnadze had also called to ask more about our peace proposal, inquiring if it epitomized Arafat's views or not. In order to appear completely unaware of what had been written in the document, Arafat turned to me and said, "Bassam, what did you write in the article? The minister is asking about it." Then he motioned for me to come closer, so that that Shevardnadze would hear every word of my answer to Arafat, as if I were only then filling him in on what I had included. I understood that Arafat wanted Shevardnadze to know that he had no idea about what I had written. He also wanted the Soviets to understand that if they were interested in knowing the truth about whether Arafat was in favor of the proposal or not, they would need to guarantee that they would support the establishment of an independent Palestinian state with the Palestinian people governing themselves. Arafat informed Shevardnadze that he would discuss the matter later and let him know what the leadership's position was.

We went next to Romania, where, as in Yugoslavia, there was great interest. Arafat was pleased to find out that the officials in Romania were also supportive of our peace proposal.

At the end of our stay in Romania, we headed for Arafat's headquarters in Baghdad, where he invited the members of the PLO's Executive Committee and the Central Council to convene in Baghdad within a week after our return.

This was Arafat's first effort to bring the discussion of the document I had published to the open PLO arena, thus paving the way for the ideas in the document to be turned into an official position of the PLO. Arafat had realized that this agenda would open the way to international recognition of the PLO as the legitimate representative of the Palestinian people. It would perhaps even lead to further political negotiations once the world realized that the official stand of the PLO was a peaceful one, not one based on terrorism as had previously been thought by the West.

Arafat's calculations had been precise. By not putting his stamp of approval on the document I had published, he had created the opportunity for public discussion between supporters and opponents of the document to take place within the various organizations under the umbrella of the PLO, without any concern over whether they were taking a stand contrary to that of Arafat. He had also allowed time for international, regional, and Arab reactions to emerge. He had been certain from the very beginning that the Palestinian leaders inside the Occupied Territories would be very much in support of it. Once everything was neatly in place, he decided to move the discussion to the PLO organizations.

Arafat did not want me to attend the Baghdad meetings because he knew they would be rowdy with malicious discussions. He knew I could get hot-headed in such situations and didn't want me to add fuel to the flames. He asked me instead to visit officials in the UAE and try to get financial support for the Intifada that was still taking place throughout the Occupied Territories. By the time I returned with UAE donations, the meeting in Baghdad had ended. Some friends came to warn me of the current flammable atmosphere and to advise me against reacting too strongly to some of the statements that had been made in opposition to the peace proposal. I had a history of being a fighter, and no one wanted me to get into heated arguments about what I had written. I found out later that some of the members had actually accused me of treason.

Arafat had ended the meetings by suggesting that a committee be formed from the members of the Central Council to question me personally about the article and its outcome. This was one of his ways of bypassing crises and ending arguments. Of course, no one contacted me and I was never questioned; it was assumed that since Arafat was turning all the questions over to me that what I had written was more than likely in accordance with Arafat's wishes, and no one wanted to get on his bad side. No one knew yet whether he had endorsed the peace initiative or not, but they didn't want to take the chance.

Arafat decided to return to his other headquarters in Tunisia to hold preliminary meetings prior to the convening of the Palestinian National Council (the Palestinian parliament) in November 1988. During the PNC meeting, the peace initiative was accepted by an overwhelming majority. It was obvious that he did not wish to lose this opportunity for peace through any hesitation. Despite there being no tangible guarantee of what the Palestinian people would gain, he sensed the importance of approving this new political path to open the doors of hope for our people.

After the peace proposal had been approved at the PNC and people were still speculating about whether Arafat had approved of it himself or not, I accepted many speaking invitations in Europe. I could sense the relief they felt knowing that the basis for all the ideas were international and centered on UN resolutions, especially the UN Security Council Resolutions 242 and 338.

In England, Oxford University invited me to give a lecture on my article and to answer questions afterward; the lecture hall was packed to capacity. Both the Palestinians and the Israeli right had rallied their supporters as if the lecture were a showdown. The director general of the British foreign ministry attended, as did many Arab ambassadors. In the question-and-answer session, extremist Zionist Jews focused on what they regarded as the PLO's terroristic nature, while peace supporters focused on finding a peaceful solution. At the end of my lecture, the director general invited me to the foreign ministry to meet with some of the ministers. He hinted that a private and official meeting might be arranged between me and the foreign minister, which would have been one of the first official invitations I would have received to discuss our proposal. It was hinted at, but never came to pass.

In London, an invitation came from The Royal Institute of International Affairs (RIIA), also known as Chatham House, a strategic research center with close ties to the British foreign ministry. In Paris, I spoke at the Research Institution of Evry and at the University of Political Science, both of which were known to have connections with the French foreign ministry. In Germany, the first meeting was with a research center connected with the German foreign ministry. I knew that people in these centers and institutions would most likely be in touch with their foreign ministers, and somewhere along the line, someone might set up a meeting for me with one of them. I was proven to be right when I finished my lecture in Germany. Shortly after I had completed my talk, I was invited to meet with the deputy minister at the German foreign ministry, during which time the Germans expressed clear and official support for the establishment of an independent Palestinian state.

I reported on all these experiences to Arafat and described the general nature of the stands of these European countries, both on official and unofficial levels, which was proving to be extremely positive. He was pleased and told me to continue as I had been doing, which I did, spreading the word through my lectures, indirectly and sometimes directly, to representatives of many European nations as I traveled from one place to the next.

The publication of the "Abu Sharif Document" had opened doors that had previously been closed.

Arafat had been right to wait.

27

GIVE PEACE A VISA

Toward the beginning of December 1988, while we were in our headquarters in Tunis, Tunisia, President Arafat called me and said, "Go to the airport straight away." This sudden request did not surprise me in the least, for I had become accustomed to his spontaneous decisions. In anticipation of such calls, I always kept a small suitcase packed wherever we were so that I would be ready to go at the drop of a hat.

The Swedish government had officially invited Arafat and his entourage of six to visit Stockholm to participate in a peace dialogue with Jewish leaders from the United States for two days, from December 6 to 7. The meeting was meant to allow for a meeting of minds to find a suitable formula that would allow for direct talks between the PLO and the United States. The Swedish prime minister, Ingvar Carlsson, and Sweden's foreign minister, Sten Andersson, were sponsoring the talks. Arafat was also told that five Jewish peace activists were scheduled to meet with him: Rita Hauser, the head of the International Center for Peace in the Middle East and a former U.S. representative on the UN Human Rights Commission; Drora Kass, executive director of the Center for Peace in the Middle East; Menachem Rosensaft, founding chairman of the International Network of Children of Jewish Holocaust Survivors; Stanley Sheinbaum, an economist and publisher; and Abraham L. Udovitch, a professor of Middle East history at Princeton University. Ms. Hauser was known to be in direct contact with the U.S. secretary of state, George Schultz. It was unlikely that the Swedish prime minister would have undertaken such a sensitive initiative without American approval, even if only implicit, and it seemed clear that this visit held political possibilities that could turn into major opportunities if it succeeded. This could be the chance Arafat had been looking for to gain U.S. recognition of the PLO, but only if all went well.

Relations between the PLO and the United States had been strained following the Reagan administration's refusal to grant Arafat a U.S. visa earlier, on November 26, 1988, when Arafat had been invited to appear before the United Nations in New York City to speak at their "Question of Palestine" meeting. It was there that he wanted to propose the peace initiative that he had approved for me to write up. In December 1988, I wrote an article for the *Mideast Mirror* entitled "Give Peace a Visa." Following the U.S. refusal to grant Arafat a visa on the grounds that he was an "accessory" to terrorism, the UN decided to convene at its headquarters in Geneva, Switzerland, on December 13, so that Arafat could address the General Assembly there.

On the flight to Stockholm, Arafat took from his file the draft agreement put together by Khaled Al-Hassan, a member of the Fateh Central Committee, during a meeting he'd had in Stockholm with the Jewish American delegation two months earlier as preparation for the meeting he was about to attend. Arafat asked the PLO delegation members on the flight, including me, to read the draft to form an opinion and suggest any modifications we might find necessary.

We were flying to Sweden about three weeks after the meeting we had just had in Algeria, from November 13 to 15, with the full Palestinian National Council. That meeting had been a historic one. A heated discussion went on for two days regarding a proposal to adopt a new political agenda for the PLO. Its strategic goal had been the establishment of peace with the state of Israel in return for the establishment of an independent sovereign Palestinian state on lands occupied by Israel in 1967. Eighty-seven percent of the council members had voted for the proposal. With that, the PLO had created a new political agenda, one that chose peace and a political settlement based on international legitimacy resolutions, starting with Resolutions 242 and 338. It included the existence of both states on the historical land of Palestine and the mutual recognition between the PLO and Israel to live in peace, cooperation, stability, and security.

We still had about twenty minutes before landing in Arlanda Airport, just north of Stockholm, when Arafat asked, "Is the proposal I am going to present to the U.S. Jewish delegation reasonable or do you recommend any modifications?" He listened carefully to each person's ideas, making amendments where he saw fit according to the advice he was receiving. Arafat always wanted his views to represent those of the people who had been elected to represent the Palestinian people.

As the plane descended toward the airport, we could see that it had been snowing. There was snow everywhere, except on the runways. Once on the ground we climbed into a van that transported us all to three waiting helicopters. It was well below freezing when we arrived and we were all shivering. Naturally our clothing wasn't warm enough because, as usual, we had not had any idea where we were headed when we had been ordered to travel, so we hadn't packed the right items.

The helicopters landed half an hour later on the grounds of a castle outside of Stockholm. The castle had once belonged to a Swedish king but had been renovated into a luxurious hotel where official meetings would often take place. Its stones were dark, and coated here and there with a sprinkling of snow. The castle garden was completely hidden under the snow, except for some tall rose branches that stood like stick figures above the blanket of whiteness.

After settling into our rooms, we gathered again in Arafat's suite. Talk resumed regarding what would be discussed at the meetings that were scheduled to take place with representatives of the U.S. Jewish organizations. Arafat commented, "This will not be an ordinary meeting. Sweden is pushing to make this work, and a delegation of American Jews cannot meet the leadership of the PLO without notifying the U.S. State Department. Therefore, we need to pay careful attention to what will be discussed. Let's not jump the gun. Let's see what they bring with them to the table." The hope was that whatever transpired would be a positive indication to the United States that the PLO was ready to negotiate in order to reach a compromise with Israel.

As soon as Arafat said that, Sten Andersson, the Swedish foreign minister, arrived. He explained that the goal of the meeting was to come out with a joint statement calling for a political solution to the Palestinian-Israeli conflict, adding that this idea had been drawn up by his government based on the new agenda the Palestinian National Council had approved at the November meeting in Algiers, in which the PNC had agreed that: the PLO, the sole legitimate representatives of the Palestinian people, would enter into peace negotiations under the auspices of the UN to establish a Palestinian state; the PNC accepted the existence of Israel; it rejected terrorism in all forms and called for a solution to the Palestinian refugee problem in accordance with international law.

"Will we be formulating a joint statement by the PLO and Sweden?" Arafat wanted to know.

"Sweden is merely sponsoring this meeting," the foreign minister replied.

"But this group of American Jewish leaders has no official capacity. It does not represent the U.S. administration, nor does it represent the Israeli government," argued Arafat.

Arafat's comment had a deeper meaning, which the foreign minister fully understood. He knew that Arafat was anxious to have official recognition by the United States, so an unofficial meeting with people not authorized to represent either the U.S. or the Israeli governments meant that whatever they were doing would be a waste of time. Mr. Andersson said that the prime minister would be joining them shortly and wanted to meet with Arafat alone. This was the minister's way of indicating that the matter went far beyond a mere joint statement, and that the prime minister would need to discuss the significance of this meeting with Arafat alone. After Prime Minister Carlsson spoke privately with Arafat for a few minutes, he invited us all to the dining room. The Swedes had arranged for our first meeting with the American Jewish leaders to take place over dinner. We arrived at the dining room before the Americans and noticed that the seating had been cleverly arranged so that all of us would be forced to mingle; this was to ensure that we could get to know one another informally before we sat down to serious discussions. Seconds later the doors opened and the Americans walked in, accompanied by the Swedish foreign minister.

At dinner, the talk was generally about the political situation and the need to find a solution for the conflict. Before dinner was over, the prime minister suggested that a small group from each side meet in the conference room to begin discussing matters in a more private and practical manner.

All but four people from each delegation retired to the conference room. Representing the Jewish side were Hauser and Kass; the Palestinian side consisted of Arafat, Yasser Abed Rabbo (a member of the PLO's Executive Committee), Mahmoud Darwish, and me. Hauser praised the draft proposal that Arafat had shown her and said that she felt it was ready to be announced. Arafat replied that he welcomed this discussion, but that some points needed modifying. Arafat left the meeting and headed for his suite while the rest of us stayed to discuss the modifications. Kass was in charge of writing up the notes after the two sides agreed. The modifications were focused mainly on making sure the text referred to the establishment of an independent Palestinian state on the lands occupied by Israel in 1967. The revised document was taken to Arafat, who requested more revisions to remove any ambiguity about the Palestinians' goal of establishing the Palestinian state as well as the sovereignty of that state. Without going into endless detail about what we changed and how various phrases were rewritten repeatedly in order to please both sides, it took us a great deal of time, writing and rewording each sentence.

We were working on further edits when we were all surprised by the unexpected arrival of the prime minister and the foreign minister, who wanted to speak with Arafat. They had come to deliver a message from U.S. secretary of state George Schultz, which stated that he had informed the Swedes that there was great interest in this meeting, and that, if an agreement was made, the United States would study it to decide whether or not it would pave the way for U.S. recognition of the PLO. This was huge! The United States had not yet officially recognized the PLO and yet here was a message from Shultz saying we had the chance. If the United States was pleased with the results of our meeting, then Arafat might just get the chance he had been hoping for: If the United States officially recognized the PLO, the Palestinians would be that much closer to achieving their sovereign state, which would put an end to the oppressive occupation of Israel.

The situation was different now than it had appeared when we had first spoken to the Swedish prime minister. This was the first time the United States had offered a political agreement through a country like Sweden. The communiqué from Schultz stipulated that the announcement include the following three points: a rejection of violence; the recognition of Israel's right to exist within safe, secure, and recognized borders; and the recognition of the international legitimacy resolutions of 242 and 338.

It was clear that the meeting would have important political ramifications. Arafat asked for a letter to be put together, which would be sent by the Swedish prime minister to Washington, explaining the following: our agenda, our goals, our willingness to make peace based on international legality, and our acceptance, within this framework, of the Americans' three points.

The reply from Schultz surprised us all mainly because it appeared that the United States was willing to make some compromises. In his reply, Shultz did not mention a U.S. rejection of the establishment of an independent Palestinian state, which is something we expected the United States to balk at. It also did not contain any comments regarding the beginning of the letter, which had stated that the Executive Committee of the PLO would act as a temporary Palestinian government until an independent Palestinian state had been established. It did, however, ask that Arafat emphasize at a press conference the three conditions that the Swedish Prime Minister had brought from the U.S. administration. The letter pledged that if Arafat announced these three items at a press conference in Stockholm, then thirty minutes later Shultz would announce the United States's recognition of the PLO. It was clear that Arafat wanted to be flexible enough to meet the American demands, but he also wanted to make sure he had the approval of the majority of the PLO Executive Committee to preserve the democracy of the decision-making process that was inherent in the PLO. No one person could make blanket decisions without the consensus of the majority of the PLO members.

Suddenly Arafat's face lit up. He had an idea.

"Let's hold a press conference here in Stockholm. We can wrap up our work with the American group and issue a joint announcement based on what we have agreed to here. We can separate the statement we make here in Stockholm from the one Shultz has requested from us. I want to include what he wants to hear when I make my speech in front of the UN General Assembly in Geneva on December 13."

His idea was met with approval by all of us present. It was also decided that, out of respect, we needed to persuade the Swedes to accept this idea, for they had been eager to hold the historic press conference in Stockholm. The Swedes, however, were understanding of Arafat's point of view and realized that his speech before the UN General Assembly would be his proposal for a peace initiative, not just a statement about what had been agreed to with the representatives of the pro-peace Jewish organizations. Arafat also asked the prime minister to send a delegation to follow up on matters between us and the American administration in Geneva, which he graciously did.

On the evening of December 7, we celebrated the issuance of the Stockholm Peace Declaration between the PLO and the leaders of the Jewish American organizations, who also included a statement indicating that they saw no reason for dialogue between the PLO and the U.S. administration to be delayed any further. We headed back to Tunisia the next day, where Arafat gained the immediate approval of the majority of the Executive Committee for his political move to include the three points Shultz wanted to hear before the General Assembly. He also was applauded for the Stockholm Peace Declaration, which had been based on the new agenda of the Palestine National Council that had been formulated in Algiers just a month before.

Preparations began immediately for the meeting of the UN General Assembly, which was only five days away, and a committee was formed to write the speech that would include the three conditions upon which Secretary Schultz had insisted.

Unfortunately, the best laid preparations don't always go as planned.

28

THE DIFFERENCE A PARAGRAPH CAN MAKE

The group that had been assigned the task of writing Yasser Arafat's UN speech had to work fast to meet the twenty-four-hour deadline he had given them. Arafat carefully studied the communiqué he had received from Schultz through the Swedish prime minister. I wanted to make sure the points would be clear and prominent in his speech, which could be summed up as the "Palestinian Peace Initiative."

When we had finished editing the speech, he said, "We need an accurate translation from Arabic into English, for this is a sensitive matter." I suggested the *Mideast Mirror* in London, for they had an efficient team of translators, led by Fawaz Najia, who knew how to address the West. I told Arafat that I could take the speech to London the next day and have it translated quickly. As soon as I arrived, I met with Michelin Hezzo, who did a superb job of translating the speech within a very short period of time.

While I was in London, I called a friend of mine, Jeffrey Archer, the well-known British author who had also been head of Margaret Thatcher's election campaign in 1979. We met at his house near London. I told him about Arafat's upcoming speech in Geneva. He was very interested in it and immediately shared the information with Prime Minister Thatcher, who was equally interested. She asked to see the speech before Arafat presented it and promised that if she found it to be heading in the right direction with regard to recognizing Israel, she would be the first to support it. Of course, this was impossible until Arafat had approved the translation of the text and of sending her a copy of it.

Back at the PLO headquarters in Tunisia, those who were unaware of the importance of this opportunity tried to persuade Arafat that sending the speech to Thatcher would ruin the element of surprise. I was shocked by their attitude. Many leaders could only dream of having such an opportunity, but the decision was not mine to make. Nevertheless, Arafat decided to send his speech to Thatcher. I sent it to Archer first, to get his opinion. Unfortunately, he was not home to receive it, which meant it did not get sent to the prime minister in time. All Thatcher had wanted to do was to make sure the English Arafat was going to use would be clear; she had wanted to let the Palestinians feel she was close to them by advising Arafat on the political language he should use in his speech. She was disappointed not to have been of help to Arafat in his great moment before the UN General Assembly. Archer had told me later, "It could have been written in a much better way, but the point was clear."

I returned the next day to Tunisia with the English version, knowing that it would have a positive impact. The translation was so precise it left no margin for misunderstanding. All of us who had worked on his speech knew it was going to be one of the most important meetings in the history of the United Nations with regard to the Middle East.

Arafat sent a large group of his delegation ahead of him to Geneva so that they could follow up on arrangements related to the presentation of his speech, which included setting up a press conference immediately afterwards.

I arrived in Geneva on December 11, 1988, the day before Arafat was expected. Security was exceptionally tight. In the lobby of the Intercontinental Hotel, a huge number of reporters and cameramen had already gathered to wait for Arafat. This was a big event and coverage of it would be extensive. The major U.S. television stations were covering the event live, and I have no doubt, from my long experience working in the media, that the content of what Arafat was going to propose had already been leaked to them.

After getting settled in my hotel room, I scheduled a meeting with the Swedish delegation that was attending the UN general Assembly for later that evening. The Swedes were still our official contact for our dealings with the United States, and it was vital for us to remain in contact with Washington in order to ensure the implementation of the U.S. pledge to officially recognize the PLO. Then I headed toward the lobby to meet with the reporters and journalists, most of whom I knew. They began to grill me in an attempt to find out what Arafat was going to say; some even asked to see an advance copy of the speech. Unbeknownst to them all, I was carrying Arafat's speech in my folder, but I dodged those questions and restricted my answers to the new agenda that the Palestinian National Council had approved on November 15 in Algeria.

In the evening, after I met with the Swedes and the press, I met with the other members of the PLO delegation, setting the following schedule: Arafat would speak on December 13, the opening day of the session, and follow-up questions would take place on December 14.

The night had been long and exhausting for me. In addition to the meetings, I had taken part in live televised debates with politicians representing many countries regarding the PLO's new agenda. The most important one had been with Binyamin Netanyahu, at that time Israel's ambassador to the UN, who accused the PLO of terrorism, saying that the UN had no right to allow Arafat, the head of a terrorist organization, to give a speech before the General Assembly. The debate was broadcast live on ABC's late-night news program *Nightline*, hosted by veteran newsman Ted Koppel. Netanyahu was proven wrong when I spoke of our new agenda to establish peace and a two-state solution. Following that debate, the PLO's new agenda became the focus of the international media once again. This was also clear from the high level of the delegations that would be present when Arafat spoke. Even though we had made these points many times, from the proposal I had published, to the PNC declaration in November, to the Stockholm declaration in December, no one believed what we were saying.

When Arafat finally arrived in Geneva, I could see that he felt worried and anxious. He wanted to know if the Swedes were there. I assured him that I had been in constant contact with them since my arrival. He relaxed a bit, but I could still see signs of tension carved into his face. He was going to be making perhaps the most important speech of his entire career, one that might ultimately lead to U.S. recognition of the PLO, an initial step toward achieving his dream of an independent Palestine. A great deal rested on what he said in front of the

General Assembly. Would the United States be true to its word? Arafat had been let down before and worried that he might be disappointed once again by false promises.

Basil Akil, the director of the Palestinian Welfare Organization, which helps the poor, asked for an advance copy of the speech, and Arafat agreed because he respected Akil's opinion. In the evening, Akil returned to Arafat's room and told Arafat he believed the three conditions Schultz had requested should be spread over three paragraphs instead of just one, so that they would come as less of a shock to the Palestinian people.

I strongly disagreed and told Arafat that I thought it a huge mistake to separate those provisions since the United States would be listening to his speech and expecting to hear them. In case Schulz did not have time to listen to the whole speech, we had to make sure that he heard what he wanted to hear.

Unfortunately, Arafat chose not take my advice.

On the morning of December 13, Arafat's motorcade drove from the Intercontinental Hotel to the nearby UN headquarters. The tension of the previous day was gone, and he was filled with energy, which was typical when he was about to do something of great importance to our cause. He felt that a great victory was at hand. The United States had pledged to finally recognize the PLO after fourteen long years and to begin serious dialogue with us aimed at finding a political solution for the conflict, one that he believed would eventually lead to stability and peace. And it all depended on Arafat's speech that day.

I did not accompany him to the UN, but stayed in my hotel room to watch the live coverage on television. When Arafat stepped up to the podium, he was greeted by a standing ovation. During the speech, he was interrupted more than once with applause, and when his speech was over, Arafat was thanked unanimously with another standing ovation.

Anticipating positive reactions, Arafat returned to his suite, surrounded by a large number of leading Palestinian figures and businessmen. Although he listened to all the enthusiastic talk going on around him, in truth, he was worried. I knew he was thinking about the pledge he had made to Washington. Would the United States be happy with his speech?

Half an hour passed, and still there was no word from Schultz.

I went to Arafat's suite, which was packed with people. Arafat was making phone calls to a number of Arab leaders, informing them of what he had included in his speech and how positive the response had been. He also asked them to take positive political steps to support the Palestinian initiative so that this opportunity would not be lost.

What we finally learned was a great shock and disappointment to Arafat, but it was what I had feared would happen. The Swedes told us that the officials in Washington were upset that Arafat had not mentioned the agreed-upon three points. It was clear that the Americans had not listened to the entire speech. Putting the items in separate paragraphs had indeed been a huge mistake.

I asked the Swedes to ask the American officials to fax us exactly what they wanted to hear from us, since there was still a chance to rectify any misunderstanding during the press conference. Finally a fax came through; it was just one paragraph containing the three items. During his press conference, Arafat read the three conditions together. The reporters were peppering Arafat with many questions, but he was not in the mood to answer them with great enthusiasm. He had wanted his speech to prove he really wanted peace, but through a lapse in judgment he had lost that opportunity. Now it would appear to the U.S. government as if Arafat had tried to get out of his agreement, and that the only reason he had accepted it was because he had been bullied into doing so. He was angry with himself for not having stuck to the original plan. After the press conference, Arafat decided to leave Geneva immediately, knowing that the Americans would find out that he had left in anger. He did not wait for the U.S. response, but left directly for his office in Tunisia. He asked the delegation to follow up on the matter and inform him of any developments.

When I returned to my room, an old American friend of mine, who was very close to Schultz, called to tell me that in half an hour Schultz was going to make an important announcement. Then she said, "*Mabrook*" (congratulations). I headed immediately for the suite of Jamal Al-Sourani, a PLO Executive Committee member, where a number of the Palestinian delegation members had gathered, all of whom were, understandably, very angry. They felt the United States had once again reneged on a promise.

I turned on the TV to CNN, and Al-Sourani shouted at me, "Is this the time for television, Bassam?"

I replied, "Don't you want to hear what Schultz has to say?"

With great sarcasm, he sneered, "Do you still trust Washington? Schultz isn't going to say anything."

Without missing a beat, I smiled, "Oh, yes he is, and I suggest you prepare to celebrate our victory."

Other delegates anxiously asked if I was certain of that, so I told them about the phone call I had received. I wasn't surprised when the group immediately split into skeptics and optimists, heatedly arguing their own points of view.

We were soon united in our relief. Schultz announced on CNN, in an official White House statement, the United States' recognition of the PLO as well as its plans to begin serious dialogues on finding a political settlement that would form the basis for peace-making in the Middle East.

Arafat had managed to regain a historic political opportunity after having it almost slip through his fingers. Back in Tunisia, I headed straight for Arafat's office.

"You were right," he admitted. "But I really thought they would listen to the whole speech." Then he grinned. "Of course, I should have known they wouldn't. Even I just read summaries."

29

THE AMBASSADOR'S LOST OPPORTUNITY

Sometime toward the beginning of 1989, Karma Al-Nabulsy, the PLO media and public relations advisor in London, called and urged me to visit her there. She described the general atmosphere in the United Kingdom as being very positive in terms of parliamentarians, British Jewish organizations, and some British foreign ministry officials with regard to the PLO.

I promised to call her back once I had discussed the matter with Arafat, but she sensed I was not enthusiastic, perhaps seeking a bigger political victory on a wider scale. She spoke to Yousef Allan, who had for many years been a mediator between Palestinian labor unions and English ones, and asked him to convince me of the importance of coming to London. He had managed over the years to create very important ties, not only with members of Parliament (MPs) in Britain's Labour Party, but also with influential political parties interested in the Middle East. Allan urged me to make that visit. He told me he could arrange meetings with the Labour Union, with Labour MPs, and with parliamentary committees that were related to foreign policy and the Middle East, including other important British figures.

I told him that if he could arrange a meeting with either the foreign minister or the minister for foreign affairs, then I would go to London. Two days later, he called to say that the minister for foreign affairs, William Waldegrave, would meet with me.

I sent my passport to the British consulate in Tunisia to obtain a visa in a normal manner, like any other citizen. I was asked by the consul-general the purpose of my visit, so I told him that I just wanted to see some friends and colleagues in London for a few days.

My application was turned over to the British ambassador in Tunisia, Thomas Day, who had also been the governor of Yemen during the 1960s when it was under British rule. He called to tell me that since I was a political official in the PLO, London needed to know the real purpose of my visit before they would grant me a visa. We agreed to meet in his residence to discuss the matter more fully. At 7 a.m. the next day, we were having breakfast on the balcony of his mansion. Not believing that I was going to London for a personal visit, Ambassador Day asked me directly if I would like to meet officials from the foreign ministry, as though he were offering to set such a meeting up for me.

I smiled. "I would be pleased to meet with the minister, as well as any other officials who specialize in the Middle East of course."

The ambassador looked at me closely as I calmly sipped my English tea. "Interesting," was all he said.

I later learned that the ambassador was not enthusiastic about my having a cabinet-level meeting in London. He wanted the relationship to develop slowly.

As I was leaving the ambassador's home, I said, almost as an afterthought, "In any case, I hope you can grant me the visa today, because I already have appointments with some colleagues in London, including the heads of some British Jewish organizations."

Trying to disguise his obvious surprise, he said he would see what he could do. That afternoon, he phoned me to say that my visa was ready, but that I would not be able to travel that day because of the security curfew that had been placed on Tunis due to Colonel Qaddafi's visit. It would be impossible for me to get to the airport. I told him not to worry; I would manage to get out somehow.

I flew to London that same evening.

Prior to my arrival, Yousef Allan and Karma had already set up appointments for me, working around my meeting with the minister. As for Ambassador Day, he had already informed the British foreign ministry of our conversation. I checked into the Grosvenor Hotel; I liked the idea of staying in the same hotel where Shimon Peres (the Israeli vice premier and minister of finance at that time) had stayed when he had come to London to meet with the foreign minister.

My meeting with the foreign minister was to be at 11 a.m. the next day. I called the Palestinian ambassador in London, Faisal Oweida, to inform him of my arrival and of my meeting with Minister Waldegrave. I asked to meet with him at 10 a.m. so that we could go over some details before the meeting.

"Impossible," he laughed. "They are lying to you. The minister cannot possibly meet a Palestinian official at this stage. I have tried many times to arrange meetings for Farouq Qadoumi [head of the PLO political bureau] and I have always been unsuccessful. The British said meetings such as these might happen at a later stage."

"I do believe them, and I am inviting you to come. You are our ambassador here and it is expected for you to be present."

"I will see you tomorrow afternoon because I am occupied from morning till noon." Thus ended my phone call with our ambassador. He didn't want to be bothered with a meeting he was sure would not materialize.

At 10 a.m., I informed Arafat of my impending meeting with the minister and told him that Karma and Yousef Allan would also be accompanying me. He told me it was a good start as a precedent, and then added, "I am depending on you to represent our views."

William Waldegrave, Sir David Gore-Booth, and Simon Fraser sat at one end of the table, and Karma, Yousef, and I sat at the other. Waldegrave spoke briefly about London's great interest in the new political agenda that the Palestinian National Council had adopted, and said that he had also been impressed with the speech President Arafat had given at the UN general assembly in Geneva. He said that there had been a decision to develop Britain's relations with the PLO based on all of the positive developments they had seen in the past year, and that this meeting, the first of its kind at cabinet level, was an indication of that. He then read aloud a paragraph he wanted me to consider, which included the PLO's rejection of violence, Israel's right to live within secure and recognized borders, and that negotiations were the way to creating stability and peace in the Middle East.

He looked pointedly at me. "If you agree to announce this paragraph to the general public, then I in turn will announce the following: Based on this positive attitude by the PLO, Her Majesty's government has decided to recognize the PLO and deal with it to achieve peace in the Middle East, taking into consideration international resolutions and the national rights of the Palestinian people." Since the United States had already started to negotiate directly with the PLO, the British government was now taking official steps to do the same. All they wanted was a restatement of what we had said already one year earlier in Algiers as well as what Arafat had said in his speech in Geneva.

I told him that I wanted to request one addendum to that statement before agreeing to read it: that an independent Palestinian state be mentioned. Allan, who I later found out was the eyes and ears of Prime Minister Margaret Thatcher, left the room briefly. When he returned, he spoke quietly to Waldegrave, who then said, "We prefer the statement to remain as it is." We had been asking for an independent Palestinian state but no one had officially agreed to our demands. We were still negotiating that concept and the United Kingdom certainly didn't like the idea of giving their official approval to a statement that was still under discussion.

I asked how we would make the announcements and he informed me that a press conference had been arranged at the entrance of the ministry. If I agreed to his terms, we would go together to meet with the reporters and then each of us would read our own part of the statement.

"I agree. Let's go."

The door to the ministry was opened, and we came face to face with a sea of reporters and journalists. Minister Waldegrave invited me to speak first, which was both a polite gesture and a precaution, making sure that I would read every word as it appeared in the statement that he had handed to me earlier before he committed to reading his.

I thanked him and stepped toward the microphones, holding the statement. I looked at it, and then folded it carefully before stuffing it into my suit pocket. Waldegrave looked horrified. I began to speak, thanking him and the British government for giving the PLO the opportunity to hold a meeting at the cabinet level. I went on to say that we hoped to develop the relationship for the sake of peace in the Middle East, mentioning the three points that were in the paper, but in my own words, not theirs. When I reached the point about Israel's right to live in peace and within safe borders, I added, "Of course, this is also the right of all countries of the region, including Israel and the coming Palestinian state that will exist side by side peacefully with Israel."

When I was done, Waldegrave read his statement. Back inside the ministry, he took hold of my arm. "You scared me when you put the paper away in your pocket, but your remarks were much better than what we wrote."

"And I also put in the part about an independent Palestinian state."

He beamed. "Yes, in a good diplomatic way."

"Now it's on record."

Over a cup of coffee, I invited him to visit Tunisia to meet with Arafat. He said he would be glad to, but that he first had to discuss such a trip at a government session.

From that moment on, we immersed ourselves in meetings with pro-peace Jewish organizations, the most important of which took place with a leading member of the British Jewish community, who emphasized the support of the Jewish community for the right of the Palestinian people to establish their own state.

The Western and Arab press requested interviews both about the meeting and the prospects for peace. Arafat and I were optimistic. He asked me to return as soon as possible so that I could go over all the particulars of our meeting with him. It was very important that we use this meeting as a basis for raising the level of the relationship between the PLO and the British government while also raising Palestinian representation so as to better support our people and our cause.

Maintaining strong media coverage in Britain remained high on my agenda. I visited London several times afterward and met with British officials, parliamentarians, and members of the House of Lords. A meeting was arranged between me and the committee for Foreign Relations in the British parliament. During this meeting, the head of the committee laid a challenge before me: "The PLO claims to be willing to establish peace with Israel based on international resolutions. Are you ready to meet with the Israelis to implement this practically?"

I called his bluff. "Of course we are ready. I would like you to arrange this matter as head of this committee."

"Allow me to phone the Israeli ambassador immediately." He was expecting the Israeli ambassador to welcome the idea, but when he returned all he could say was, "The ambassador will call Tel-Aviv and will let me know their reply."

Israel refused.

The attitude of the head of the committee changed as he began to appreciate that Israel's claim of the Palestinians neither wanting peace nor a chance to negotiate was simply not true.

Not long after, I was once again invited to give a speech on peace before thousands of students in the Grand Lecture Hall of Oxford University, while extremist Jews rallied their forces and again attempted to limit the effect of my address. But they failed once again, for the number who wanted to listen to my words far exceeded the capacity of the hall; all of the attendees were fully aware of the importance of the topic of peace in the Middle East and the PLO's agenda for a political solution.

Such activities continued until the level of the relations between the PLO and Britain reached a point at which I was granted a meeting with the foreign minister as well as Ministers William Waldegrave and David Gore-Booth.

The Palestinian ambassador, Faisal Oweida, wasn't going to make the same mistake twice; this time he made sure he attended the meeting.

30

THE POWER OF
AN EMBRACE

In the very beginning of 1989, shortly following the launch of the Palestinian peace initiative in mid-December 1988, Egypt, the largest Arab country and the first to have signed a peace agreement with Israel, supported the plan and began rallying Arab, regional, and international powers to support it, too. Within this framework, President Mubarak thought it necessary that Jordanian-Palestinian relations, which had been strained since the 1987 cancellation of the Amman Agreement, be repaired so as to provide additional impetus to the Palestinian peace initiative. He worked hard to turn the stagnation between Jordan and the PLO into action, even if it was gradual. However, he soon realized that the barriers between the two countries were not going to be easily broken down. It would be up to him to instigate a political move that would reestablish links between Jordan and the PLO. Although King Hussein and Arafat had made friendly moves toward each other, no official statement had ever been made that indicated they were officially on good terms until the Amman Agreement, also referred to as the Hussein-Arafat Accord. When Arafat had refused in 1987 to accept Resolution 242, Hussein broke ties with Arafat and nullified the agreement. The following year, the PNC had also cancelled the agreement.

Since the Israeli occupation of the rest of Palestine in 1967, I had deleted such terms as "weekend" and "vacation" from my personal dictionary. However, in July 1989, my family insisted on going to the shores of the Mediterranean near Alexandria, Egypt. My father-in-law owned a comfortable villa near the Egyptian-Libyan border. The waters were clean and the sands of the beach were dazzlingly white. My children, Karma and Omar, were so happy, for it was one of those rare times when I was able to spend several days with them and their mother without being engrossed in never-ending work. I enjoyed our family time together in that breathtaking spot on the Mediterranean shore.

After four days of relaxing on the beach and listening to great Arabic music, I was surprised to see an Egyptian police car arrive at the outer gate of our villa. An officer approached me.

"Bassam Abu Sharif?" he asked. "President Mubarak is inviting you to his quarters in Burj Al-Arab tomorrow morning at 7:30 a.m."

Burj Al-Arab was one of Mubarak's summer homes, just outside of Alexandria. I knew at that moment that my relaxing family vacation had come to an abrupt end.

The next morning I entered the grounds of what appeared to be an army encampment. I was surprised to see beautifully groomed rosebushes colorfully dotting the garden located in the center of the camp. The buildings were set in a square formation with a courtyard in the center. Guards were busy fulfilling various orders, briskly walking from one building to another, some carrying what appeared to be important papers. In between the buildings I could see the Republican Guard standing at attention in their striking red and black uniforms.

Dr. Osama Al-Baz, President Mubarak's advisor for political affairs, greeted me in his distinguished, high-pitched voice outside an old, yet simple building. Moments later, the doors opened and a number of security officers came out, followed by President Mubarak. When we were left on our own, President Mubarak explained the reason for his invitation to me.

"I want you to go to Tunisia and deliver the following message to President Arafat: 'Someone who does not go for what he needs will remain forever in need.'"

"I'm sorry, but I don't understand what you mean."

"President Arafat will know. Just tell him the proverb."

Since I could see that Mubarak wanted to give advice to Arafat, I felt I could offer some advice to him as well. I brought up the subject of Libya, since I knew that Mubarak and Qaddafi were still at odds about Egypt having made peace with Israel during the days of Sadat. So I gave my opinion about how I thought Egypt could better handle its ongoing conflict with Libya.

"Your Excellency, I believe Libya, and by this I specifically mean President Qaddafi, should not be dealt with using blows as you have been, but instead with embraces. Egypt is a large country which is able to handle what small countries cannot. Libya is rich, but small, so it needs the support and protection of Egypt. If you embrace Qaddafi instead of striking him, he will feel not only that his country is safe, but that he is important to Egypt. Your benefit would be the establishment of joint economic projects between the new nations. Let's not forget that Libya has the money to back Egyptian projects."

President Mubarak showed great interest in what I had to say. At one point, he called for Osama Al-Baz to come hear what I had said and how they could better handle their relations with Libya. From that day onward, President Mubarak followed my advice by treating Qaddafi with respect; his change in policy led to positive results for both countries, which also benefited the whole Middle East in the long run.

The next day, I left for Tunisia, where I delivered Mubarak's message to Arafat. Once I had completed the proverb, Arafat's eyes lit up and he smiled. He began to make immediate arrangements for us to go to Egypt.

Because it was the holy month of Ramadan (see Key Terms), meeting times were planned after sunset so as to coincide with the traditions of the holy month. Arafat's discussions with Mubarak opened with talks about political efforts being made toward attaining the Palestinian peace initiative, ending the occupation of Palestine, and establishing an independent Palestinian state, side by side with Israel. Then Mubarak focused on his real reason for having that meeting: He wanted to persuade Arafat to mend the rift in Jordanian-PLO relations. "You need the support of all the Arab countries," he said, "You must be the one to initiate good will and not wait for others to do it." It was then that I fully understood the proverb: The one who wants help must be the first one to pave the way for it to take place, or else remain in need forever.

Arafat agreed. Mubarak then called King Hussein and suggested that he and Arafat conduct direct and open talks about their political visions, including the political movement needed to pave the way to peace in the region. His Majesty also agreed. Arafat wanted me at his side during these meetings because he knew that I would tell him what I honestly thought. I was not afraid to disagree with him, and he liked that about me.

It was then arranged for Arafat and King Hussein to meet in Jordan at dawn the next day for *suhour* (the last meal before the start of the Ramadan fast at dawn). Arafat brought up a security problem: "We have confirmed reports that the Israelis are tracking the movements of my private plane. If we cross into the air space over the Gulf of Aqaba, our plane will become an easy target for Israeli missiles."

"In that case," Mubarak replied, seeing no problem, "you will head to Jordan in an Egyptian military plane." We flew to Amman with Dr. Osama Al-Baz and Palestine's ambassador to Egypt, Said Kamal.

We arrived at 3 a.m. and were personally greeted by King Hussein, a gesture that not only showed us all how much he wanted to repair the split, but also how very welcome Arafat was. His Majesty was dressed informally in slacks and a sport shirt, which added to the friendliness of the atmosphere. King Hussein invited Arafat to ride with him as he drove to his palace. Al-Baz, Kamal, and I followed in an unofficial motorcade.

As we ate *suhour* in the palace, a cautious yet diplomatic discussion took place between the two leaders. They discussed what each could do with regard to the Israeli government's evasive stand regarding Middle East peace negotiations. Although both King Hussein and Arafat appeared pleasant and cheerful, an unspoken tension could be felt in the room the entire time. Keeping in mind that this was the first meeting between the two men since King Hussein had nullified the Amman Agreement in 1987, it was understandable that they would feel a bit awkward. King Hussein sensed this, so he decided to break the ice by asking Said Kamal how he thought Israel could be brought to the negotiating table. Though Said was surprised by the question, he gave an opinion that was not in compliance with Arafat's pint of view. He was vague about who should represent the Palestinian people, which was actually closer to the Egyptian point of view. I could see that Arafat was visibly angry, although he didn't say anything at the time. Then His Majesty turned to me. "Let's hear Bassam's opinion." I said, "Your Majesty, my opinion is the same as that of President Arafat. The future of the Palestinian people should be in their hands as determined by their legitimate representative." I also included my views that, in the end, the decision would be an American one after all, but that somehow we should find a way to exert pressure on the United States to start the ball rolling.

Both King Hussein and Arafat were pleased with what both Kamal and I had said. This encouraged me to suggest the creation of a joint Jordanian-Palestinian institution that would be responsible for wielding pressure in Washington.

Although the meeting ended without any tangible results or decisions, the tension between the two leaders had eased, and I felt that there was a chance for a resumption of better relations between our two men in the near future. We were hoping that this meeting would provide the opening of a new door we needed for both continued dialogue between us, and hopefully cooperation.

Yasser Arafat continued to work on keeping all avenues of communication open between Jordan and the PLO. President Mubarak's suggestion for us to repair our rift with Jordan was very similar to Arafat's desire to rally Arab powers to support both his peace initiative and political negotiations.

Besides, Arafat also knew that having both Egypt and Jordan on the side of the PLO meant that Palestine could not be isolated again.

31

TWO WAGERS

We Palestinians had always identified closely with the situation of the black South Africans. Our refugee camps were similar to the townships in South Africa, and we too had been a majority who had been occupied by a foreign minority. The Israeli iron-fist policy under which our people were being forced to live was a prime example of apartheid. Because of the close similarities between our two situations, the release of Nelson Mandela on February 2, 1990, was not only a politically historic event, but it also was an emotionally moving one for all of us. Africa's great leader had spent over a quarter of a century in prison, but he maintained his dignity and commitment to his people, becoming a respected international symbol of the fight against apartheid.

As the news agencies hurriedly telegraphed the news of his release, I was in Arafat's office in Tunisia. Arafat was encouraged by the fact that Mandela would finally be leaving prison, something that so many people in Africa and around the world had wanted for so long. He called Mandela's release "a strategic transformation in South Africa." Arafat believed it would "reflect on the international political atmosphere in the direction of solving deadlocked problems in different parts of the world, such as our own."

We had always likened the Israeli treatment of Palestinians to the apartheid system in South Africa. Being treated as second-class citizens in our own homeland, being used as cheap labor, being the indigenous people who are treated as strangers within our own land, being unfairly treated and kept in poor living conditions were but some of the conditions we had in common with the blacks of South Africa. In my opinion, Arafat should have been one of the first to congratulate Mandela on regaining his freedom. He wanted to emphasize to Mandela that the struggle of his people and ours were one and the same, connected by every human being's right to live freely in his or her homeland. Arafat was not making this call for public relations; he sincerely felt Mandela's struggle and ours were very similar. What Mandela had achieved was Arafat's dream for his own people as well.

But how were we going to contact Nelson Mandela? He had just come out of prison and had undoubtedly gone to meet with his supporters and the people of the Soweto, a suburb of Johannesburg. I searched for the number of my friend Scott McCloud, the director of *TIME* magazine's office in South Africa and the former director of its Middle East office. Scott gave me several leads, including the number of Thabo Mbeki, a close friend of Mandela who later became the president of South Africa following Mandela's retirement in 1999.

Mbeki was very amenable to the idea of Arafat meeting with Mandela, and he gave me Mandela's personal phone number in Soweto. After many attempts, I was finally able to get through to his wife, Winnie Mandela, who greeted me with great enthusiasm, promising to awaken her sleeping husband immediately. Arafat and I excitedly waited to hear Mandela's voice on the other end of the line. Two giants of liberation were about to speak. Although his voice was hoarse from exhaustion, Mandela spoke to Arafat for several minutes, and the two men promised to meet at the earliest convenience of both. I began to make the arrangements.

Scott told me that African leaders, including Prime Minister Frederik Willem de Klerk, would be meeting in Namibia to congratulate Mandela on his release. Since the PLO was a member of the Organization of African Unity, it would be vital for us to attend such a gathering as well.

Arafat, his guards, and I landed in Lusaka, Namibia's capital, on February 15, 1990, to join the African leaders in welcoming Mandela. Considering the major significance of Mandela's release, the media was well represented, including my friend Scott. We made a wager as to what the headlines would be: Scott bet that they would focus on Mandela's release, while I bet they would spotlight his meeting with Arafat. The loser had to take the other one out to dinner.

Mandela's welcome was huge. African music played while hundreds of young men and women danced joyfully in the streets. When the newspapers came out the next day, Scott called me to say that I had won the bet. All the photographs and the headlines were of Arafat and Mandela hugging.

Complex negotiations began in South Africa to establish a new democratic system to replace apartheid: one based on freedom, democracy, and political diversity that preserved both the rights of the indigenous African people and of those who had settled in South Africa. Sam Nujoma, the leader of the Namibian Liberation Movement (started in the 1950s to gain independence from the apartheid rule of South Africa), was a close friend of Arafat; both men supported the other's efforts to win freedom for his people. As a result, Arafat had been able to isolate Israel economically from the countries of the African continent, despite all of Israel's generous offers to help African countries in such fields as agriculture, medicine, and foreign investment. The Palestinian cause was even considered by the Organization of African Unity to be one of its own. The PLO was successful in persuading Arab countries and Arab investors to cooperate with Africa by establishing strong economic ties, signing mutual business agreements to help African countries, and strengthening ties between Arab and African countries economically, politically, and socially. Arafat insisted that all Arab countries should think strategically by investing in African countries with projects that would bring benefit to the African people, all of which had a very positive impact on the economic development of Africa. He also made sure we never forgot that the largest Arab countries, such as Egypt, Sudan, Iraq, Algeria, Libya, Morocco, Tunisia, and Mauritania were all African countries as well.

Arafat had played a crucial role behind the scenes in mediating negotiations between African countries, many of which would otherwise have led to war. Because of this, he was among the first of the invitees to Namibia to celebrate the establishment of their constitution, which finally led to their complete independence in March from South Africa.

Important world leaders, such as British prime minister Margaret Thatcher and U.S. secretary of state James Baker, were invited to attend the ceremony on February 15, 1990. It was seen as the first of many examples of ending racist regimes in Africa. By gaining independence from the apartheid rule of South Africa, Namibia had proven that what was best for its people was to be ruled by its own people, not by a white minority who were only exploiting the people for their own benefit. Also among the invitees was Frederik Willem de Klerk, the prime minister of South Africa, which, while still an apartheid regime, was undergoing radical changes to become democratic.

On our way there, I felt as if we were going to the independence ceremony for Palestine because we had such a close affinity to the Namibian struggle. I was reminded of the day Nujoma had been invited to the Libyan city of Sirt to attend a conference called for by President Muammar Qaddafi. Because there were no commercial flights available from Namibia that day, it appeared Nujoma would not be able to attend. Arafat asked me to rent a small private plane for Nujoma and his delegation, adding that it was vital for me to travel with him, not only out of respect to him as a great leader, but also to facilitate everything for him once he reached the city.

Although Namibia had never before witnessed an international event of such magnitude, great efforts were made to make everyone comfortable, from organizing the landing of planes to directing guests to the stadium where the reception was being held. We headed quickly in a presidential motorcade to the stadium, where the crowd was even bigger than I had expected. The security was so tight, I felt claustrophobic as we were crushed between U.S., British, African, and Palestinian security men.

Palestinian security men surrounded Arafat, forming a human shield around him, as he entered the wing of the stadium reserved for presidents, prime ministers, and ministers. He sat next to Egyptian president Husni Mubarak, British prime minister Margaret Thatcher and U.S. secretary of state James Baker. On the main platform sat Namibia's newly elected president, Sam Nujoma, with UN secretary general Javier Perez de Cuellar along with South African prime minister de Klerk.

It was a long ceremony that included speeches, music, dancing, and an announcement from the ministry regarding the problem of indigenous and nonindigenous peoples. As the guests began to leave for the official reception, I whispered in Arafat's ear: "Shake hands with Sam now in front of everyone." It had been announced earlier that congratulations would be received in the reception hall, not there, so I knew Arafat would have an excellent opportunity to have the spotlight on him.

Arafat headed straight for Nujoma, who stood up quickly and addressed him as "my brother." Not only did Arafat publicly congratulate the Namibian leader before anyone else even had a chance, but he also shook hands with Prime Minister de Klerk for the first time.

When we were walking toward the reception hall, I ran into my friend Scott. "I suppose you're going to tell me that the photo and headline this time will be about Nujoma and Arafat."

I couldn't resist another wager. "Double or nothing?"

While we were in the official reception hall, de Cuellar, the UN secretary general, and de Klerk came over to speak to Arafat. De Klerk began the conversation. "We want you to help us persuade Mandela not to be extreme."

Arafat smiled. "And we want *your* help in persuading the Israelis to withdraw from our land."

Arafat asked how the negotiations were going, and de Klerk said he was optimistic that an agreement was imminent. While everyone listened, Arafat spoke to de Cuellar about the tragic situation in the Occupied Palestinian Territories. De Cuellar promised to consult with member countries about increasing UNRWA (United Nations Relief and Works Agency for Palestine Refugees in the Near East) aid to Palestinian camps.

As the presidents and ministers moved slowly toward the dining room, Nujoma hugged Arafat. "Your name is on the main presidential table, seated next to Mrs. Thatcher."

I was sitting close to James Baker. I smiled, saying loudly enough for everyone to hear, "Now it's Palestine's turn."

He nodded. "I hope so."

We returned to Tunisia the following day, feeling that we too had scored a major victory. As soon as I got back to my office, I called Scott. "You owe me two dinners now." The front page of the *New York Times*, among many others, had the photograph of Arafat shaking hands with de Klerk and Nujoma.

"I don't know how he does it, Bassam, but President Arafat always manages to steal the show."

"Get used to it, Scott. Wherever he goes and whatever he does, there is bound to be a headline."

32

––––––

U.S. TRAP

O nce the eight-year war between Iraq and Iran (also called the Persian Gulf War) came to an end on August 20, 1988, with a cease-fire agreement between Saddam Hussein and Ayatollah Khomeini, political scuffles between Iraq and Kuwait began in the two years that followed. Iraq, which had suffered great financial losses during the war (some estimates were more than $500 billion), demanded payment for all the oil that they accused Kuwait of having extracted from Iraqi wells through slant drilling. Kuwait, on the other hand, said Iraq owed them $40 billion in unpaid debts, which they felt entitled to get back by harnessing Iraq's oil revenues. Iraq accused Kuwait of using "economic warfare" against them, but Kuwait refused to stop the drilling, saying the oil was theirs in the first place because Iraq owed them so much anyway.

Saddam Hussein tried to exert pressure on Kuwait to stop the drilling through Saudi Arabia and the Gulf States, but all his efforts had failed. His last attempt to get Kuwait to stop what he saw as illegal drilling operations came at a conference held in Jeddah, Saudi Arabia, on July 31, 1990, which was attended by Kuwait's prime minister Sheikh Sa'd Al-Jaber. However, Saddam Hussein was once again unsuccessful in getting Kuwait to agree to stop their drilling.

Saddam Hussein summoned the U.S. ambassador in Iraq, April Glaspie, to ask her to request U.S. aid in resolving the argument before it escalated into a military clash. Ambassador Glaspie returned the following message to the Iraqi president: The United States's policy regarding disputes between the Arabian Gulf countries was one of nonintervention.

Like a fly in a web, Saddam Hussein fell into the trap Washington had set for him. He took Washington's reply as a tacit support for him to deal with the crisis in his own way; the United States had made it perfectly clear it would not interfere. Saddam Hussein had good reason to believe Washington. The United States had supported Iraq both directly and indirectly during its war with Iran (and, as was discovered in the Iran-Contra scandal, had also supported Iran with arms from 1983 to 1988). This had convinced him that the United States regarded Iraq as a regional power. What Saddam Hussein failed to realize was this was only part of the U.S. plan: By supporting both sides in the war, the United States had not only wanted to make a profit on the war, but also had allowed the two oil-rich countries to remain engaged in a war that weakened them both militarily and economically within the region. Hussein failed to foresee that the United States sought only to control the oil wells in both Iraq and Kuwait in order to serve its own strategic interests.

Thinking that the way was clear, Iraq began planning its invasion of Kuwait.

At the same time, the United States wanted to find a political solution to the Israeli-Palestinian conflict. It was clear to the world that the Israeli government was stalling for more time to build up their illegal settlements on the West Bank and did not want to find a political solution, despite the Palestinian peace initiative of a two-state solution, the acceptance of UN Resolution 242, as well as the acceptance of Israel's existence and the renouncement of terrorism that had been put forward two years earlier. U.S. secretary of state James Baker had informed the U.S. administration of the Israeli position of intransigence, and, unlike other U.S. politicians, he was not afraid to make his displeasure known regarding the Israeli government's negative stand with regard to anything the Palestinians put forward.

Arafat followed what developed between Iraq and Kuwait with great interest. He understood the scope of the negative economic and political repercussions on the Middle East as a whole, and on the Palestinian cause in particular, that would arise from using a military option to solve the oil dispute. It was vital to him to be able to maintain international pressure on Israel to accept the Palestinian peace initiative, something that would not be possible in the event of a war between Iraq and Kuwait. Such a conflict would become the media's main concern, with Palestine's future fading into oblivion.

Arafat decided to move quickly, making a diplomatic shuttle between Baghdad and Kuwait in an attempt to defuse the war. Because I was working as his senior advisor, Arafat took me along on all of these meetings. He and I met first with President Saddam Hussein in July 1990, reminding him of the dangers of a military solution. Arafat asked the Iraqi president to give him a chance to find a solution to the problem, but Saddam was adamant. "We are seeking our rights and not bloodshed among Arabs. We want our rights: no more, no less. If Kuwait refuses to stop its slant drilling from our wells, then let them know their country will be in our hands in less than two hours."

Arafat and I then flew to Kuwait. We arrived at dawn, and headed to the guest palace to wait for the meeting between him and Emir Sheikh Jaber Al-Ahmad Al-Sabah. During that time, we also followed closely the escalation of Israeli aggression in the West Bank and the Gaza Strip. The Israelis were increasing the level of their reprisals against the Palestinians with the bulldozing of homes, mass punishments, prisoner torture, and shooting live ammunition into crowds of protesting youths. The situation was very dangerous for our people.

Our meeting with the Emir was short and tense. The Kuwaiti foreign minister, Sheikh Dr. Mohammad Sabah Al-Sakem Al-Sabah, was not present as he usually was during official visits. Arafat spared no effort in his attempt to persuade the Kuwaiti leader to find a peaceful solution to the dispute. He suggested trying to find a compromise that would please both parties, such as forgetting or at least reducing the debt owed by Iraq since the country was still trying to recover after the eight-year war with Iran. I remained silent the entire time, but I will never forget the expressions on each man's face. It was apparent to me the Kuwaitis did not want to resolve the matter politically because they believed they were right and that Iraq was trying to blackmail them. It was also obvious that the Emir did not want Arafat to interfere.

Following our half-hour meeting, we visited Prime Minister Sheikh Sa'd Al-Jaber, with whom Arafat had had close ties since he had graduated from Cairo University as an engineer. Again, nothing could have been clearer: the Kuwaiti decision had been made. Sheikh Sa'd told us that their military experts had reported that Iraq would not be able to invade Kuwait for four days and clearly hinted, without mentioning names, that other countries would have intervened by then. Arafat replied that the fundamental issue was to avoid war. Sheikh Sa'd changed the subject by speaking about the Intifada, as if to say that Arafat should mind his own business and concentrate on his own problems.

War was inevitable.

On August 2, 1990, Iraq invaded Kuwait with tanks and infantry. Disputes escalated throughout the Arab world as to which side was right, and this left the door wide open for the Western powers to take control of the area, its oil, its natural riches, and its strategic location by sending in vast numbers of troops and establishing permanent military bases.

This was what Arafat had feared most and why he had sought so hard to prevent the war; he wanted to preserve at least a modicum of Arab unity. Even after the invasion had begun, Arafat continued to try to find a political solution by remaining in constant communication with the two leaders. When the United States began to mobilize its troops under the banner of "freeing" Kuwait, he knew this was just a ruse to target Iraq and its oil. Arafat worked relentlessly, traveling from one Arab capital to another in a race against time to prevent any foreign troops from landing on Arab soil to wage war against Iraq. He came up with a viable political solution to the problem, which he hoped Saddam Hussein would accept. He knew it was not going to be an easy task, because his solution started with the immediate withdrawal of Iraqi troops from Kuwait.

Saudi Arabia was against allowing the United States to intervene, militarily or otherwise, and initially refused to allow American troops to enter its borders or to give the U.S. Air Force access to its airports. The United States, however, used all means possible to persuade Saudi Arabia to change its mind.

On the last visit Arafat made to Saudi Arabia to persuade the government to put whatever pressure it could on Kuwait to adopt a political solution, his plane was stopped on the runway for thirty minutes so that Cheney's plane could land before Arafat arrived. The United States was also in a race against time. It appeared that the United States was dead set on fueling the flames of war and didn't want anyone, especially someone like Arafat, to put the fire out.

Even so, Arafat did not give up. He made several more trips to persuade Arab leaders that war must be avoided; he also made quick tours to Africa and Europe to establish international backing for his political solution, which simply asked for an Iraqi withdrawal in order to allow negotiations to take place between Kuwait and Iraq in order to settle their disputes. He spoke to wealthy Saudi businessmen, including Adnan Khashuqji and Harb Al-Zheir, and begged them to carry his plans for a nonviolent solution of Iraqi withdrawal and diplomacy to Saudi leaders. Prince Sultan bin Abdel Aziz was very responsive to using reason, sincerely wanting to find a political solution, but he, too, could convince no one.

Arafat's efforts were on the brink of success when it was agreed by all members of the Arab Summit to convene an emergency meeting in Cairo on August 10, 1990. The Arab countries' representatives were to approve a political solution in which they, through a committee formed by the summit, would play the main role in implementing the agreement. The U.S. pressures, however, threw a spanner in the works. The emergency Arab summit sessions in Cairo took place without Arafat even being able to propose his political solution because of two quirks: a twisted use of the rules of discussion and the way in which proposals were presented. The standard procedure at our summits was for proposals to be presented to the general assembly, after which they would be thoroughly discussed in smaller groups first, then discussed again before the whole assembly before being voted on by all members. This time, however, nothing went as it should.

The discussion began with one watered-down proposal made by the Egyptian representative, which limply condemned Iraq for its invasion of Kuwait. It was hurriedly voted on, agreed to, and then the whole session was adjourned before Arafat had even been given a chance to speak. The entire place exploded into angry turmoil, with Arafat shouting that the procedure followed had been illegal. The assembly had been adjourned without even asking if there was any further business. It seemed that he was not meant to be heard.

In my opinion, the powerful influence of the United States had reached many of the representatives there, making it impossible for Arafat even to present his proposal for a vote. The final decisions made at the summit were, as I said, diluted proposals that included: Kuwait's sovereignty, independence, and territorial integrity should be protected and maintained (how this would be accomplished was never decided); a public condemnation of Iraq's invasion of Kuwait should be issued; multinational Arab forces should be sent into Saudi Arabia to defend its borders from foreign invaders.

Leaving the Summit feeling discouraged that nothing really positive had come of it, Arafat decided to try one last time through the European Union to see if anyone was willing to listen to his idea of using diplomacy to get Iraq to withdraw from Kuwait. He asked me to go to Rome and relay a message to the Italian prime minister Giulio Andreotti. Italy at that time (from July to December) was the country that held the presidency of the Council of the European Community, so Arafat felt that Andreotti would the best person to speak to in order to get the word out to the other European countries.

In the meantime, the U.S.-led Allied Forces had completed their preparations and were ready for battle. Time was running out. War was definitely on the horizon.

I made it to Rome on the morning of January 14, 1991. Arrangements were made for a meeting between me and Andreotti, and, as protocol requires, I also called the Palestinian ambassador in Italy, Nimr Hammad, to inform him of the meeting and the purpose of my visit.

I told the prime minister that we were desperately trying to prevent the war; we were proposing that a delegation from the European Union (Troika—see Key Terms) be sent to Iraq immediately. We also needed to formulate a political proposal adopted by Europe and some Arab countries that would be implemented immediately to bring about the withdrawal of Iraqi troops from Kuwait.

Andreotti, speaking in French with me so as to bypass the interpreter, explained the difficulty of the situation. He assured me that Italy also hoped war could be avoided. He then led me to the balcony of his office, where he was sure we would not be overheard either by the interpreter or any possible devices planted in his office of which he was not aware, and whispered, "The U.S. decision is war. No initiative to stop the war will succeed. God help Iraq."

Ambassador Hammad and I left our meeting with Andreotti very discouraged. It was obvious that nothing could stop the U.S. war machine, no matter what was said or done. The war was going to happen, regardless of our political and diplomatic attempts to intervene. We returned to our hotel very disheartened. As we entered my room, I received a phone call from my secretary in Tunisia; she was sobbing uncontrollably. Abu Hol and Abu Iyad, two leading Fateh members, had just been assassinated at Abu Hol's house. The killer had taken refuge on the top floor and held his wife and children hostage. The assassinations had been carried out by a Palestinian double agent who turned out to be part of Abu Nidal's (see Principal Characters) gang, a group that was adamantly opposed to any Arab proposals that called for a peaceful settlement with Israel. To gain the release of the hostages, the Tunisian government had stepped in and offered the man free passage out of the country if he would just release his hostages. This of course was just a trick to get the hostages released safely. The assassin was later turned over to us for interrogation. It was discovered that he had infiltrated Fateh and had become a trusted bodyguard. After he had gunned down Abu Iyad, he then did the same to Abu Hol. By that time, however, he was unable to escape because the other guards had surrounded the house. His only way out, he thought, was to hold the grieving family as hostages. He was executed in the end.

Arafat returned to Tunisia on January 15, 1991 to attend the burial ceremonies for Abu Iyad and Abu Hol. After the funerals, the PLO leaders met in Arafat's office, feeling the enormity of the situation. The assassinations were a great shock to everyone. Although we were saddened by the deaths of our two valued colleagues, we also knew we still had a great deal of work to do.

Worry over the anticipated war against Iraq was suffocating everyone, despite the fact that a number of leaders were convinced that the United States would not wage war against Iraq for fear of their own losses. I, on the other hand, believed that war was imminent. I was convinced that the United States would use its aerial and missile arsenals against Iraq rather than engage Iraqi forces on the ground.

At dawn on January 16, a friend of mine in France called from a pay phone (to avoid a trace on the call) to tell me that a U.S. attack by air and cruise missiles would begin in the early morning hours of January 17. The target was to be Baghdad, not Kuwait.

I reported this to Arafat, and he wanted to relay the news immediately to Baghdad. Some of Arafat's men still did not believe that the United States would ever launch an attack against Iraq because of their history together. They said that Arafat could go ahead and tell the Iraqis, but it would just cause unnecessary alarm because nothing would happen. Arafat, however, was of a different opinion. We had a piece of information that might be useful to the Iraqis, and the citizens of Baghdad needed to know about the impending attack so that they could take the necessary precautions and evacuate to secure bomb shelters. According to the tip we had received, the missile and aerial attack would start at 3 a.m. Baghdad time, which would have made it midnight in Tunisia.

At midnight on January 17, 1991, we gathered in Arafat's office to watch CNN. Nothing was happening. Some of the men began to smile, thinking that the tip had been wrong as they had predicted and that the United States was not going to wage war against Iraq. Just moments later came the breaking news: Baghdad was being bombed by the United States.

Arafat's attempts to prevent the war had failed. Now we had to deal with a new, more dangerous chapter facing our region.

33

LAST-MINUTE MODIFICATIONS

After the end of the first Gulf War (Iraq's invasion of Kuwait), President George H. W. Bush delivered a speech on March 6, 1991, to the U.S. Congress about what the United States had achieved in the Gulf War. His speech was met with great bipartisan approval. During this "New World Order" speech, in which he referred to the Gulf War as a victory of U.S. and Allied Forces over Iraq, Bush received five standing ovations. The longest standing ovation came when he announced that the time had come to find solutions both to the Arab-Israeli conflict and the Palestinian situation. We couldn't help feeling that it was about time.

The United States then opened the doors to the start of a Middle East peace process aimed at establishing stability and peace based on the UN Security Council Resolutions 242 and 338. It was also decided that the United States and the Soviet Union would sponsor a Middle East international peace conference for Syria, Lebanon, Jordan, the PLO, and Israel in Madrid, starting on October 30 that same year. The hope was for two outcomes: Jordan, Syria, and Lebanon would sign peace treaties with Israel; and a plan could be set up for an interim self-government for the Palestinians, which would eventually become permanent.

At that time, Yitzhak Shamir of the rightist Likud party was head of the Israeli government. Israel remained opposed to any peace agreement based on Resolution 242, which called for the complete withdrawal of Israel from Palestinian lands occupied in 1967. Shamir refused President Bush's invitation to the Madrid conference on the grounds that he would not negotiate with the PLO. Israel, he said, did not negotiate with terrorists. The truth was that he vehemently opposed both the Security Council resolutions. He would be willing, he said, to hold negotiations with local Palestinians from the West Bank and Gaza Strip, but only if they had no Jewish blood on their hands.

Shamir insisted that the Israeli government approve the names of the Palestinians participating in the conference. Understandably, Arafat was not pleased with the idea that Israel could dictate who would and who would not be allowed to participate in the conference: Who was Israel to decide about attendees when they weren't even hosting the event? The Bush administration was worried that the PLO might just pull out of the conference because of this, so they tried hard to persuade the PLO leadership that they must not miss this opportunity to achieve their dream of a self-governed Palestine. Despite wanting to participate in the conference, Arafat and the other leaders decided they would find some way to please the Israelis while also getting what they wanted. This was their way of dealing realistically with the obstacles Shamir had put up, knowing full well that he was doing his best to kill the project. Communication lines between Washington, Moscow, and Tunisia were very busy as we worked hard to reach an agreement that would be satisfactory to both the PLO and Shamir.

The Bush administration was told by the Israeli prime minister that it would agree to the participation of a Palestinian delegation that represented the Palestinian people in the West Bank and the Gaza Strip on the condition that Israel play the main role in selecting its members. If he had any objections based on strong evidence that anyone among them had been involved in any terrorism whatsoever against Israel, he would let President Bush know. The United States then asked the PLO to draw up a list of forty Palestinians from the West Bank and the Gaza Strip so that the selection process of who would be allowed to attend could begin. Israel took a few names off the list and others were put forward by the PLO until both sides were happy with the list. The actual selection process did not take very long since the PLO had ready a long list of alternate names, knowing that the Israelis would try to delay the process. The executive committee decided to send a number of high-ranking Palestinians, including me, from Tunisia to Madrid to observe the conference sessions and to remain in constant contact with the official Palestinian delegation that had been allowed to go. We in turn were to keep in close contact with Arafat, who remained behind at his headquarters in Tunis. All of the delegation members were working on the speech that would be delivered at the opening session because they knew it would be very important to set the stage of the conference from the very beginning.

Although the executive committee had asked me to go as an observer to Madrid, Arafat requested that I remain with him in Tunisia in order to follow up on the events of the conference. I later discovered, however, that a number of Fateh leaders had already made it clear that they did not want me to attend. A group of them wanted to exclude me from the center of action now that political, diplomatic, and media efforts had been successful in shaping this first tangible step since the peace initiative. It seems they were afraid to have me attend for fear of what direction I might take the conference since I was known to be a bit of a renegade.

Those who had been late to catch the "peace-initiative train" mistakenly thought that secret diplomatic work would push the process forward. I knew what a sharp weapon the media could be in the political arena, and that public opinion could be a true force in exerting pressure on governments. The PLO had put forward their peace initiative, which rejected violence, but they still needed the media to get the peace initiative going, to make sure our political and diplomatic agenda was heard. The excuse this group of Fateh leaders used was that I was media-oriented, and this made me harmful to the political movement and diplomatic activity of the Palestinians. They seemed to fear that too much media coverage would be bad for them, and I would most definitely have brought the conference into the media spotlight. Somehow they felt it was better to arrive at solutions between the PLO and Israel in the dark of secrecy than to bring it into the spotlight of the media.

The first part of the conference concentrated on trying to get Syria, Jordan, and Lebanon to find some common ground on which they could finally arrive at a peaceful agreement with Israel. They met for three days without much luck in that arena. Our conference was to begin on November 3, immediately following the first session.

On the morning of the opening session of the Madrid conference, Arafat gave me instructions to join him as he headed to the airport. As usual, I set off with him as instructed, not knowing my final destination, only to find out later that he and I were flying to Morocco at the invitation of King Hassan II to watch the conference proceedings from there. With us on that visit were Farouq Qadoumi and Abdallah Horani, two other PLO executives.

As soon as the plane took off toward Morocco, Arafat handed me a document written in English, and explained that it was the text of the speech drafted by the Palestinian delegation from the West Bank and Gaza, which they felt should replace the speech that had been written and approved by the executive committee. I read the speech carefully and could not hold back my anger and surprise at what they had written. "This speech apologizes for our struggle and announces our repentance as if we have committed a sin. The speech neither mentions the PLO as the sole legitimate representative of the Palestinian people nor does it refer to the leadership of the Palestinian people. It doesn't even mention the international resolutions related to our land."

Arafat asked Horani, Qadoumi, and me to modify the speech based on our concerns. Our changes focused on the following: the Palestinian people's national rights; the international resolutions that guaranteed the return of some of our land; and a confirmation of the PLO as the sole legitimate representative of the Palestinian people, with the PLO as the governing body of the Palestinian people. We also highlighted the two-state solution, which had also been left out.

When we landed in Rabat, Arafat cut the welcoming ceremony short in order to avoid wasting time. He headed immediately to the Guest Palace, where our group was to stay. We settled in and continued to work on the speech while Arafat got in touch with Dr. Nabil Sha'ath, who was in charge of coordination between the delegation inside Palestine and the Russian team that was cosponsoring the conference. In no time, we had completed our modifications, and Arafat passed them on to Sha'th, who then sent them to Dr. Haidar Abdel Shafi, the head of the Palestinian delegation and also the man who would deliver the opening speech. We had made sure that the speech he was going to deliver said what needed to be said. The other speech would have been a political disaster. It appeared to us that the delegates in Madrid were afraid to present a strong case before the Israelis and had watered down the initial speech so as not to make waves.

Minutes later, Arafat was told that Sha'ath needed to speak to him urgently. The Russians, to whom Sha'ath had shown the revised speech and who had undoubtedly shared it with the Americans, were afraid that the Israeli delegation would withdraw if the modifications were allowed.

I disagreed with him. "Shamir did not go to the Madrid Conference just to withdraw." I then told Arafat, "This conference is the wish of the Americans.

The Israelis would not put themselves in an awkward situation with President Bush. Plus, we have no idea what Shamir is going to say in his speech, although I suspect it will be extreme, rejecting the peace project altogether."

Arafat agreed with me, saying so to Nabil Sha'ath, despite his worry that the conference would collapse. Sha'ath sent word to the Russians that we were adamant about the content of our speech. We appreciated their concerns, but we would take that risk. This was the first tangible step in what would undoubtedly be a very long journey toward the establishment of an independent Palestinian state. This was the first time the United States and the Soviet Union were in agreement with regard to the possibility of an independent Palestine, governed by Palestinians. What I had published three years earlier, "The Abu Sharif Document," was a baby step compared to what was taking place at the conference.

Sha'ath was to inform the delegation of Arafat's instructions. Haidar Abdel Shafi' gave the speech we had put together, in its entirety. To everyone at the conference, especially the Israelis, our point had been made clear: the PLO was the sole legitimate representative of the Palestinian people.

That was one of the most important political moments for each one of us. Imagine the irony of it all. After Shamir had insisted, week after week, that the PLO could not participate in the conference, adamantly making sure that he had the right to veto any candidate for the Palestinian delegation, and then having to sit there and listen while the Palestinian delegation that he had approved confirmed the PLO as the sole legitimate representative and leader of the Palestinian people. It was a coup, without a doubt!

King Hassan II and Arafat agreed that our battleground had shifted. We were now fighting on a political, media, and diplomatic field, with our first goal being the transformation of our aims into tangible results. The new swords would be our pens, and the new bullets would be our words.

34

LOVE AND HATE

T he discussions at the Madrid conference had been a complete waste of time. The entire Middle East peace process was paralyzed. Despite attempts by the Bush administration to change his mind, Shamir refused to modify his position, which effectively put an end to the Bush peace initiative. Israeli obstinacy continued to such an extent that Secretary Baker gave out the White House phone number at a press conference, saying to the Israelis, "When you're serious about peace, give us a call."

However, a turning point took place when, on June 23, 1992, Yitzhak Rabin, head of the Labor Party (the center-left-wing party in Israel, opposed to the Likud Party, the radical right-wing party), was elected Prime Minister. Because of the good relations between the Norwegian government and the Israeli Labor Party, Norway was able to persuade the Israelis to attend secret discussions in Oslo. These discussions led to the Oslo Accords, which provided for the creation of a Palestinian Authority that would have responsibility for administrating the territory under its control. The accords also included the complete withdrawal of Israel from the Gaza Strip and the West Bank.

On September 13, 1993, Yasser Arafat and Yitzhak Rabin traveled to Washington, D.C., where they signed the agreement and then shook hands in front of the White House, with photographers snapping pictures, and a jubilant Bill Clinton, Bush's successor as U.S. president, looking on.

Palestinians began to prepare for their journey home. On July 1, 1994, Arafat returned to the Gaza Strip in Occupied Palestine. On September 28, 1995, one year later, a new agreement called "Oslo 2," which was a follow up to the Oslo Accords, included issues related to the West Bank, Palestinian elections, the transfer of land, trade conditions between the two countries, and the release of Palestinian prisoners.

But if the Oslo Accords were a significant step forward in Palestinian-Israeli relations, everything changed again following the assassination of Yitzhak Rabin on November 4, 1995, by Yigel Amer, a radical left-wing Zionist who was angry that Rabin had taken any steps toward making peace with the Palestinians. Shimon Peres, who temporarily took over as prime minister until elections could take place, took a negative position on the implementation of the Oslo Accords. Proving to be an extremist within the Labor Party, Peres launched over 1,100 air raids against Southern Lebanon on April 11, 1996, targeting the city of Qana in South Lebanon. He called this mission "Operation Grapes of Wrath"; it was his attempt to quell the Hezbollah (see Key Terms) rockets that kept hitting Northern Israel. His sixteen-day blitz included hitting a UN installation and killing 118 Lebanese civilians and injuring countless others. He also decided to postpone the implementation of the Oslo Accords, ignoring the approved timetable set out in the accords, failing to hand over the West Bank city of Hebron at the scheduled time.

The Likud returned to power on May 29, 1996, after the Labor Party lost the elections. Binyamin Netanyahu was elected prime minister of Israel, and he renewed the commitment to the Shamir iron-fist policy. Netanyahu made it that clear he too rejected the formation of an independent Palestinian state as a basis for peace between the Israelis and Palestinians, which meant we were once again back to square one.

Arafat and I discussed Israeli intentions. We knew that the Israeli officials with whom we would have to negotiate from now on did not and would not accept the idea of a sovereign independent Palestinian state with Jerusalem as its capital. We also knew that they wanted the PLO to have limited self-rule, with Israel as the chief decision maker and policeman of all the Palestinians. Arafat was determined: "Not everything that they want will happen. We will establish our independent state."

Netanyahu gradually began to implement Shamir's iron-fist policy, ignoring the Oslo Accords and returning to the use of even stronger military force to subdue the Palestinians. Netanyahu prepared the needed infrastructure that Sharon had used in order to reoccupy Palestinian territories through bloodshed, destruction, and mass arrests of Palestinians. Palestinians were being kept in a police state with absolutely no rights whatsoever. Their olive trees would be uprooted if the Israelis felt Palestinians might use the groves as a place either to hide in or from which they might launch attacks against Israeli citizens. Entire Palestinian neighborhoods were bulldozed if it was suspected that just one Palestinian living there might have committed a crime of protest against an Israeli. People were left homeless as the Israelis began to build settlements on the foundations of Palestinians' obliterated homes. Palestinians were dragged from their homes in the middle of the night, arrested, and taken to prisons without any given reason. Families neither knew where their loved ones had been taken nor what was happening to them. Palestinians were being put through a hell created by the Israeli government that wanted to "cleanse" the entire land of them.

The following entry in my journal on December 9, 1996, expresses my deepest concerns and thoughts during that time.

The conflict that Yasser Arafat is facing now is a bitter and difficult one. He is directly facing the Likud's plan aimed at annexing the West Bank to Israel, gradually driving the Arabs out of it, and Judeaizing Jerusalem. Arafat is fighting the beast face-to-face.

At first glance it would seem that the balance of power of this struggle does not hold any indications of overcoming the beast, but some indications appear to favor Arafat, if we plan well.

There are many reasons for this being a difficult situation, the main one being Netanyahu, his government and all they represent in terms of obstinacy, land confiscation, expansion of settlement activity and the halting of the peace process. Since Netanyahu became Prime Minister of Israel, obstacles to the peace process have been appearing one after the other. 300,000 dunams [4 dunams = 1 acre] of Palestinian lands have been confiscated by Israel under various excuses, such as construction of roads for settlements and various security reasons. A decision was made to expand a number of settlements by establishing 50,000 new homes. The Israeli government built up its military presence in the West Bank to its previous state by adding three thousand soldiers to the troops based in the West Bank. This caused many doubts amongst us regarding the validity of the entire peace process.

From another aspect, Israel's stands have led to a deteriorating economic situation in the area. International pledges have stopped because Israel is deliberately blocking any attempt to break the economic siege against us as well as allow any project

that could save the area from its depression and paralysis. There has also been no comprehensive plan for economic development on the Palestinian level that could be implemented even in stages. Besides that, there has never been a quick plan that could set
up small projects to provide fast revenue for us such as job opportunities for thousands
of unemployed Palestinians or anything which might energize the economic cycle in our
society.

Another factor is that we are transitioning from the stage of revolution to that
of statehood with all the consequences this produces. This phase is an anxious and difficult one in which confusion reigns. It is hard to distinguish between struggle criteria as a measure for ruling and making evaluations and technical and professional
criteria as a measure for establishing new institutions. This creates several internal
contradictions and generates states that might appear satisfactory after a short period
of time, but are hindered in their administrative and institutional development.

Back to the topic of Arafat and the beast. Despite the existing difficulties, I feel
Arafat is the stronger one, the master of the lair; he must use all this information, despite its complexity and difficulty. The Israeli government is causing its own isolation
through its expansionism and rejection of the "land for peace" formula of which the
entire international community, including the US, has approved.

The Israeli government's agenda has roots that extend deep into the Jabotinski-
Likud policy which considers Judea and Samaria to be the land of Israel. This is clear
in what Israeli Prime Minister Netanyahu said to Robertson. "Hebron is the heart.
It is the cradle of our forefathers and Judea and Samaria are the lungs. How can you
expect us to give up our heart, our lungs and our head?"

Europe, which attempted to revive the peace process and mend rifts during the US
elections, discovered the truth and now completely supports Arafat. This was apparent in the many comments made by French President Jacques Chirac and his Foreign
Minister de Charette. It was also clear in the statements of Italian officials following
Mr. Dalima's visit to Israel, Palestine, and the Middle East.

Arab countries also realize that there can be no peace with Israel without the
Palestinians. This was made clear in the statements of Omani Foreign Minister Hasan
Alawi during his meeting with the Tunisian Foreign Minister and when the Arab
states announced they would suspend ties with Israel if it did not implement agreements made with the Palestinians. The recently held summit of the Arab Gulf countries echoed the same position.

The general political circumstances of the region are all moving in this direction.
Iraq will soon begin to pump its oil implementing the Security Council Resolution

defining the "oil for food" formula which will enable Iraq to be an Arab power which can pump blood into the veins of Arab solidarity, all of which is part of Arafat's plan.

The meeting between Iraqi Foreign Minister Sahhaf and King Hussein of Jordan the day before yesterday, which was followed by a quick visit by King Hussein to Abu Dhabi to meet with Sheikh Zayed bin Sultan, undoubtedly directly touches on the concept of reviving Arab solidarity.

On the US front, Clinton, in his second term, now has more freedom, despite the Congressional chains placed on him by the Republican majority. These restrictions could be used by Israel to prevent President Clinton from taking any steps to exert pressure towards completing the implementation of agreements signed with the Palestinians. They could also stop him from crossing into the second phase of the negotiations which include discussing the future of Jerusalem and the settlements built on confiscated Palestinian lands in the West Bank and Gaza Strip.

Matters may not go Israel's way with regards to the Republicans going along with all that Netanyahu asks of them. During my meeting last week in Paris with Ronald Leeds [Deputy Head of the Republican Party], *I was informed that the Republicans see the Palestinian position as a moderate and reasonable one that they support. They regard Netanyahu's position, however, as a deviation from signed agreements to which the US was a partner. Leeds informed me that this matter would be proven soon in the party's next conference.*

Even all this is not enough. Plans need to be made to confront the beast. The best of these plans might include the following points:

1. *Strengthening Arab positions calling for suspending ties with Israel until problems on the Palestinian track are solved. This would keep the Arab world as a strong opposition force against Israel.*

2. *The development and revitalization of small and medium agricultural, industrial and tourism businesses in Palestine.*

3. *On the international level, there must be wide-spread activity to persuade European and donor countries to approve needed guarantees for Palestinian banks. The most important thing is to deal with Palestine as a country as the laws of European investment do not provide aid to their companies unless they are dealing with a country. Dealing with Palestine on the basis that it is not an authority of self-rule prevents these companies from obtaining enough guarantees for their investments. Europe could play this card to support Arafat and confront Netanyahu.*

4. *In France, for example, the "Kovas Institution," which guarantees the invest-ments of its country's companies abroad, provides sufficient guarantees for the projects. The same with the Italian Export Bank with regards to Italian compa-nies which invest in other countries, especially developing ones.*

5. *If Europe dealt with Palestine as a country and provided all these guarantees for the investments of its countries, the economic situation in the region would change, which, in turn, would provide the Palestinians with greater power against Israeli obstinacy. It would also create an economic cycle in Palestine that would make all of us Palestinians feel that the peace process would bring bene-fits to all.*

6. *The most pressing matter is the formation of a political agenda made up of the PLO, the Labor Party, and the Israeli leftist parties to oppose the plans of the current Israeli government and Netanyahu. This would cause Netanyahu to face a joint Palestinian-Israeli camp, no longer making the confrontation simply a Palestinian-Israeli one. By expanding the circle, the confrontation of the joint peace camp against Netanyahu's plans would become more prominent, thus iso-lating the extremist minority in the Israeli community.*

After the Clinton administration had put pressure on Netanyahu's extremist gov-ernment, Israel finally agreed to hand over 80 percent of the city of Hebron to the PLO. This was the only step Netanyahu ever took within the framework of the Oslo Accords. Israeli-Palestinian meetings were discontinued after that for close to seven months.

I was to accompany Arafat to Hebron on January 19, 1997, when he would be handed back the historic site. We left from Gaza in Arafat's helicopter, with an Israeli military helicopter flying in front of us. Israelis, to this day, determine the flight patterns anyone can take over the skies of Palestine. They, not us, de-cide who can and cannot fly over our country.

We flew over Tel Aviv and then the West Bank. Arafat pointed to the Israeli settlements surrounding Ramallah. For the first time, I saw with my own eyes the settlement colonies that had been set up by the Israelis on Palestinian land in the West Bank that had been confiscated from its owners. "These are military posts," Arafat said, "and they are controlling our towns and villages."

As we approached Mount Hebron, we could see the continuous chain of set-tlements that had been built on Palestinian hills surrounding Hebron. That had been the Israeli plan: to surround Palestinian cities and towns with military settlement colonies that would keep them under siege at all times, thus enabling the further Israeli expansion of settlements.

The helicopter hovered over Hebron and approached the *Muqataa* (government) building, which houses all the departments of the government, where Arafat was to give a speech celebrating the liberation of Hebron. Thousands of people had already gathered there to welcome President Arafat. As we stepped out of the helicopter, I could see that people were crying. All of us who had traveled with Arafat walked behind him, but he was swallowed up by the crowds, everyone wanting to embrace their leader. One of the National Security officers saved us from the same predicament by giving us a ride in his car. We slowly tried to plow our way through the throngs of people so that we could reach the *Muqataa* building. A special stage had been set up from which Arafat was to address his people. Seas of people waved Palestinian flags. I could see young men up on telephone poles, women and children dancing in the streets, people crying and hugging each other. Arafat waved his "V for Victory" hand signal to the crowd, shouting "Yes, it's true! The city has been liberated!" Arafat was overwhelmed with emotion; he had not been in Hebron for the thirty years it had been occupied by Israel. In his speech he vowed, "We will have our Palestinian state. A promise made is a promise to be kept." He went on to say, "Hebron will be the beginning of more Israeli withdrawals from the Occupied West Bank and a step closer to achieving peace in our region. It will not be an easy road, but we Palestinians will be victorious in the end! You, the people of Hebron, are the true heroes who will lead us all to peace!" The people started to chant over and over again "Long live Palestine!" When they started to quiet down, he added, "I want all the Jewish settlers who have chosen to remain to know this: Palestinians do not want confrontation with you. We want a just peace and nothing less."

During our journey back to Gaza, Arafat was deep in thought. There had been touching moments for him that day. "Israel handed over 80 percent of Hebron with great reluctance," he said. "I see trouble on the way. They do not want peace. They will go back on their pledges and will not honor their agreements."

The events and meetings that took place at the Aspen Institute's Wye River Plantation in Maryland between President Arafat and Netanyahu on October 23, 1998, proved Arafat right. The Israeli government was bent on reneging on all its commitments to Palestinians. He was also trying to get President Clinton to release Jonathan Pollard, a U.S. naval intelligence officer who had released classified information to Israel. The head of the CIA threatened to resign if Pollard was released from prison. Netanyahu resentfully agreed to withdraw from 13 percent of the lands of the West Bank, even though the original agreement had called for a second-phase withdrawal of 35 percent. He and Sharon, who was then Netanyahu's foreign minister, agreed to do this only after pressure was applied by the United States. However, behind closed doors, Sharon and Netanyahu were conspiring not to honor their agreement with President Clinton.

President Clinton and President Mubarak called for a summit to take place at Sharm Al-Sheikh on October 4, 1999. Nothing much came from the meeting between Ehud Barak—who beat Netanyahu in the next elections in 1999—and Arafat except that they agreed to keep trying to find a solution. Barak and Arafat were invited, on July 5, 2000, by President Clinton to Camp David in order to build on the first Camp David Accords, which took place in 1978 under Jimmy Carter. It was hoped that the two men could continue negotiations on the Middle East process, from July 11 to 25, but unfortunately no agreement could be reached. Barak made it clear through his evasive actions that Israel was still unwilling to honor its previous commitments. About all that came from that meeting was another agreement by the two leaders that they should keep trying and that the only way to arrive at a peaceful solution would be to abide by UN Resolutions 242 and 338.

On September 28, 2000, Ariel Sharon and armed guards entered Al-Aqsa Mosque during prayer time, which was a serious breach of convention. Naturally, Sharon's violation of the sanctity of one of Islam's holiest sites led to clashes inside Al-Aqsa between worshippers and the heavily armed soldiers. Demonstrations broke out all over the West Bank and the Gaza Strip, protesting Sharon's violation of the sanctity of Al-Aqsa Mosque. The Israeli army responded to these peaceful demonstrations with live and rubber bullets as well as canisters of tear gas, but the clashes continued through February 2001. Sharon's visit marked the beginning of a new phase of Israeli aggression and settlement expansion.

At Taba, Egypt, from January 21–27, 2001, the Israeli and Palestinian negotiating teams would have reached an agreement if Barak had not been fearful of losing the upcoming elections. To sign a peace agreement with the Palestinian Authority would have seriously hurt his chances to win the next election, so he refused to agree to anything that might appear to be a move toward peace. Even though he tried his best to avoid peaceful negotiations, he still lost the elections in February to Ariel Sharon, whose election heralded an escalation of barbaric aggression against the Palestinian people throughout Palestine.

After rejecting the Mitchell Report (see Key Terms)—the result of an American fact-finding committee that was released in April 2001—Sharon called in the Israeli army reserves and mobilized thousands of Israeli soldiers in vehicles and tanks in a battle to reoccupy the Palestinian territories. Before that, he had rejected the Tenet Plan (see Key Terms) and later flatly refused even to consider the suggestion made by the G8 countries (see Key Terms) on July 19, 2001, to send international observers to supervise a ceasefire that could bring an end to the bloody clashes between the Palestinians and the Israelis.

Sharon rejected all U.S. and international attempts to bring an end to the fighting and to initiate a return to the negotiating table. In fact, he had plans for further aggression already in place. I learned from very reliable Israeli sources that Sharon planned to besiege Arafat's headquarters at the *Muqataa* in Ramallah, where the Palestinian Authority had set up its government offices. When I was in Ramallah, I called Arafat and told him I needed to see him immediately, and then I headed directly to his office.

I told him that I had received information that Israeli tanks were preparing to storm his office and were planning on reaching all the way to his door, not just the wall outside. I also warned him that Israel was calling for his assassination or deportation, whichever came first.

At dawn on December 12, 2001, Israeli tanks invaded Ramallah, imposing a curfew on the entire city. Dozens of tanks surrounded President Arafat's headquarters at the *Muqataa*.

Israeli troops took over the houses surrounding Arafat's office, holding men, women, and children prisoners in their own homes. Snipers armed with light to medium weaponry set up positions on nearby rooftops. Tanks shelled the *Muqataa* relentlessly, while military helicopters flew overhead.

The siege on Arafat had begun.

35

UNDER SIEGE

It was 5 a.m. on December 12, 2001. Dozens of Israeli tanks stood at the entrance to both my home and my office next door, less than a hundred yards from President Arafat's headquarters.

I watched from the window of my home as dozens of soldiers poured out of armored personnel carriers. The door from my home to my office was open, so I could hear the heavy sound of scores of soldiers pouring in. What sounded like a hundred armed soldiers pushed their way inside my office and at least half that number took up positions on the roof of my building.

I opened the front door to my home. Dozens of machine guns were pointing directly at my face. I asked the soldiers what they wanted. One of them pushed me back, pinning me against the wall with the butt of his machine gun. Then he knocked me down onto the floor—three soldiers aimed their guns directly at me. The rest of the soldiers forcibly entered my home and proceeded to deploy themselves for combat in my bedroom, kitchen, and bathroom, tearing down curtains and dragging the chairs to the windows, positioning themselves for sniper fire.

Keeping their weapons trained on me and my wife, Maha, the soldiers ripped out our phone and destroyed my computer. While the soldiers were busy getting situated, Maha sneaked into my office and miraculously managed to smuggle my laptop back into our home while the soldiers were busy securing it for a battle.

Unfortunately, she was spotted setting up the laptop before she had a chance to plug it in; they threw it against a wall, destroying it, and threatened her with their bayonets. Several soldiers used their bayonets to push her back into the room. They had pushed her so hard she was left with small cuts and bruises all over her chest, back, and sides. Some of the soldiers urinated on our furniture, walls, and floors in an attempt to humiliate us.

As the soldiers continued to take up combat positions, I whispered to Maha, who always kept her cell phone in her pocket, to try to use it to call a friend of ours who was a retired Israeli general. I knew no one could help us get out of our dire situation except one of their own, and luckily we had a good friend who was not only influential in Israel, but was someone we could depend on for help. She asked one of the officers if she could use the toilet, and after some heated discussions amongst them, one of the soldiers finally allowed her to go into the bathroom alone. Maha dialed our friend and managed to get through to him. Some of the soldiers overheard her speaking and broke down the door, but not before she had told him that our home had been taken over by Israeli soldiers. As they rushed toward her, Maha held out the phone to one of the men, bravely saying, "General XXX wants to talk to the officer in charge."

It was obvious the officer in charge knew to whom he was speaking. He had lost some of the color in his face, and I could tell he was not pleased with us for having made the call. However, and more importantly, it was also obvious he knew the reputation of our friend and that he was someone who was in a position to cause serious problems for the officer if he did not leave our home immediately. Following his brief conversation with the general, the officer shot a nasty look at Maha and me and then barked out orders to his men in Hebrew, telling them to pack up and get out. Our home had been left in a shambles, but at least they were leaving. As they were going, the officer in charge turned to us with a sarcastic smile and sneered, "You're going to hear the sound of huge explosions in a few minutes."

Within seconds of their leaving both my office and our home, the tanks surrounding our home began to shell the walls and courtyards of the *Muqataa* building that held the headquarters of President Arafat, the ministry of interior, and the security agencies in the city of Ramallah. The tanks and bulldozers had intentionally destroyed the electricity poles and blown up the water pipes that supplied the entire neighborhood, causing the building to lose electricity and water instantly.

I cannot even remember how many days and nights this relentless aggression continued because it never stopped. All I can remember is a blur of bomb blasts and machine gun fire. During this time Israeli soldiers took over many homes in our neighborhood, terrorizing men, women, senior citizens, and children, breaking their possessions, throwing discarded food and wrappings on their floors, and even defecating on their furniture. No one was allowed to leave his home; we were all under house arrest. What food and bottled water we had in our homes was all we had to eat and drink. No one was allowed out to get medications; people with chronic illnesses such as diabetes, high blood pressure, or heart problems just had to get on without if they ran out of their medications. If anyone got ill during that time, they couldn't get out to see a doctor. Food rotted in our refrigerators because we had no electricity; and we weren't even allowed to throw out the stinking food. We couldn't flush our toilets or take baths or even brush our teeth because we had no water. During one of those terrible days, I made the following entry in my journal:

> If the scientist Pavlov were alive today, he would know for certain that his theory of Conditioned Response was absolutely correct, especially with regard to sound and its relation to a certain psychological state.
>
> In Ramallah, thousands of children, women and men will now associate the clamor of tank chains with death, bombing, shelling and humiliation. In the minds of children especially, the sound of the tanks will forever be linked to the terror which causes them to tremble and cry for long periods of time accompanied by an instinctive attempt to hide in their mothers' laps.
>
> This is terrorism.
>
> President Yasser Arafat has been put under siege and tanks have destroyed what was left of his compound. They have also occupied the surrounding buildings. Ramallah now lives the life of Second World War concentration camps. Everyone is under curfew; we have no normal life.
>
> The Israeli occupation forces have cut off electricity and water to many neighborhoods in the city since they first entered on the 12th of December [2001]. Anyone who has not experienced having the water and electricity cut off cannot comprehend the full meaning and consequences of such a situation. No TV, no computers, no light at night, no heat during these cold, stormy days and nights, no water to drink or wash with. We can't even use our toilets. Without electricity, our food is starting to spoil.
>
> Ramallah is shrouded in a veil of darkness and grief.
>
> Before the siege, I used to like fog and loved walking through it, especially on the streets of Oxford. I now hate it. Pavlov was right. We do get conditioned quickly.

Thousands of children, women, men and the elderly now sit in their homes without heat; fuel is nowhere to be found even if anyone does manage to slip out unnoticed.

Since morning, Ramallah has been hit with harsh, cold, and violent wind, almost Shakespearean in its rage against what the Israelis are doing. Yesterday, the grieving citizens of Ramallah buried twenty-one bodies during the two hours when the curfew was lifted. The bodies had been found in the streets, a number of them unidentified. The Israelis refused to allow religious rites to be conducted, ordering the bodies to be buried in a mass grave, each in a plastic body bag. They were all buried in the garden of the hospital because it no longer has refrigeration for the morgue. The smell of death is everywhere.

Tanks are patrolling the streets, and the silence of death can be heard in all the houses, buildings and huts. Even the birds that used to sing every day, swaying on the branches of the fig and oak trees around my home, have stopped singing. Perhaps they too are scared and too sad to sing.

Our neighbor's rooster has stopped crowing in the morning, his hens are hiding in the shed. The walls around my office have lost their splendor. They were demolished by the occupation forces and turned into rubble. The rose bushes I had planted in the spring have been crushed by soldiers' boots. Now I won't see them bloom in the spring.

How sad is the view.

The occupation forces stormed the hospital [the Medical Care (Al-Ri'ayya Al-Tibbiya) Hospital near the Manara Square is a modern, specialized hospital], *putting the lives of all the patients in danger. They insisted on going into every room, including the children's rooms, the doctors' clinics, and the operating theaters. They did this after they had confined the medical staff in one room, forcing one doctor to show them each room, each department. They also stormed the Ramallah Hospital, accompanied by police dogs. They took the dogs with them into the neo-natal ward of all places!*

The Israelis continue to prevent ambulances from removing the dead bodies lying in the streets or from taking the wounded to the hospitals, leaving them to bleed to death on the sidewalks, in the streets and inside their homes.

The soldiers have stormed private homes, destroyed food supplies, broken furniture and intimidated children and adults. How can people be so inhumane? The Israeli forces are waging a psychological war against us by trying to seize complete control over us all. They keep firing their weapons into the air for no apparent reason other than to keep us all on our nerves. They have cut off water and electricity to more parts of the city and have set unreasonable curfews in order to intimidate and suffocate us in our own homes, in our own country. Some of the men who work in Jerusalem can't make it home on time to beat the curfew, so they have to sleep in homes of friends, sometimes of complete strangers. Ironic how living in such misery can make us all bond together even stronger.

On my battery-operated radio I found out that medical and food relief is not being allowed to enter. Relief trucks are being targeted by the Israelis, as was the case yesterday with the UN convoy sent by [UN secretary-general] Kofi Annan. An Israeli military roadblock near the village of Qalandia prevented the UN convoy from getting into Ramallah. When the UN person in charge of the convoy insisted on going through, the Israeli soldiers shot him dead.

The scenario was repeated when a convoy of aid arrived that had been sent by Israeli Arabs and Jews from within the 1948 Israeli border. It was stopped at the same roadblock. The people accompanying the convoy tried to talk their way through, but to no avail. In protest, they staged a sit-in there and demonstrated. At the time of this writing, they are still there, refusing to go back.

Isolating us from the outside world is another form of Israeli psychological warfare aimed at subduing all of us Palestinians. What they don't seem to understand is that the worse they try to make our quality of life, the stronger our will to survive becomes.

Today the Israeli press published a story about a tapped phone call between Sharon and [IDF chief of staff Shaul] Mofaz in which they talked about eliminating Yasser Arafat physically. Of course, I don't find it at all strange that this is coming from either Mofaz or Sharon. Such threats must be taken very seriously because both Mofaz and Sharon are professional criminals with an insatiable appetite for killing. Sharon in particular has complete disregard for others, even for the promises he made to President Bush that he would withdraw from our occupied land.

Israeli soldiers now occupy the very floor of the building where Yasser Arafat is. They are standing face to face with the President's personal guards. The Israeli soldiers are changed every six hours, whereas the President's guards cannot change over, or even sleep more than a few minutes every now and then. They are completely fatigued.

Water and electricity have also been cut off to the compound, which means no toilets, no bathing, no washing before prayers, no food, no light.

While Sharon is continuing his war of physical elimination in all the West Bank cities, he has stepped up his psychological war as well. My question is this: What is the long-term aim of this physical and psychological war, in addition to the aims already mentioned? It can be for one reason and one reason only: eviction and annihilation.

Sharon openly believes that large numbers of Palestinians must be evicted from the West Bank and Gaza Strip so that the percentage of those remaining is the same as or close to the percentage of Israeli settlers. This way he would be able to bring over a million new Jewish immigrants from Latin America to counterbalance our numbers.

We have not had a drop of water for days, absolutely no electricity, no phones, no fuel, and no food. What Arafat is suffering is what I must suffer as well because I live and work so close to his headquarters, which is completely surrounded by barbed wire, tanks and armored personnel carriers.

Sharon recently announced that he had completed the first phase of his plan to "fight terrorism" in Palestine, and that he would continue in his campaign to fight "terrorism" using various means, which, as far as I can see, means he will continue to use his own brand of state-approved terrorism to annihilate us all if he can.

It appears that he has decided to continue occupying the countryside, storming village after village, home by home, arresting as many of us as possible while assassinating activists of all factions. On top of all this, he is destroying the infrastructure of the Palestinian Authority and our security services.

It is certain, as events have indicated, that the withdrawal announced by Sharon, based on President George W. Bush's request, is but a political tactic aimed at quieting the indignation of the international community and pleasing President Bush. In reality, he has transformed the Palestinian cities, towns, and villages into concentration camps similar to what the Nazis had used.

At the same time, the Israeli occupation's war against the Palestinian people on the psychological front continues. Destruction, murder, and massacre have always been Sharon's methods, but they have never succeeded in subduing us from continuing in our struggle to achieve our human rights.

Sharon and his rightist-leftist government, however, seek, through this war of destruction, murder, and mass crimes, to destroy our will and strike a blow to our pride and dignity by attempting to humiliate us. Perhaps, this is with the aim of implementing Sharon and [Israeli minister of strategic affairs Avigdor] Lieberman's plan to force a great number of us living in the West Bank and Gaza Strip to leave. Such a move would enable the Israeli government to annex 52 percent of the West Bank and 57 percent of the Gaza Strip before bringing in Jewish immigrants from Latin America to colonize these confiscated lands.

In my opinion, this would be Sharon's way of turning those of us who remain in the West Bank and Gaza Strip into slave laborers for the new settlers. But Sharon's calculations will not succeed. We Palestinians, who have been subjected over the years to countless injustices at the hands of the Israeli occupation force, will not surrender. We deserve our freedom and independence just like anyone else. We have paid dearly already, but we are ready to pay an even higher price to regain our liberty.

Matters have gone so far as to have Nobel Peace Prize—winner Shimon Peres blackmail Europe into turning their backs on us in our worst hours of need. He continues to remind Europeans of what the Nazis did to the Jews, making them feel guilty about something they were never a part of doing.

[Former Israeli prime minister] *Ehud Barak is no better. Here he is, one of the participants in the Camp David and Taba negotiations, and yet, yesterday, as I was listening to the news on my little battery-run radio, he announced at the AIPAC meeting in Washington that Israel does not intend, and does not accept, to remove any of its settlements.*

As for Sharon, he has asked his office personnel to begin circulating the idea of annexing 50 percent of the West Bank, and that he will not give up the synagogue in Jericho or Joseph's Tomb in Nablus, although these cities are both located in Palestine.

As long as we remain steadfast and endure all these tragedies and crimes for the sake of gaining our freedom, we will eventually influence international and regional compassion towards our cause. Our endurance is the most effective weapon we have.

President George W. Bush has stated that the basis for stability in the Middle East region is two-fold: the establishment of a Palestinian state and for Israel to enjoy security. He said that Sharon was "a man of peace" and that history would prove that, but I know better. He said that Prince Abdullah bin Abdel Aziz [of Saudi Arabia], has, by launching his initiative before the Arab Summit, provided a framework that will guarantee security and peace for Israel with its Arab neighbors.

International legitimacy resolutions have crystallized as being more accurate in terms of the establishment of an independent state, which is related to Resolutions 242 and 338. They clearly defined this when they broached the matter of an independent state following the Israeli withdrawal to the borders of June 4, with Jerusalem as its capital. In my opinion, the U.S. must use its great influence over Israel to make it abide by the implementation of these resolutions so that we all can all enjoy security and peace.

Sharon and his government want all of us Palestinians along with our leaders to surrender so that our expectations and ambitions can be lowered, thus forcing us to submit to 50 percent of his political program.

But this will not happen.

The historic deal, land for security and peace, will only be achieved if the right price is paid:

1. *An independent Palestinian state on the lands occupied by Israel in 1967, which means an Israeli withdrawal back to the borders of June 4, 1967.*

2. *Jerusalem as our capital.*
3. *Withdrawal of occupation forces from the Syrian and Palestinian Golan.*
4. *Withdrawal from the Shaba'a farms and their return to Lebanon.*

In order for this to be achieved, Prince Abdullah bin Abdel Aziz and King Mohammad the Sixth [of Morocco] must insist on the following while they are in Washington: an immediate Israeli withdrawal (a practical, not a theoretical one) from areas under the control of the Palestinian Authority; the implementation of the Tenet Plan and Mitchell recommendations within a week; the proposed Washington conference must include all parties interested in the Middle East peace process; and to discuss the implementation of the international legitimacy Resolutions 242 and 338 and other related United Nations resolutions which relate to the establishment of the independent state of Palestine.

I am convinced that Sharon would not have launched this barbaric attack against us if the U.S. administration had not given him the okay in a message delivered by U.S. Vice President Dick Cheney when he visited Israel on March 18, 2002.

Such was but one of my countless journal entries during the nightmarish time that was inflicted upon us by the Israeli forces.

On April 13, strong Arab and European criticism of the siege finally convinced Israel that enough was enough. The siege against Yasser Arafat was lifted, and the tanks that surrounded us withdrew. A meeting was held between President Arafat and Colin Powell, the U.S. secretary of state, who had carried the message to Sharon from President Bush that requested an end to the siege. In my opinion, the United States was not asking for him to withdraw for humanitarian reasons. I believe they felt a continued confrontation would undermine U.S. efforts to line up solid European and Middle Eastern support for their war on Iraq. Whatever the reasons, Israel was forced to withdraw, which I am sure made Sharon angry because he had not achieved his two aims: to get Arafat to agree to go into exile and to arrest about fifty people within the compound for "terrorism."

36

HOUSE
ARREST

By January 2002, after one month of siege, we were all worn out, but as soon as the Israeli tanks drew back, hundreds of the citizens of Ramallah rushed to the *Muqataa* to check on President Arafat. Although the siege had been lifted on the city, Arafat was still not allowed to leave his headquarters, and snipers could be seen on rooftops with their guns aimed at the building. He had been cut off from all communications, except for the rare times when we had been able to talk to him via a cell phone connected to the Israeli television networks. To prove they had not assassinated Arafat, Israeli networks would often be allowed to film him. When they did, we would sometimes get permission to speak to him via cell phone, our only means of communication with him.

We found him in good spirits, discussing his plans to visit other cities in the West Bank that had also been suffering from Israeli incursions. But before going anywhere, he had to wait until he was allowed to leave the compound. George W. Bush arranged for him to be able to move relatively freely within the city and, when permission was granted, he could visit the other cities of Palestine. Once he was allowed to leave the compound without fear of being killed by a sniper, he spent the next couple of months working on the rebuilding of Ramallah and his compound. In April, he made plans to visit the Jenin refugee camp in the north of the West Bank, which had been under blockade since 2000 and continuously besieged for five months in 2002 by tanks, bulldozers, and air strikes. The Israelis were engaging in mass arrests of Palestinians, murdering anyone they suspected of terrorism while also using psychological intimidation against the residents. Homes were demolished and the basic infrastructure was completely destroyed. Israeli soldiers also denied humanitarian aid to enter the camp. In the end, over 3,000 people were left homeless and hundreds had been slaughtered. Arafat wanted not only to see the damage with his own eyes, but he also wanted the people to know they were not alone. Arafat wanted to console the survivors and see what could be done to help.

A number of his security officials tried to discourage him from traveling, advising him to wait until it was safer to move about the West Bank and into Gaza, but he was not to be dissuaded. He issued orders to prepare for more visits to the hospitals and camps of Ramallah, after which he would proceed to Jenin. The Israeli aggression continued unabated, as did Palestinian resistance to it. Armed Palestinian fighters carried out operations that targeted Israeli civilians in a sort of "eye for an eye" reprisal for what was happening not only in Jenin, but also in Nablus and Beit Sahour as well. It seemed as if the whole of Palestine was under siege and the people had had enough. Arafat and the entire Palestinian Authority condemned these attacks against Israeli civilians. In spite of this, Israel responded by escalating its aggression, shelling Palestinian neighborhoods as well as assassinating many of our high-ranking leaders by entering Palestinian cities and killing them in broad daylight. They were often targeted them from the air, without a care as to how many others might die. They would be considered "collateral damage," according to the Israelis. Events spiraled into a never-ending cycle of violence and counterviolence.

The Israeli government carried out a plan to isolate Yasser Arafat on the grounds that he was a terrorist who openly supported terrorism, making him an unsuitable partner in the peace process. No matter what he had tried to do, from his peace initiative to Oslo to Wye to Camp David to any of his promises and declarations, even to the UN, he was never regarded as anyone other than what the Israelis had continued to see him as: the epitome of a terrorist. I am convinced that the main aim of these accusations and isolation was to disrupt the peace process, which had been the wish of the Israeli government all along. Sharon's government continued to accuse Arafat of being behind every bombing in Israel, holding him personally responsible. Arafat had always been the more moderate of the PLO leaders. He had been the first to recognize that peace was the only way to establish his dream of Palestine. He had started off believing in an armed struggle in 1967, and then after twenty years had developed into a statesman who supported the peace process, but Israel could never accept that he had changed. When he offered them an olive branch, all they could see was a gun.

The Israelis fabricated reports to the Bush administration, saying that Arafat was behind the attacks on Israeli civilians, hoping the United Sates would stop recognizing him as the legitimate representative of the Palestinian people, but that did not happen. If any politicians or diplomats had arranged to meet with Arafat, Sharon would refuse to receive them, saying that any official who wanted to visit the Palestinian Authority while President Arafat was still its head was not welcome in Israel. This was his way of exerting pressure on the European Union and the UN so that they would fall into line with the United States and Israel, allowing Israel to continue its attacks in the name of self defense, while also blaming Arafat for any acts of terror committed against Israeli citizens. The irony was that everyone, including the Israelis, was fully aware of the fact that Arafat continued to publicly condemn the targeting of both the Israeli and Palestinian civilians. Arafat's path remained clear: he was seeking a political solution that would lead to peace and stability for the entire the region.

Sharon said more than once that he regretted making a pledge to President George W. Bush that he would not harm President Arafat, openly stating that he still considered killing him. Israeli newspaper *Haaretz* quoted him as saying, "I wouldn't propose that any insurance company give them [Arafat and Nasrallah] coverage. Anyone who kills a Jew is a marked man. Period." He had also said in an interview with the Israeli daily newspaper *Yediot Ahronot:* "Israel is determined to 'remove' Arafat one day." He went on to say again that he regretted promising Bush that he would not harm Arafat physically. The reporter for the newspaper wrote: "by 'remove,' he could mean either Arafat's expulsion or his assassination. But I had a strong feeling he meant the latter." Sharon circumvented his pledge to Bush by getting the Israeli cabinet to vote to eventually deport Arafat from the Palestinian territories, once a decision on how to do it could be made. Meanwhile, I had received information from one of my sources in Israel that, in an inner Cabinet meeting, a cabinet member had told Sharon that he believed that the time was right to "dispose" of Arafat. Sharon reminded Mofaz of his pledge to Bush that Arafat would not be harmed, but added, unless, of course, there were "other means" of accomplishing that goal.

I wrote to Arafat immediately. Following is a translation of my letter to him.

> *September 19, 2002*
> *President Abu Ammar*
>
> *Palestine greets you.*
>
> *The meeting of the inner Cabinet at noon today did not take a decision, as I had informed you. It will convene in an hour to discuss what decision to take. The two proposed options include isolating you as well as expelling you from the territories.*
>
> *I beg you to be extremely careful. Please be vigilant with regard to what you eat and drink: drink only from a bottle you open yourself; eat only canned foods with valid expiry dates which you open yourself, but be sure they have been bought to you only by those you trust. I am prepared to ask my wife Maha to do this for you on a daily basis. I have information that the Israelis will try to poison you.*
>
> *Also, I ask you again to safeguard the funds. You must revoke the authorization any other person has to deal with the money. The Israelis have decided to besiege you financially as well as physically. What I am warning you against is based on very reliable sources in Washington. This is a serious matter. There is a conspiracy which aims at taking away your control of the money under the pretext that you are buying weapons to fund terrorism. They wish to abolish your control of security so they can be in control of it.*
>
> *I hope that you keep in mind what I had said to you before the siege: Survival is victory. I pledge my loyalty and allegiance to you, Abu Ammar. You are not only our leader, but the symbol of our struggle.*
>
> *May you remain always for Palestine.*
> *Your brother,*
> *Bassam Abu Sharif*

Arafat's reply was pragmatic. "This is not the first time. Sharon has already tried to assassinate me eighteen times, and he will no doubt continue to try. But I am not an easy target."

In subsequent letters, I drew Arafat's attention to the second phase of Sharon's plan, which was to besiege him again in his headquarters in Ramallah, and then to hold him under house arrest, isolated from his people and from the world so that they could eliminate him permanently by "other means."

The next day, September 20, Israeli tanks and military helicopters again began heavy shelling of the buildings at the *Muqataa*. Eighteen buildings were destroyed and their contents looted by the Israelis, who took many gifts President Arafat had received from heads of state over the past four decades. After destroying a part of Arafat's office, the Israelis surrounded his personal quarters and placed him under house arrest for the second time.

Israeli Ministers demanded Yasser Arafat's deportation. They threatened to have his office stormed all the way inside this time, and then to have him forcibly removed from his office and flown out of the Palestinian territories, some going so far as to say they would dump him in a Libyan desert. Arafat scoffed at such threats. "I will neither be a fugitive nor a prisoner, but a martyr, a martyr, a martyr!"

I also had it under good authority that Israeli security services had begun active preparation of the "other means." Before they had threatened; now they were acting on it. Food was allowed to be brought to the compound in a van, but then the driver would have to leave the van while the Israelis searched each and every container, each can, and each carton of milk. I believe it was during those times that they managed to put poison into his food.

President Arafat remained steadfast and strong, infusing hope and the spirit of resoluteness into all of us through the speeches that he broadcast over the phone or by satellite from inside his compound. All those of us who were allowed to visit him felt that he was a giant, a model of patience and persistence, and someone who was a far greater person than all his enemies. Arafat would say to me, "All our people are under arrest, besieged, surrounded, and starving while their homes and farms are being demolished. I am one with the Palestinian people. Together, we must remain unwavering and enduring because we will triumph eventually in the end."

It was also a measure of the man that he was able to run the affairs of the Palestinian Authority from a room that never saw the light of day. He was ever vigilant in attending to the needs of his people, who were suffering under Israeli military escalation, from Jenin to Nablus to Gaza to Beit Sahour, all cities that had been surrounded by Israeli tanks and continually bombed from the land and air. Homes were bulldozed regularly, people were assassinated by helicopter strikes, orchards of olive trees were destroyed on a daily basis, and no one in the international community appeared to care. All was accepted as long as Israel claimed it had the right to defend itself; but we Palestinians never seemed to have that same right or it would be seen as terrorism. Arafat saw to the needs of those who had lost their homes to Israeli bulldozers while he continued to send help to the families of martyrs and prisoners. He backed his compassion with action, smuggling whatever food or medicine he could to help his people through their trying times.

Though under siege, he never hesitated to rally his people when he sensed their frustration. Once he said to a high-ranking Palestinian, "This is not the first time we have been besieged or had battles waged against us. Our people are mighty. We will hold firm, establish our state, and raise our flag over the walls of Jerusalem."

However, although he spoke bravely, I sensed that he was hurting deep inside. This siege prevented him from moving freely in the West Bank and the Gaza Strip, making it impossible for him to visit his people. It also hampered him politically by reducing his contact with regional and international governments. He could only move about within Palestine if he had permission to do so. The number of official visitors who came to see him was also limited since Israel was threatening not to receive anyone who visited him. In one of our private meetings, President Arafat said to me: "The Americans have betrayed us. Each promise they have made to us has eventually been broken, and they have never held Israel to its word after Oslo and Camp David. They have obviously given Israel free rein to do what they want to us, not holding them accountable for any of the human rights violations they are committing each day, accusing us of terrorism but not seeing that what Israel is doing is state-supported terrorism at its highest degree. There can be no stability in the region until our people gain their freedom and independence."

For the next two years, Arafat lived under siege but never gave up hope.

EPILOGUE

THE FINAL FAREWELL

Since January 1, 2004, the anniversary of the start of the revolution, I had begun to notice unusual signs of fatigue and exhaustion in Arafat. He was losing weight, his skin was very pale, almost transparent, and his energy levels had dropped significantly. His breath smelled strange and it had nothing to do with onions or garlic. His doctors attributed his fatigue to his tirelessness; they said that he was exhausted because he refused to stop pushing himself, never getting enough sleep, oftentimes working throughout the night without taking a rest, without stopping to eat. Arafat never thought of himself; his people always came first and they were suffering.

When I visited him, Arafat would often offer me fruit, even though what he had was limited to whatever the Israelis would allow in, but I always refused.

"What, are you afraid?" he would joke.

I would always respond, "I don't know what's in it." I wish he had been as careful about his food as I was.

On August 4, 2004, his birthday, those signs of exhaustion were much more obvious, and by October, Arafat was frail, as if his entire body had atrophied. He had always been a physically sound and strong man, but he was walking as if he were a hundred years old. He could hardly make it from one side of the room to the other without sitting down to rest. His skin was like tissue paper. He reminded me of a brittle piece of old, dried-up wood that had rotted from within.

On one of my visits to him, we sat together for approximately thirty minutes, talking about our future, the difficult circumstances we were still facing with the unbelievable Israeli siege on his headquarters still in place, the U.S. decision to back Israel without question in anything it did, and the inability of the Arab countries to unite under one banner. He seemed incredibly tired. His passion and love for Palestine were both still burning brightly behind his eyes, but I could see it was an immense effort for him to even talk.

When it was time for me to leave, he embraced me five times, something he had never done before.

"Abu Ammar," I asked, him, "are you alright?"

"Yes, Bassam, but I am exhausted."

A number of days later, in August, one of his aides informed me that Arafat was "very tired," an Arabic euphemism for "exceedingly unwell, on the brink of death." I went immediately to his headquarters. As I greeted him, I could see that he was even weaker than he had been when I had last seen him only a few days earlier; he was barely able to grasp my hand when I extended it to him.

"What's wrong, Abu Ammar?" I asked.

"Severe flu," he answered, "it seems it has affected my intestines, too."

I didn't believe that it was the flu. I had seen these symptoms before, when, almost thirty years earlier, the Israelis had poisoned Dr. Wadi' Haddad. I had learned the truth about Haddad's death many years after the fact. I had been in Rome visiting with an old friend of mine, an Israeli officer, who had had too much to drink. He started to brag to me about how they had killed Haddad with a poison that had destroyed his red blood cells. His body had been sent to Germany for an autopsy, and a German doctor who had been part of the autopsy team confirmed to me that Haddad had ingested the poison through his taste buds. He went on to say that the poison had literally slowly eaten away his insides over time. I feared the same thing was happening to Arafat now. I did not tell him my fears for I didn't want to alarm him, but I did insist that get medical help. I wanted him to go to the hospital immediately. "Your face is colorless, Abu Ammar."

"You mean I look pale?"

"No. I mean that you have no color at all in your face." I was sure his red blood cells were being destroyed, just like Wadi's had been. "You need to see a specialist."

"We'll see," was all he said. He was an independently stubborn man and I knew I couldn't force him to do anything he didn't feel was necessary.

Arafat's condition continued to worsen, and all of us who were close to him were anxious and worried. The leaders of Tunisia and Egypt sent their personal doctors to examine him, and Arafat saw his own private doctor as well. Everyone was searching for the real reason for this accelerated collapse, but none of the doctors had access to the labs they needed to do the tests that would have proven my worst suspicions to be true.

But I was sure Arafat was being poisoned just like Wadi' Haddad. I was positive they were poisoning his food on a daily basis and doing it right under our very eyes.

I could not sleep for days. Finally, I decided to act. Late at night on October 25, I contacted the French consul-general, Regis Koetschet, and told him that President Arafat was very ill. I asked him to call the minister of foreign affairs, Michel Barnier, and ask him to help arrange for Arafat to be medivacked to the best hospital in Paris for tests. Koetschet called me back to say the minister could arrange for him to be taken to Percy Military Hospital in Paris and that he would get the ball rolling immediately.

On October 29, two Jordanian helicopters arrived at the compound to transfer the president and his guards to Marka Airport in Amman, Jordan, where a medically equipped French plane had landed and was waiting to transfer him to Paris. Officers and high-ranking officials headed to the helipad at the *Muqataa* to see him off. I stood in the back row, my heart heavy.

Arafat, although very weak, walked on his own out to the helicopter and boarded without any assistance. He wanted his people to see that he was strong and still able to lead them. When he saw all of the people that had turned up to bid him a safe journey he was overwhelmed and very touched. I watched him board the helicopter with tears streaming down my face. President Arafat stood at the entrance of the helicopter, turned to us all and struggled to raise his hand to his mouth so that he could throw a kiss to everyone. I knew in my heart that this was his final farewell.

I returned to my office, sobbing uncontrollably.

The next day, I asked the French consul-general for a visa to France so that I could visit the president. He said that it would be easy for me to get the visa but that Arafat was in the intensive care unit and his doctors were not allowing any visitors in to see him until his condition had become stable. When I started receiving conflicting information regarding his health, some saying he was getting better, others saying he was deteriorating, I knew he was dying. I would never see President Arafat again.

On November 12, 2004, following state funeral ceremonies in both Paris and Cairo befitting the stature of this giant, an Egyptian helicopter landed in Ramallah, carrying the remains of President Yasser Arafat. He had returned home to his beloved Palestine for the last time.

The world—and I—will never be the same without Arafat. But his dream for an independent Palestine, in which Palestinians can thrive, safely and securely, lives on in my heart and in the hearts of his people.

ACKNOWLEDGMENTS

I would like to thank my family and friends who continued to encourage me throughout the process of writing this book. I would like to take this opportunity to thank in particular my daughter, Karma Abu Sharif, who put a great deal of effort into making sure my words were not only clear, but that this book would find its way first to a reputable publisher and then to the people who deserve to know the truth. To her, I am forever grateful not only for her encouragement, but also for her unconditional belief in me.

I would also like to thank all the editors at Palgrave Macmillan, especially Alessandra Bastagli and Virginia Faber, who made absolutely sure that what I had written included enough examples and proof of what I had experienced so that readers unfamiliar with the Middle East and its labyrinth of information and convoluted politics would better be able to comprehend the complexities of this part of the world. I would also like to extend special gratitude to Colleen Lawrie for coordinating all the information that needed to be processed between Jordan, the United Kingdom, and the United States.

A very special thank you to Adrienne Denaro for being patient in taking so many pictures of me in order to finally get just the right one that caught me smiling naturally; and thanks to her husband Nasri Mukhar, who made sure she got to my home in time for the "golden hours" for that perfect shot. Last, but certainly not least, I would like to thank Katherine ("Kay") Barwick-Mukhar, without whom this book would never have made it to the publisher on time. Her willingness to spend countless hours with me in order to get the right answers to all the questions Alessandra and Virginia had sent, her hours on the Internet seeking historical background to my experiences as well as her long days and nights sitting before her computer as she typed everything up, proofreading over and over again—I cannot thank her enough for all she has done. I also need to thank her husband Elias for understanding the time she needed to spend away from him as she worked so hard to ready my book for publication, even working on my book on their farm in the Jordan Valley.

But above all, my very special gratitude goes to the man who was not only my friend, but my hero, without whose existence the dream of Palestine would never have crystallized. Thank you, Abu Ammar, for being such an important part of my life, for sacrificing every day of your life for our people and for giving your life for our homeland . . . our beloved Palestine.

INDEX